D0820365

Medieval
Foundations of Renaissance
Humanism

Medieval Foundations of Renaissance Humanism

WALTER ULLMANN

Cornell University Press
Ithaca, New York

In memoriam

CUTHBERTI EMERY

et

THEODORI PLUCKNETT

First published 1977 by Cornell University Press

International Standard Book Number 0–8014–1110–6
Library of Congress Catalog Card Number 77–278

Printed in Great Britain

Contents

Preface

Renaissance humanism has always exercised a peculiar attraction for the general reader and the student of history as well as for the professional historian. On the other hand, it is undeniable that the subject itself is accorded little more than a small niche in books dealing with the history of the period, and in the teaching of history no less than in examinations in history. Renaissance humanism leads, so to speak, a life of its own, is relegated to the periphery of the period and not related to the general historical development. One of the reasons why the vital role of renaissance humanism has not been fully acknowledged appears to be the commonly accepted view that it was a cultural, literary or educational movement that had little concern with, or bearing upon, the historical process. It was a movement which developed apart from, and irrespective of, the actual social and political conditions. By viewing it in this severely confined framework, the observer not only deprives himself of a good deal of relevant historical information, but also brings to bear an unhistorical approach upon a thoroughly historical subject. Indeed, it would seem somewhat naive to think that so crucially important a movement as renaissance humanism indubitably was can be profitably investigated, so to speak, in a vacuum.

If on the other hand one attempts to see renaissance humanism as an historically conditioned phenomenon and to look at it from an historical perspective, one soon comes to realize how strongly embedded it was in the antecedent medieval past. One can go further and say that renaissance humanism and all its relevant manifestations are incomprehensible without the ecclesiological background. Precisely because renaissance humanism evolved from its medieval environs, it moulded the complexion of society and decisively shaped its thought processes, its outlook and philosophy. And this very effect persuasively proves the receptivity of contemporary society for the substance of humanist themes which therefore was not only an historically, but also a socially conditioned movement in so far as it was a response to postulates and needs which emanated from society itself.

Considered on the purely historical level, renaissance humanism demonstrates itself as a vital strain in the fabric of the late medieval and early modern period.

In its original, pristine and unadulterated form renaissance humanism presents itself primarily as a politically motivated and socially orientated phenomenon – the literary, cultural, educational kind of humanism was a sequel to the political conception of humanism. Provided that strictly historical methods are applied, renaissance humanism can be subjected to historical–genetic criteria, which means that one of its earliest roots was the secularization of governmental structures in the high Middle Ages. Together with the corresponding secular features unmistakably observable as they were throughout Western society in the twelfth and thirteenth centuries, the soil was prepared for the appropriate theoretical and philosophical groundwork. This eventually evolved into a fully-fledged political humanism, perhaps the most outstanding consummation of a historically conditioned intellectual movement. At the cradle of the literary and cultural humanism stood political humanism. It was man's essential *humanitas* that now became the primary object of attention: activated in a political sense, his humanity first emerged as citizenship: the citizen (as distinct from the subject) was an autonomous member of the autonomous State, and it was the citizen whose public concern and activity was summed up in the concept of politics. This political humanism was in fact one of the strongest begetters of modern concepts, such as the nation as the basis of the State, the national State, State sovereignty, international law regulating the relations between sovereign national entities, individualism and pluralism replacing collectivism and corporatism, and so on.

I am fully aware that this is an at first novel, if not startling, presentation of renaissance humanism, but neither the sources nor the actual development nor the contemporary intellectual scene can reasonably bear any other interpretation. And here a feature of modern historiography on the Middle Ages calls for a comment. The vast majority of medievalists give insufficient attention to one of the most crucial topics without which the medieval setting can only imperfectly be understood. And this concerns the idea of rebirth, of renaissance, effected as it was believed to have been through baptism which had unquestionably vast juristic and constitutional consequences and implications. It is indeed one of the most extraordinary lacunae of modern writings on medieval subjects that this most crucial of all crucial topics is hardly ever envisaged or even seen, let alone treated, because it alone renders meaningful the complexion, the fabric and the evolution of medieval society which – it is agreed on all sides – was in substance and tenor and scope ecclesiological and therefore thoroughly impregnated with the idea and consequences of baptismal rebirth. It is as if future historians of the present age were to leave aside the effects of the steam and combustion engines, telecommunications, money economy, industrialization, and so on. Baptismal rebirth was the explicit and implicit assumption upon which the medieval outlook rested: its comprehensive effects concerned man from the cradle to the grave, in every walk of private and public life and in all socially and constitutionally relevant respects.

Renaissance humanism was conditioned by baptismal rebirth, but expanded and modified and developed it and in this way yielded an infinitely richer and wider world outlook than that which baptismal rebirth had originally provided. But the growth point was the idea of rebirth in its as yet not fully acknowledged variety, and it is this point which should be borne in mind. This conclusion seems to me the only one that an unprejudiced observer can draw from the evidence which is at once persuasive and full and abundantly available in the records. The simple reason why this explanation of renaissance humanism has not been attempted before is that, with some notable exceptions, the medievalist generally takes only a perfunctory interest in the humanist age, and the humanist a similarly perfunctory interest in the medieval period proper. But if it is true that the object of historical pursuits is to discover what we were before we became what we are, renaissance humanism should be accorded the historic function which is its due. For renaissance humanism was the antechamber of the modern world, in which a good many medieval elements are still operative. Renaissance humanism supplied the infrastructure of the age of transition from the fourteenth to the sixteenth centuries. It effortlessly explains the smooth transition from the late medieval to the early modern period and is capable of furnishing a satisfactory explanation of the profound changes which came about in this age. But, above all, because renaissance humanism necessitated a consultation of the ancients, it set in train a systematic recourse to ancient writers as sources of information, with the consequence that already existing links with the ancient world were strengthened and new links established. Renaissance humanism functioned as a vital connecting element between the ancient and the modern worlds.

The gratifying invitation by the publishers to write a book on a subject of special interest to me was most welcome, because it provided me with an opportunity to set before a wide and interested public the new approach to renaissance studies and humanism on which indeed over the years I had touched in a number of my publications and in lectures and addresses to universities, academies and learned societies both in this country and abroad. Nevertheless, the book can hardly do more than stake out the areas and signposts of one of the most fascinating topics and movements in history. In order to save space I have kept the footnotes to an irreducible minimum and left in the final draft only those which were necessary for purposes of verification or to guide the interested reader to further sources or literature. It is once more a very pleasant duty to thank not only the numerous friends and colleagues who by their spoken words and in their written works have greatly stimulated me, but above all my students – undergraduates and graduate research students alike – who have in our lengthy discussions, in seminars, classes, and informal gatherings, in fact focused my attention on the subject itself. To them – some of them now eminent academic teachers and fruitful researchers in this country and elsewhere – my sincere and appreciative thanks are due. And lastly, it is my wife once more who deserves, as on previous occasions, my deepest gratitude for her exemplary patience, understanding, wise counsel and devoted help based on sound critical sense throughout the chequered, worrying and lengthy period of preparation of this book.

Cambridge,   W.U.
Summer 1976.

Abbreviations

ACW	*Ancient Christian Writers* (London, 1946–)
AHR	*American Historical Review*
AKG	*Archiv für Kulturgeschichte*
CC	*Corpus Christianorum*
CL	W. Ullmann, *The Church and the Law in the Early Middle Ages*, Collected Studies I (London, 1975)
CR	W. Ullmann, *The Carolingian Renaissance and the Idea of Kingship* (London, 1969)
CSEL	*Corpus Scriptorum Ecclesiasticorum Latinorum*
EETS	*Early English Text Society*
EHR	*English Historical Review*
ET	English translation
FC	*Fathers of the Church* (London and New York, 1947–)
FT	French translation
GT	German translation
Hist Jb	*Historisches Jahrbuch*
HZ	*Historische Zeitschrift*
IS	W. Ullmann, *Individual and Society in the Middle Ages* (London, 1967)
IT	Italian translation
JEH	*Journal of Ecclesiastical History*
JHI	*Journal of the History of Ideas*
JTS	*Journal of Theological Studies*
LCC	Library of Christian Classics
Loeb	Loeb Classical Library
LP	W. Ullmann, *Law and Politics in the Middle Ages* (London, 1975)
LT	Latin translation
M.A.	Middle Ages; *Moyen Age; Mittelalter*
MGH	*Monumenta Germaniae Historica*
Misc	*Miscellanea*
PG	W. Ullmann, *The Growth of Papal Government in the Middle Ages*, 3rd/4th edition (London, 1970)
PGP	W. Ullmann, *Principles of Government and Politics in the Middle Ages*, 3rd edition (London, 1974)

PGr	J. P. Migne, *Patrologia Graeca*
PL	J. P. Migne, *Patrologia Latina*
PPI	W. Ullmann, *The Papacy and Political Ideas in the Middle Ages*, Collected Studies II (London, 1976)
Rin	*La Rinascità*
SB	*Sitzungsberichte*
SHP	W. Ullmann, *A Short History of the Papacy in the Middle Ages*, 2nd edition (London, 1974)
SR	*Studies in the Renaissance*
SS	*Scriptores*
SSRRGG	*Scriptores Rerum Germanicarum*
SSRRII	*Scriptores Rerum Italicarum*
ULC	University Library, Cambridge
ZKG	*Zeitschrift für Kirchengeschichte*

All other abbreviations are self-explanatory.

Introduction

Although renaissance humanism has been the subject of literally speaking countless studies and publications, although special departments in many universities exist for the better pursuit of this subject, and several disting-uished series of monographs and scholarly journals are solely dedicated to the better understanding of it, there is no commonly agreed view of what renaissance humanism stood for or what it represented.[1] Hardly any other topic has attracted so much talent and erudition and intellectual energy.[2] Was renaissance humanism a scholarly, literary, educational system that rested on the study of the classical authors?[3] Was it chiefly, if not ex-clusively, concerned with the revival of classics?[4] Was it philosophical in content and orientation?[5] Was it perhaps a predominantly educational movement that affected many intellectual disciplines?[6] Was its core philological?[7] Was it possibly the cult of rhetoric and oratory and had it in

1   The best historical introduction is still Wallace Ferguson, *The Renaissance in Historical Thought: Five Centuries of Interpretation* (Cambridge, Mass., 1948).
2   For surveys of recent literature see P. O. Kristeller, 'Studies on renaissance humanism' in *SR*, 9(1962), 7ff.; A. Buck, 'Italienischer Humanismus' in *AKG*, 52(1970), 121–40. The surveys in *Renaissance Quarterly* give a good conspectus of the annually published literature.
3   Cf. R. R. Bolgar, *The Classical Heritage and Its Beneficiaries* (Cambridge, 1954); P. O. Kristeller, *The Classics and Renaissance Thought* (Cambridge, Mass., 1955). The vocation of the humanist concerned the acquisition and manipulation of Ciceronian style in speeches, letters, poems and books, according to the *Evangelisches Staats-lexikon*, ed. H. Knust and S. Grundmann (Stuttgart, 1966), s.v. 'Humanismus', p. 776.
4   Cf., e.g., G. Voigt, *Die Wiederbelebung des classischen Altertums oder das erste Jahr-hundert des Humanismus* (reprinted Berlin, 1960).
5   Cf., e.g., G. Saitta, *Il pensiero italiano nell' umanesimo e nel rinascimento* (Bari and Rome, 1949–51); C. Trinkaus, *In Our Image and Likeness: Humanity and Divinity in Italian Humanist Thought* (London, 1970), at I.18: humanism in part was 'simply a turn toward other branches of ancient culture in poetry, oratory, moral philosophy'.
6   Cf. W. H. Woodward, *Studies in Education During the Age of the Renaissance* (Cam-bridge, 1924); N. W. Gilbert, *Renaissance Concepts of Methods* (New York, 1960); H. O. Burger, *Renaissance, Humanismus, Reformation* (Berlin and Zürich, 1970), pp. 28, 37 (educational programme; educational movement).
7   Cf. on this D. Weinstein, 'Interpretations of renaissance humanism' in *JHI*, 33 (1972), 167. Cf. also the quotation below, p. 173, n. 83.

fact evolved from the medieval art of composing letters (the *ars dictaminis*) or prose composition?[8] Or did it not, as has also been claimed, simply mean a liberal education, provided agreement can be reached on what liberal education meant in the fourteenth and fifteenth centuries?[9] Was it perchance a philosophical method of rational enquiry and hence at base epistemology? Could its essence possibly be aestheticism that saw the world without regard to reality, as indeed its main proponent, Giovanni Gentile, averred when he said that the humanist lived 'in mondo che agita nel suo cervello'?[10] Was the encouragement of literature as a cult for its own sake the hallmark of renaissance humanism?[11]

These are just a few questions which have been debated and will go on being debated, precisely because renaissance humanism meant different things to different people at different times. Each of these characterizations sets out from one premiss and focuses on one single strain of renaissance humanism, with the consequence that the substance of humanism recedes into the background. Indeed, renaissance humanism was all that has been claimed for it, and much else besides. Similarly, questions have been asked and debated and answered concerning the development of renaissance humanism. They too reveal an astounding variety of standpoints and explanations, such as: Why was medieval rhetoric abandoned in favour of the renaissance classics? What was the 'cause' of the renaissance?[12] Why were the humanists dedicated to philology, linguistic form and style? The overriding question evidently is why the educated world began to study the classics at all. Yet, this very question may reveal the absence of a historical dimension, for it is indisputable that most of the classics and their works had been available throughout the preceding centuries. To be sure, this fact is recognized by some modern authorities who go a step further and say that renaissance humanism was little else than the revival of Latin grammar, syntax, prose and oratory, holding as they do that the medieval antecedents of renaissance humanism were the grammatical and rhetorical traditions.[13] It was the stereotyped world outlook fostered in the

---

8   See P. O. Kristeller, *op. cit.* (above, n. 3), and *id.*, *Renaissance Thought: The Classic, Scholastic and Humanist Strains* (New York, 1961); further, H. H. Gray, 'Renaissance humanism: the pursuit of eloquence' in *JHI*, 24(1963) 497ff.; J. Siegel, *Rhetoric and Philosophy in Renaissance Humanism* (Princeton, 1969).

9   Cf. Wallace Ferguson, *Renaissance Studies* (New York, 1970), p. 95.

10 G. Gentile, 'Il carattere del rinascimento' in *Opere complete*, 4th edition, XIV (Florence, 1969) at p. 33. Cf. also p. 43: 'L'umanesimo divenne il naturalismo del rinascimento.' Cf. in this context the pungent remarks by Denys Hay, *The Italian Renaissance in Its Historical Background* (Cambridge, 1961), p. 8.

11 See A. Buck, *Zu Begriff und Problem der Renaissance* (Darmstadt, 1969), p. 4 (*Eigenwert*).

12 Cf. H. Weisinger, 'The renaissance theory of the reaction against the Middle Ages as a cause of the renaissance' in *Speculum*, 20(1945), 461–7.

13 In this sense P. O. Kristeller, *art. cit.* (above, n. 2), p. 20.

medieval period which, it is claimed, bonded man to pure formalism: it revelled in juggling concepts and notions far removed from reality, which explains the emergence of what is called renaissance humanism. It was characterized by the concentration on classical works which promoted the formation of 'civilized' man – the so-called *homo civilis* – whose pre-occupation in life is said to be the cultivation of aestheticism and the relevant literature.[14]

A feature of renaissance humanism that is sometimes thought to have been characteristic of it concerns the relationship between the humanists and Christianity. The humanists were said to have been cool towards, and detached, if not estranged, from, Christianity. Some modern expositors go even so far as to claim that there was a revival of paganism, supposedly the inevitable result of the intensive study of the ancients. This humanist attitude towards Christianity is deduced from the attacks on scholasticism[15] which was one of the characteristic features of humanism itself.[16] That there was anticlericalism, mainly aimed at monks, bishops, cardinals and so on, is evidently true, but this was also true of the eleventh and twelfth centuries. The difference is not one of degree, let alone kind, but merely one of form and expression. The humanist, having a much better command of Latin at his elbow than the anti-Gregorian or the Ghibelline or the member of a proscribed heretical sect, was able to give vent to his view coloured as it might be with sarcasm and scorn in a subtler, and also more refined, way, but there was little difference in the substance of his arguments. Furthermore, the number of people who expressed themselves adequately in these matters was infinitely greater in the fourteenth and fifteenth centuries than in the eleventh or twelfth. And, finally, their works were much better preserved than those of their predecessors. What would have been much more effective would have been either silence or a frontal attack on Christianity, but this was precisely not the case. On the contrary, a glance at the artistic and literary productions of the period reveals no animosity against Christianity. Indeed, the former were overwhelmingly inspired by religious motives. And, by way of contrast, many a statement made by a pope in the fifteenth century was identical to those made by the so-called 'antireligious' or 'anticlerical' humanists. That a number of

---

14 By stressing this aspect one incurs the danger of dressing the movement up in its Sunday best. See J. Huizinga, *Das Problem der Renaissance* (Darmstadt, 1971), p. 39: 'Es ist nicht zu leugnen: die Renaissance war ein Sonntagskind.'

15 Cf. P. O. Kristeller, *op. cit.* (above, n. 3), pp. 70ff.

16 For a balanced assessment of this problem cf. P. O. Kristeller, *Renaissance Concepts of Man* (New York, 1972), pp. 1–3; H. Baker, *The Dignity of Man: Studies in the Persistence of an Idea* (Cambridge, Mass., 1947) (=*The Image of Man* (New York, 1961)), p. 206, has pointed out that the schoolmen were condemned for their method rather than for the truth which they sought to establish by their method.

humanists opposed the medieval schoolmen and theologians is again incontestable, but on the other hand some of the worst excrescences in theological and philosophical literature can be witnessed during the period of renaissance humanism: these productions continued to come forth in ever bulkier quantities (not necessarily matched by quality) from the scriptoria and the new printing houses long after renaissance humanism had spent its force.

If indeed renaissance humanism was little more than a *Bildungsideal,* a purely academic, educational, scholarly ideal that was to recreate ancient 'ideals' by imitating their literary and artistic works, it could assuredly be applied only to small select circles. This elitist standpoint might conceivably be entertained, though even so its barrenness, its superficiality, its tinsel complexion stares the discriminating observer in the face and forces him to ask further questions. Can an intellectual movement that has so many social ramifications and applications and implications as the renaissance undubitably had, be restricted to elitist groups or classes? Can any movement make progress in a vacuum, that is, without regard to environmental factors, without the focal point provided by society itself, although this movement is strongly suffused with elements which are directly relevant to society? Are not in fact movements of this kind a response to the needs of contemporary society? That the humanists had certain educational aims is self-evident, but were they an end or merely a means to an end? And this seems to be a crucial question which faces the enquiring observer.

Assuredly, loving care was devoted to the cultivation of Latin prose, syntax, style, but this was something of an ivory tower affair remote from the exigencies of everyday life. Latin had been a dead language since the sixth century and certainly nobody thought of resurrecting the dead Latin from its grave. Generally speaking the rulers, dukes and princes, prosperous merchants, the lower aristocracy, still less the ordinary people, had no more fluency in, or familiarity with, Latin than they had had in previous centuries. There is no evidence that Latin enjoyed greater popularity in the sixteenth or seventeenth centuries than in the antecedent millenium. Apart from the ecclesiastical institutions, the only circles in which Latin still had a firm hold were academic in the strict sense of the term, since lectures were given in Latin, examinations were conducted in Latin, and books, glosses, monographs and special orations were written in Latin. But this was a feature that was to continue until the end of the nineteenth century – and in some countries and institutions well into the twentieth – and nobody would for this reason call the eighteenth and nineteenth centuries ages of humanism. Yet, although the cultivation of Latin prose, oratory and style was supposed to have been the educational ideal of the humanists, it left few traces among those who did a very great deal of writing for fairly large circles, such as the professional jurists, theologians, the writers on political and related topics, philosophers in the fifteenth century, let alone chroniclers (and significantly the numbers writing in Latin were decidedly decreasing). What is still more interesting is that quite clearly there were 'humanists' among the jurists in the fifteenth century (for instance, Franciscus de Accoltis, or Marianus Socinus) who themselves read and advocated the study of the ancients for linguistic and educational reasons. But their own juristic work shows no trace of classical influence: the study of the ancients was obviously reserved for leisure hours. For the most part the professionals continued to write in the old traditional manner.

It is not without significance that at this very same time the vernacular began to permeate new disciplines which only a generation earlier would have seemed immune to it. And, what is more, there were several 'humanists' of renown who themselves wrote in Latin as well as in the vernacular. Indeed, it was this very age – the fourteenth century – that witnessed the rapidly growing production of vernacular literature which has commanded respect to this very day, not because of the language in which it was written, but because of its intrinsic worth – its happy combination of beauty of form and profundity of matter. Nor were they exceptions, as were the *Nibelungenlied* or the *Chansons de geste* in the century before. No doubt the authors now writing in the vernacular knew Latin well enough without having necessarily 'cultivated' it, but what should be borne in mind here again is that there was no rivalry between two camps, the classical and the so-called simple vernacular, but that they complemented one another and in this way gave a specific complexion to the age. Dante, Boccaccio, Chaucer, Gower, and so on, were just as much 'humanists' as Petrarch or Bruni.

There is one point, however, which is and always has been agreed upon by scholars of all shades of opinion. It is unanimously recognized that there was such a thing as renaissance humanism, whatever its meaning may have been. This is a historical fact. Once this is admitted – and it would be very hard to deny it – this historical phenomenon must have a historical background because such movements as renaissance humanism do not come about *ex nihilo*. This simple consideration forces the enquirer to adopt a very much broader standpoint than has hitherto been common. What is required is an integrated approach that at least attempts to see the movement in its historical setting and as a whole. Such an integrative view was put forward in a great number of most stimulating works[17] by Eugenio

---

17   Cf., e.g., E. Garin, *L'educazione in Europa 1400–1600* (Bari, 1957) (GT *Geschichte der Pädagogik*, 1966); 'Die Kultur der Renaissance' in *Propyläen Weltgeschichte*, ed. Golo Mann, VI (1964), pp. 431–534; *Italian Humanism* (Oxford, 1965); Introduction to *Giovanni Pico della Mirandola* (Berlin and Zürich, 1968).

Garin, for whom humanism was the philosophic expression of the renaissance itself. Another broad view was put forward, from an entirely different angle, by Hans Baron for whom, most significantly, the essence of humanism was 'civic humanism', best observable in early fifteenth-century Florence.[18] It was, for Hans Baron, politically motivated humanism. The adoption of a wider view was furthermore urged by Marvin Becker, according to whom humanism had a social base in the rise of lay piety within the communal world: humanism began with the predicament of man, and the humanists were spiritual counsellors to the laity.[19] Whereas these scholars – and their followers – have profoundly advanced the understanding of renaissance humanism, its historical roots have still not received much attention. To say this is not to revive the debate of continuity or discontinuity. But there can be no denying that renaissance humanism is usually viewed as a phenomenon on its own, isolated from its historical environs and detached from its manifold roots which lie deeply buried in the past.[20]

There is every justification for advancing the thesis that what is commonly called renaissance humanism was an epiphenomenon, a concomitant feature and integral part of the overall ecclesiological, philosophical, governmental and political thinking that pervaded the age. The impact which renaissance humanism made upon society at large then becomes intelligible, because only historically conditioned movements can achieve such deep and profound influence. Renaissance humanism was a European movement that was firmly anchored in the past.[21] It gave that age and succeeding ages their particular physiognomy. It cannot be restricted to purely 'educational' or linguistic 'ideals' culminating in the prose and style of a dead language. Renaissance humanism was a veritable rebirth and for this reason constituted an infinitely rich, pregnant and fruitful phenomenon capable of evolving in many varied directions. For it is a common historical experience that all influential movements as well as

18   Hans Baron, *The Crisis of the Early Italian Renaissance* (Princeton, 1966); and especially *Humanist and Political Literature in Florence and Venice at the Beginning of the Quattrocento* (Cambridge, Mass., 1955); further, his contributions to *JHI*, 19(1958), 26–34; 20(1959), 3–22; 21(1960), 131–50 (review article).

19   See Marvin Becker, 'Observations on the rise of early humanism in Italy' in *Civiltà dell' Umanesimo*, ed. G. Tarugi (Florence, 1972), pp. 51ff.; *id.*, 'Individualism in the early Italian renaissance' in *SR*, 19(1972), 273–97. Cf. now also J. M. McCarthy, *Humanistic Emphases in the Educational Thought of Vincent of Beauvais* (Leiden and Cologne, 1976), who sees a strong link between this thirteenth-century scholar and the so-called humanist educational programme (p. 151).

20   For the continuity of certain medieval philosophical strands in renaissance philosophy see P. O. Kristeller, *Renaissance Concepts* (above, n. 16), pp. 110ff. Cf. also from a different angle E. Garin, *Medioevo e rinascimento* (Bari, 1954), pp. 15ff., 66ff.

21   A brilliant example is E. Cassirer, *The Individual and the Cosmos in Renaissance Philosophy* (ET Oxford, 1963).

institutions are intrinsically linked with social conditions, so much so that educational 'ideals', 'reforms' and 'programmes' present themselves as responses to the exigencies of society and are its emanations. Otherwise one would have to condemn the 'humanists' to an existence on the periphery of society, government and public affairs (in which they did in fact take a very great interest and play a vital role) and to maintain that they lived in a virtual vacuum and were, as Voigt once called them, solitary heroes of eloquence and elegance.[22] The concentration on well delineated, circumscribed aspects of renaissance humanism also harbours the danger of overlooking its other vital perspectives. The very name, idea and connotation of *humanitas* – a term of distinguished ancestry – should by itself be an indication that its essential meaning is, by definition, comprehensive. The arts, language, law, and so on, are merely partial manifestations of man's total humanity. Indeed the idea of 'humanity' embraces the whole of man and takes into account all his natural faculties and innate potentialities, as indeed the 'humanists' of the fourteenth and early fifteenth centuries most conspicuously did. To view the *artes* or the *studia humanitatis* only from the narrow rhetorical or grammatical level surely does not do justice to the richness, comprehensiveness and fertility of the very idea of *humanitas*. The external appearance of form should not be confused with the inner substance or matter.

Renaissance humanism consisted of many parts, embodied varied strands and was nourished from diverse sources. The name should long have directed attention to the historic environs in which it grew: for the core of this phenomenon was a rebirth which was intimately linked with that rebirth that had given the medieval period its peculiar complexion, outlook, meaning and appearance – and that rebirth was baptismal. The intrinsic meaning of baptism was to redeem man who was originally created in the image of God. This redemption amounted to a transformation and rebirth of man's being.[23] Through baptismal rebirth the ordinary natural unregenerate humanity of man was figuratively washed away by baptismal waters with the consequent emergence of a 'new creature'. That was the point of view expressed by St Paul in numerous places and that is the doctrine and, following it, practice which is witnessed throughout the patristic and medieval period. As far as public and social life went, this 'new creature', baptized man, was incorporated into the divinely founded Church: the Christian had shed his naturalness which was spoken of by St Paul as his animalic humanity or being. Thereby he moved, so to speak, on a level different from that of ordinary 'unregenerated' humanity,

22 G. Voigt, *op. cit.* (above, n. 4), II. 478.
23 See, for instance, Tertullian, *De baptismo*, 12.1–2, edition in *CC*, 1(1954), 286f., where he treats of baptism as the sacrament without which salvation cannot be achieved. Cf. also the sources cited below, p. 15, n. 2.

because he now lived according to a *novitas vitae*, that is, led a new life (to use Pauline language (Rom. 6:4)) that was designed by divinity itself. The main effect of baptismal rebirth was, therefore, ecclesiological, that is, acting, living, thinking, arguing, in terms of the corporate manifestation of Christianity which was the Church as the society of all the baptized, of all reborn men. This, as we shall presently see, was a topic of veritable cosmological dimensions: it had all the appurtenances of a world outlook with a definite programme, structure and end. The new personality was (and still is) symbolically shown by the baptismal name which originally replaced the 'natural' name. In early Christianity the change of personality was symbolized by the undressing of the newly baptized (the neophyte) and by his putting on white clothes.[24]

Humanist renaissance was in essence an expansion of this ecclesiological theme. By re-activating the atrophied natural humanity of man this humanism restored or resurrected the original *homo*, unregenerate man, and thereby his 'humanitas'. The vacuum which baptismal rebirth had left came to be filled by resuscitating natural humanity, by attributing inborn value to the unregenerate being of man. In more than one respect can one here speak of a rebirth – a renaissance – of man's true humanity, of that being that had been hibernating for many centuries because it was said to have been regenerated in, and absorbed by, the 'new man' (*homo novus*), to use another metaphor of St Paul. Hence, on the ecclesiological premisses, this neutralized or atrophied natural humanity did not and could not count in the public field. What did count was solely the regenerate, the new man, the faithful Christian as a member of the Church. It does not need much historical imagination or a particularly well developed intellectual acumen to realize that through the rebirth of natural man, through his restoration into his natural state, cosmological perspectives came to be opened up which were hitherto barely perceived: they brought with them new horizons which in their aggregate constituted an altogether new cosmology. For man's innate humanity had reacquired legitimate standing with all the attendant and necessary consequences. Natural – that is, unregenerate – man was awakened from the slumber of centuries: he was re-activated.

The full extent of the effects of baptismal rebirth in the public and social fields is but rarely apprehended. Yet only a brief reflection suffices to show that the ecclesiological society, the Church, into which the Christian was incorporated, could be ordered and governed only according to the sets of norms and rules and laws which were germane to it, had

---

24 Cf., for example, St John Chrysostom, *Baptismal Instructions*, ET in *ACW*, 31(1963), 47. See also Pseudo-Denys, *De ecclesiastica hierarchia*, cap. 2, in *PGr* 3.403 (=John Scotus Eriugena's translation in *PL* 122.1079). For a synopsis of the various Greek and Latin translations see *Dionysiaca*, ed. P. Chevallier (Paris, 1937–50), p. 1158.

actually brought it into existence and were not of human, but of divine, provenance, precisely because the ecclesiological unit itself was a divine institution. It assumed concrete shape within earthly and mundane environs and precincts. The ecclesiological society was in every respect a body public that was nurtured by the laws eventually of divine origin made known by the qualified ecclesiastical organs. The presupposition evidently was that baptismal rebirth had rendered man's natural humanity ineffective and inactive by christianizing it. That is to say, through his incorporation into the Church the Christian had, according to the undisputed doctrine and practice in the Middle Ages, become a subject of divinely instituted authority that had nothing in common with natural humanity. The ecclesiological body and its governing organs were not of human provenance, and baptismal rebirth had neutralized the Christian's natural humanity in so far as the government of the Church was concerned. It was the restoration of man's natural humanity, of his own natural being, which was the hallmark of that historic development that became renaissance humanism. And this restoration or re-activation or rebirth of natural man necessarily resulted in attributing to him precisely that which he was said to have lost through baptismal rebirth – autonomy and independence and legitimacy of standing in the public and social fields, precisely because these spheres were wholly ecclesiologically orientated. The beginnings of renaissance humanism can be traced back to the historic situation in the late eleventh century: it was this historic contingency which supplied the first concrete impulse to that development that culminated in this renaissance of 'natural' man. Differently expressed, the humanist renaissance made its first appearance within the political and governmental orbit and was throughout its development a politically inspired movement.

This is the first point that must be borne in mind in any consideration of the evolutionary aspect of renaissance humanism. The process began with the secularization of government itself and inevitably went on to engulf society at large, which indeed provided an extremely fertile soil for the dissemination of secular–mundane–human points of view. Finally it was the individual himself who, as a result of the antecedent development, experienced the rebirth or restoration of his own humanity. Throughout this evolution the political and governmental as well as social character of the movement was unmistakable. Nevertheless, this cosmology was not at all in rivalry with the ecclesiological point of view, but on closer inspection can be seen to have been its complement and supplement.[25] Evidently,

---

25 Wallace Ferguson in his *Renaissance Studies* (above, n. 9), p. 101, rightly points out that the aim of the humanists was 'to erect a secular ideal of virtue . . . alongside the Christian a lay morality . . . an ideal not so much in conflict with Christianity as independent of it'.

humanist renaissance thus understood was conditioned by the earlier ecclesiological standpoint. *Humanitas* and *Christianitas* came to be the ideological poles upon which the new world outlook was to rest.

But since on the one hand renaissance humanism primarily concerned public government and the ordering of society, and since on the other hand society had previously been directed by exclusively ecclesiological norms, the need clearly arose to discover how a purely human society with no aspirations or ambitions in regard to eternity was to be adequately ordered. Surely the new cosmology, which was so strongly suffused with political ingredients, was pure theory. What had to be learnt was how in practice this kind of concrete society was to arrange itself. It is assuredly not enough to have the intention to remodel society and its government nor is it sufficient to have a blueprint or a programme or a doctrine without the appropriate equipment, without the 'know-how' of its implementation, without the expertise to translate abstract principles into concrete political or social action. This, in parenthesis, is what happens today when advisers and consultants are called in to help to launch projects to be operated in underdeveloped countries. And the same indeed happens when newly constituted modern states replace colonies. They too draw heavily on the advice and expertise of consultants from other countries until they are mature and experienced enough to proceed on their own. As a matter of fact, in the Carolingian age this desideratum was already clearly perceived when a whole society was remodelled on Christian and ecclesiological principles: here too there was conspicuous need to acquire the right kind of knowledge relative to the principles and axioms which were to form the backbone of the (new) Carolingian society. And now within the terms of the humanist renaissance the consultation of the ancients had precisely the same function – to discover how in the ancient world a purely human ('unregenerate') society was ordered, governed and directed. This recourse to the ancients was, in a way, a reversal of the process that characterized the Carolingian renaissance. Then as now the recourse or regress to models was dictated by the character of society and pursued very topical, concrete, practical ends. For a purely human society only antiquity could offer models.[26] No doubt is permissible about the purpose of the lively searches and researches into ancient sources: this purpose was severely practical and was a means to an end, and not an end in itself.

It was only when this search and research became an end in itself that renaissance humanism entered the phase which focused attention on

---

26   Ferguson, *op. cit.*, p. 94, dealing with the problem of 'causation' or 'what caused the literary world of Italy to turn with such enthusiasm to the study of the ancients', holds that this ancient literature 'was the product of a wealthy, aristocratic, secular and predominantly urban society' which was 'non-feudal', 'in which the upper classes of the Italian city-states could easily imagine themselves at home'.

literary, cultural, aesthetic, linguistic, ethical and philosophical aspects. Above all, language as a vehicle for conveying and transmitting records, situations, ideas, etc., lost its auxiliary character, became detached from its original function and assumed the dimension of a special branch of study. From the strictly historical point of view the specifically literary and cultural renaissance was the end of a long evolution, the beginnings of which can be traced back to the high Middle Ages: this literary and cultural renaissance humanism in its various manifestations really concerns only one selected strain of the rich humanist renaissance. The literary concentration is a consequence of the main phenomenon. In figurative language, it is as if a broad river had separated into smaller streams, with the result that each small rivulet pursued its own course and followed its own paths by cutting its way over the boulders and winding itself through the various ravines, gorges and valleys. It is perhaps especially significant that the very term *humanista* made its appearance only when the broad renaissance humanism had entered upon its literary, linguistic, aesthetic, educational, philosophical specialist careers and the *studia humanitatis* had been restricted to well-circumscribed intellectual disciplines. This term of *humanista* was not known, or at any rate was not familiar, before *circa* 1490.[27]

When renaissance humanism is looked at in this light, one of the problems often raised since the renaissance became a métier of modern study seems effortlessly to resolve itself. Why, it has been asked, was it in Italy that so much of what came to be called humanist renaissance developed and found its, perhaps, most articulate expression? There are several reasons why the initial stages of the humanist renaissance came to a full flowering on Italian soil. Nowhere else in Europe was the ecclesiastical life as extensive and intensive as in Italy, and nowhere also in Europe was the scholarly pursuit of the law and government so advanced as in the Italian universities and their law faculties: the jurisprudence studied and taught there was the perfect counterpart of the ecclesiastical life, and yet provided also the presupposition for the impulse towards the new orientation. And, thirdly, Italian libraries in cathedrals, monasteries and other institutions were more richly endowed with copies of ancient authors than their counterparts anywhere else in Europe. All three features – the ecclesiastical, the academic and juristic, the abundance of copies of ancient writings – had one common focus, and that was Rome, whether in its ancient republican shape or in that of the late imperial age or in that epitomized by the Roman Church. And the one respect in which Rome

---

27 See A. Campana, 'The origin of the word "humanist" ' in *Journal of the Warburg and Courtauld Institutes*, 9(1946), 60–73, especially the Postscript, at p. 73. Other examples, pp. 61ff. The term was obviously derived from *humanitas* (*ibid.*, p. 69).

was always outstanding was its capability of ordering social life, of manip-
ulating social relations, of government, of the idea of law as the regulating
force in civilized communities.

Once this quiet simple point is grasped, its potentialities in our present
context are easy to comprehend. Law – and its academic manifestation:
jurisprudence – was understood not merely as a technical and vocational
matter (to be sure, it was this, too), but above all as an instrument of
government: only by law could a body public be governed, its aims and
aspirations be realized, its path towards its destination delineated. Law
was the one medium that concerned the whole society and gave it authoritative guidance. Law was the channel by which the government attempted
to realize the end of society, and this goes for the papal, royal, imperial – in
short for any kind of government. Legal science was governmental science,
because structurally government was the manifestation of the idea of law.
That in the ancient Hellenistic allegory of soul and body (*anima–corpus*)
the former was equated with the law which breathed life into the body
public, that is, *animated* it, only goes to show how deeply the idea of law
had permeated intellectual levels: already the Visigothic laws of the seventh
century expressed the view that 'lex est anima totius corporis popularis'
('the law is the soul of the whole body of the people').

It will readily be understood that since the law was of such overriding
importance, its creation was of the most crucial concern to contemporaries.
And the problem of who was to create law depended upon the kind of
society, the kind of body public that was to be governed by law. A communist society can be governed only by a law based on communist or
Marxist principles; a capitalist society on axioms derived from the free
deployment of capital. A purely ecclesiological society evidently was to
have a law germane to its divine foundation and aims – hence the fundamental importance of the ecclesiologically inspired law. On the other hand,
it may be remarked in parenthesis that a purely human society, such as is
represented by republican Rome, had a law that catered for its own human
needs and for no more. We thus return to the point that the character of a
society also determined its law and postulated its creating organ.

The Italian soil was in a quite specific sense destined to play a vital role
in the context of humanism. It was on Italian soil that the very institution
of a university emerged at Bologna, if we disregard, as we legitimately may,
the proximate law school at Ravenna that disappeared from view when
Bologna became pre-eminent in the early years of the twelfth century.
And at Bologna – as well as at its later satellites – the law studied was the
hallowed Roman law in its Justinianean shape. Here was a fully matured
body of law that was capable of answering the needs of a society which was
just then beginning to recover from the severe repercussions of the
Investiture Conflict. The growth of Bologna as the citadel of all juris-

prudential, governmental studies was intimately linked with the Investiture Contest which had indeed shaken the foundations of contemporary society. It was then that the full magnitude of the problem of the relations between law and society came into the open. What is of direct concern here is that Bologna was staffed by laymen who taught laymen studying the law that was issued by laymen – the Roman law. And it was as a result of the study of law in the predominantly law universities, situated as they were in Italy, that the humanist re-orientation began its triumphant career. We shall presently see that the study of Roman law initiated the secularization of government. In contemporary circumstances, this was a necessary preliminary to the full restoration of man's humanity. For just as in the Carolingian period it was the government that set afoot the renaissance of society in the ecclesiological sense, it was necessarily again the government that had to take the initiative in partly reversing the earlier process.

In modern parlance the cluster of problems attendant upon the implementation of secular or mundane or human principles of government and society would without question be called political, however inexact this designation may be, but originally it was a question of government pure and simple which did eventually and correctly become an issue of full-blooded politics, and this was indeed due to the effects of renaissance humanism. It embodied a new – and yet also, from the strictly historical angle, an old – cosmology which constituted a considerable broadening of man's perceptions, powerfully promoted old branches of intellectual disciplines and was instrumental in creating new ones. This was the long-term result of the historical–ideological contingencies in the late eleventh century which presented themselves as a challenge to hitherto unquestioned premises. And challenge has always acted as a generating stimulant, because its acceptance compels re-examination and re-thinking of premises, assists clarification and widens the horizon by opening up hitherto unknown perspectives and vistas. This is exactly what characterized the humanist renaissance in its initial phases. It was firmly embedded in the historical process, conditioned as this was by the social effects of baptismal rebirth.[28] This renaissance humanism implicitly and explicitly brought forth a world outlook at once deeper and broader, and also more complex, than the traditional medieval cosmology.

---

28 As A. Heuss once said, humanism must always be understood in a relative sense, because it is related to an already existing situation. It is a reaction to actual contingencies – see A. Heuss, 'Der Humanismus und die Geschichte' in *Antike und Abendland*, ed. U. Fleischer *et al*. (Berlin, 1973), pp. 173ff., at 174. Hence 'humanism may serve as a label for most diversified standpoints'.

I

The Background:
The Renaissance of Medieval Society

I

Baptism and the effects which it displayed in society occupied a far more prominent place in the medieval period than modern scholarship acknowledges. However much its sacramentality and its liturgy were stressed by writers in all ages, from the strictly historical and social angle there is one feature that has always accorded to baptism a special place within a Christian framework: it was considered an eminently legal act by which man entered a society that was held to have been divinely founded. Through receiving baptism man was said to have undergone a rebirth: in metaphorical language baptismal waters had washed away his natural being and transformed him into a 'new creature', into a 'new man', in a word, into a different being altogether. The effect of baptism was a regeneration, to use one more expression by St Paul, which sublimated, if it did not replace, his natural, carnal generation. Indeed, St Paul himself called this regeneration a *renovatio*, that is, a renewal, a renaissance or rebirth: natural man, or as he was also called 'animalic man', was transformed into a new being that alone was said to be capable of achieving salvation. The crucial point here is the incorporation of the new man into the Church. This incorporation was effected by divine grace which was transmitted through the appropriate officers of the Church. Man thereby not only assumed a complexion which was different from that which he had as a natural being, but also entered 'a new life' (*novitas vitae*) which in ordinary language meant that he became subjected to new norms of living, to a new style of life, to a new outlook and aim.[1]

---

1 The main passages of St Paul concerning this point are: 1 Cor. 2: 14f.; 2 Cor. 5: 17; Gal. 6: 15; Eph. 4: 23; Col. 4: 10. The *novitas vitae* is in Rom. 6: 4. The *homo novus* is in Eph. 2: 15 and 4: 24. Further, Titus 3: 5; 1 Pet. 2: 3; John 3: 4–6. For literature see A. Harnack, 'Die Terminologie der Wiedergeburt' in *Texte und Untersuchungen zur Geschichte der altchristl. Literatur*, 42(1918), 97–143; O. Heggelbacher, *Die christliche Taufe als Rechtsakt nach dem Zeugnis der frühen Christenheit* (Fribourg, 1953); and the additional literature in *PGP* p. 316; further, W. Ullmann, 'Der Wiedergeburtsgedanke in der Staatslehre des Mittelalters' in *Aufstieg und Niedergang der römischen Welt*, ed. H. Temporini, vol. III (forthcoming).

This standpoint of St Paul and of the early Christian writers was classically formulated and transmitted to the medieval world by St Augustine who spoke of two births, the 'first nativity' (*prima nativitas*) effected through carnal copulation, and the 'second nativity' (*secunda nativitas*) by divinity and grace.[2] This doctrine was held throughout the subsequent period. As a representative scholar of the high Middle Ages, Alan of Lille, one of the outstanding minds of the twelfth century, may be cited. In his work entitled *Lamentations on the Corruption of Nature* he dealt in a number of passages with the topic of nature and grace. The book itself was written in the form of a dialogue between himself and nature. One instance must suffice to show how deeply embedded in the thought-pattern of the time was the idea of baptismal rebirth. Alan made nature say that 'through my activity man is born, through God's authority he is reborn . . . through me man is created to die, through him [God] he is re-created to life,' though he makes nature add that it does not know the character of his second nativity. These views make abundantly clear the difference between the unregenerate and regenerate man, between the natural man and the Christian.[3]

Within the accepted medieval doctrinal framework, then, both the Christian and the Church stood apart from natural evolution, growth, expansion, in fact, from the laws of nature, and were governed by divine norms of living. The Church, so it was held, was a body specifically instituted by divinity which differed from all other societies in two basic respects. First, it did not follow the natural rules which governed tribes,

2 See Chrysostom (above, p. 8, n. 24), p. 139: 'The old man is broken to pieces and a new man has been produced.' Further, St Augustine, *Sermo* 121, in *PL* 38.679f.; *id.*, *Expositio in Ep. ad Romanos*, edition in *CSEL* 84.174, lines 12f. ('renovatio in baptismo est'); also his *De baptismo*, edition in *CSEL* 51.194 and 255f.; *De Genesi ad litteram*, 6.26, edition in *CSEL* 28.197f.: here he says that 'renovabimur etiam in carne'. There are many more Augustinian statements to the same effect, some of them in Gratian's *Decretum, De consecratione*, Dist. 4.1ff. ('renascitur homo ex aqua . . .'). Numerous other writers expressed themselves on these points. Cf., for example, Ambrosiaster (late fourth century), in *CSEL* 82.236 (a new being emerges who was previously merely a man: 'homo tantum'); *ibid.*, p. 56 (baptismal rebirth signifies flight from the old and is a 'renovatio'); *ibid.*, p. 104 (the Christian gives up 'the old man' and 'walks a new way of life'). See further Hilary of Poitiers (also fourth century), in *CSEL* 65.214: the Christian's life is regulated by new laws ('novis legibus'). See also the fifth-century *Quaestiones veteris et novi testamenti*, cap. 113, edition in *CSEL* 50.298: the reborn man enters a 'novellus populus', and in cap. 127, p. 408, considers the second birth to be a rebirth which is an inauguration. Cf. further Gaudentius, edition in *CSEL* 68.64, 73d, or in the sixth century Arator, who was widely read in the Middle Ages, edition in *CSEL* 72.142, lines 1147f. But there are dozens of others who dealt with the problem in the same way.
3 Alanus ab Insulis, *Liber de planctu naturae*, in *PL* 210.431ff., at 445D: 'Homo mea actione *nascitur*, Dei auctoritate *renascitur* . . . per me enim homo *procreatur* ad mortem, per ipsum *recreatur* ad vitam . . . ego Natura huius (secundae) nativitatis ignoro naturam.' This is also edited by T. Wright in *Rolls Series* (1872) pp. 429ff., at 455; ET by D. M. Moffat (New York, 1908), p. 30.

nations, ethnic groupings, and the like: it was a-natural. Secondly, its government was fixed at the very act of its institution. These two features remained undisputed throughout the Middle Ages, and partly also beyond. By entering this body, the Christian also changed his status: he became subjected to the norms which governed the Church. And in the making of these norms he had no share, because they were said to be of divine provenance.

A natural society, such as a tribe, governs itself and is guided by the unsophisticated insight, the natural judgment and assessment of the members uncontaminated as they are by any pre-existing programme, blueprint or doctrine. The path of a natural society is determined by the wants and needs of its members as assessed by them themselves. It is they who fix the aim of the society and the means to achieve it. This was precisely the grievance of early Christian writers, such as Lactantius, who blamed Homer for writing on human rather than on divine things.[4] St Augustine, whose views decisively shaped the medieval outlook, launched his attack on the ancient pagan philosophers because they held that the supreme good could be found in this life and in the objects of nature and in human virtue: 'with marvellous shallowness' (*mira vanitate*) had the ancient philosophers sought to find blessedness in this life and had 'fabricated on utterly fraudulent felicity', whereas Christians realized that *their* end could only be in a future life.[5] A divinely founded society, such as the Church, had features entirely different from natural societies. The Church was conceived as the ecclesiological manifestation of Christianity itself. As such its path was determined by divinity which also fixed the aim of its members – eventual salvation and eternal life. It had a well-formulated programme and a well-articulated set of norms. All Christians aimed at was heavenly bliss, whatever their station in life might have been. Whereas a natural society made its own programme and laid down its end and the means to achieve it, these varying greatly according to regions, geographical location, historical pre-conditions, cultural and educational standards, the end of the ecclesiological unit was predetermined by, and anchored in, divinity.

This was the principle of unipolarity – the pursuit of one aim or the orientation towards one pole – which was a hallmark of medieval ecclesiological thinking and partly also of its translation onto the plane of reality. The attainment of this one end was guaranteed – so it was held – by the harmony that existed between the ecclesiological unit and its government (Matt. 16: 18f.). Since the Church was merely the external embodiment of

---

4 Lactantius, *Divinae institutiones*, 1.5, 8, edition in *CSEL* 19.14, lines 16ff. (=ET in *FC* 49(1964), 27.)

5 Augustine, *De civitate Dei*, 19.4, where he critically views the four cardinal virtues as true virtues, because 'genuine virtues are possible only when men believe in God'.

the Christian religion, its direction could lie only in the hands of those who knew the tenets, maxims, and canons of Christianity. In parenthesis it may be remarked that modern societies operate, for understandable reasons, on exactly the same principle: a communist society cannot be directed by liberal or capitalist governors, and vice-versa. Christianity was not a natural or intuitive matter, but a highly sophisticated, thematic, rationally conceived system. Hence the government of this ecclesiological manifestation of Christianity could be in the hands of those only who had special knowledge (this was a Platonic bequest). The ordinary lay Christian was never credited with this knowledge, hence could not claim to take part in the government of the Church or in creating its law. The division of the Church into laity and clergy reflected this clearly: and within the latter there was hierarchical ordering which mirrored knowledge and hence authority. St Augustine expressed all this very clearly when he claimed that what was necessary for the attainment of the ultimate end was not so much reason as *auctoritas*, and that it was the ecclesiastical officers who pointed the way towards the achievement of the ultimate aim.[6] And sacraments could be administered solely by those who were ordained. Since only through the sacraments salvation could be attained, the role of the ecclesiastical officers as mediators of the means of salvation suggested itself.

The unipolarity standpoint explains why the pursuit of 'worldy' or 'human' ends was considered objectionable from the strictly Christian angle in the European Middle Ages. Life on this earth was not an end in itself, but merely preparatory to that life which in Augustine's terminology was 'felicity in that other world'. Earthly life was a *vita transitoria*, a mere transitory phase in man's existence to which no value of its own could be attributed – hence the proliferation of medieval tracts entitled 'On the contempt of the world' (*De contemptu mundi*), or 'On the misery of the human condition', or 'On the worldly lust and desires', and the like, topics, indeed, clearly suggested by Augustine who in no uncertain manner had spelt out the miseries and unhappiness of this human life.[7]

Because natural features played no role within the ecclesiological unit, its principles, tenets and aims could indeed be, as they were, pronounced universal. Regionalism, provincialism, tribalism, and all the numerous varieties of social naturalness, were of no consequence. There was but one society – the universal ecclesiological society that programmatically set aside biological, ethnic, linguistic and geographical peculiarities and

---

6   Cf. Augustine, *De vera religione*, edition in *CSEL* 77.2, pp. 9ff.: in regard to the ultimate end everyone depends on the ecclesiastical officers of the Church; *id., De moribus ecclesiae*, in *PL* 32.1311 (=ET in *FC*, 56(1966), 5.)

7   Cf. Rom. 12:2: 'Be not in *con*formity with this world, but be *trans*formed by re-casting your mind.' See also Augustine, *De civitate Dei*, 19.4; 22.22.

reduced them to an inferior role. As St Augustine said, Christian norms were fixed ecclesiastically for every age, every sex, every sort and condition of man. This principle of universality was evidently also reflected in the individual Christian. His own personal peculiarities, his own 'intellectual' physiognomy, were relegated to the background: what mattered (according to medieval doctrine) was his conformity to the law, the norm, the rule which – and this is the essential point – was given to him, and not made by him.

It is consequently evident that unipolarity and universality involved the wholeness point of view. Since there was only one goal for the Christian – salvation – everything had to be subordinated to this one aim: the end determined the means which clearly meant that only one norm – the Christian – could be determinative in society. Within the Christian setting, the Christian norm alone was autonomous and engulfed all other norms: there could be no distinction between political, religious, moral, social and other sets of rules each following its own programme and standards. It was the whole in every respect that mattered. It was the totality of the Christian claim that put the stamp on the incorporated 'new man'. Christianity embraced the whole of the Christian, and that related to his life from the cradle to the grave in the literal meaning of the term. This fundamental theme was expressed forcefully and unequivocally by St Paul, according to whom 'everything' was to be done by reference to Christ:[8] hence private and public, social and individual life, every category of thought and action was wholly absorbed by, and subsumed under, the norms set by Christ and made known through the Scripture as interpreted and explained by those qualified to do so. This totality principle[9] was as characteristic as the principle of unipolarity and universality. There was no splitting up or atomizing the various human activities into moral, religious, political, etc., categories.[10] The whole counted, and nothing but the whole as an integrated entity, as, indeed, St Paul himself had said as plainly as possible. This totality point of view was also sometimes expressed by *unitas*, with which the relevant medieval literature was replete. Unity of government, of life and the purpose of life – from the fourth to the fourteenth centuries these were held the immovable tenets obtaining in a Christian society. What Chrysostom and Augustine expressed at the turn of the fourth and fifth centuries, was said a thousand years later in different terms but with exactly the same meaning: the Christian religion was one.[11]

8   1 Cor. 10:31; Col. 3:17. Chrysostom, *Homiliae XII in Ep. ad Col.*, in *PGr* 62. 364, cap. 3: 'Quodcumque facitis in verbo aut corpore, *omnia* facite in nomine Domini.'
9   Priestly and monastic celibacy may have been an offshoot of the totality principle: total dedication to the service of God was demanded from priests and monks.
10 On the principle of indivisibility (or totality) cf. *PGP* pp. 33f.; *LP* pp. 12, 13, 39, 41ff.
11 See the quotation in *LP*, p. 12, n. 1.

The view of earthly life as merely a transitory stage[12] towards the eventual goal of the Christian was only a paraphrase of St John: 'Love not the world nor the things that are in the world'.[13] The Christian was only a wayfarer on his journey to heaven: he was a *viator*, as it was said from the eighth century onwards. In a word, unipolarity, universality and totality were the pillars upon which the ecclesiological unit rested. Admission to this unit was through the gate of baptism (the *ianua* or *initium*, as it was commonly called following the lead given by Pseudo-Denys[14]). Baptism was historically and liturgically as well as legally and socially a renaissance which had the most profound and long-lasting repercussion within the European orbit.

II

Little historical imagination is necessary to visualize the far-reaching individual and collective effects of baptismal rebirth. It was especially the strict adherence to, and application of, the triad of unipolarity, universality and totality which was bound to affect any organized society. The ecclesiological development came to full fruition in the Frankish age when governments themselves, notably that of Charlemagne, designedly began the transformation which effected a rebirth or renaissance of their society. And this society was to all intents and purposes Western Europe, which as a unit began its historical career in the late eighth century. It was a predominantly ecclesiological entity and developed therefore within an ecclesiological context. Here the triad became operational. Seen from another angle, one could speak of this renaissance also as a Romanization of Western Europe, because (for reasons irrelevant in this context) the

---

12 See the statement made in the fourteenth century, cited in *PGP*, p. 316.

13 1 John 2:15. Mundane things, Gregory the Great in the late sixth century said, were to be used only for the sake of achieving salvation, see his *Homilia*, 2.36, in *PL* 76.1272. This kind of sentiment was expressed right down to the fifteenth century, if not beyond. For the twelfth century cf., for example, John of Salisbury, who said that 'temporal things were the gift of God and their use was conceded in order to achieve eternal life' (*Policraticus*, 8.17). For the identity of 'worldly' and 'human' matters cf. Augustine's *Sermo*, 12.2, edition in *CC* 41(1961), 166, lines 53–8, and also his *Sermo*, 121.1, in *PL* 38.679.

14 See Pseudo-Denys, *De ecclesiastica hierarchia*, cap. 2, in *PGr* 3.392. John Scotus Eriugena's translation has: *principium* (beginning) and *principalissima processio*, in *PL* 122.1074, and *Dionysiaca*, ed. cit. p. 8, n. 24, p. 1106. For details on John see J. Szövérffy, *Weltliche Dichtungen des lateinischen Mittelalters*, I (Berlin, 1970), 653ff., and now also F. Brunhölzl, *Geschichte der lateinischen Literatur des Mittelalters* I (Munich, 1975), 469ff. and 569. In the high M.A. John Scotus was generally followed, cf. William of Auxerre, *Summa aurea* (edition Paris, 1510, reprinted Frankfurt, 1964), IV, 'De baptismo Christi', fol. 250rb; or Peter of Tarentaise, *In libros sententiarum commentaria* (Toulouse, 1651, reprinted Ridgewood, N.J., 1964), IV, 2.1, ad 7, p. 31.

Roman Church had provided most of the ideological armoury for the transformation of a more or less natural society into a 'regenerated' body. One should not forget that the peoples of the vast territory stretching from the Pyrenees in the west to the Elbe in the east and the Frisians in the north had been conquered in many military campaigns and were now to be raised from their natural unregenerated condition into a regenerated status. A basic feature of this renaissance was that the initiative, the stimulus as well as the impetus, came from governmental quarters, that is, from the rulers themselves: they acted entirely in consonance with the underlying principles of the ecclesiological-descending theme of government. This was a renaissance on perhaps the largest scale conceivable: it was the transfer of the idea of baptismal rebirth from the individual to a whole society. This social renaissance involved a good deal of amalgamation and fusion of Germanic, Christian and Roman elements, a fusion that was henceforth to give medieval Europe its particular complexion.[15]

This social renaissance, modelled as it was on the individual's baptismal rebirth, resulted in the emergence of an ecclesiological unit that was held together solely by faith and in which the triad of ecclesiological principles was signally effective. This unit was not a conglomeration of tribes or ethnic groupings somehow held together by natural bonds of kinship or blood. Just as in the individual rebirth baptismal waters had figuratively washed away man's naturalness, in the same way the collective or social renaissance welded heterogeneous peoples together by the unity of faith. In the individual as well as in the social renaissance there was a carefully worked out programme, a sophisticated blueprint, that is, a social order which effortlessly absorbed Germanic-pagan features into its system and 'baptized' them. As a result of this absorption naturally evolved customs, habits, experiences, traditions, evaluations, judgements, were to yield to the authority of doctrine and dogma. The law was no longer made by un-regenerated men but was given to regenerated man by those who claimed to have a special function because they possessed the appropriate qualifications.

In a literal sense, this social renaissance involved fundamental changes in the structure of society, of its government, in the relations of the 'subjects' to the government, and in their outlook and orientation. The new society had to be directed according to the anxious germane to its underlying cosmology and norms which were handed to mankind by those who claimed to have special links with divinity. A glance at, say, the Frankish scene in the mid-eighth and in the mid-ninth centuries shows even the most adamant sceptic what profound changes society and its

15 For details cf. *CR* pp. 1–70.

government and its public officers had undergone. The layman as such had no special qualification to take a part in the government or in the creation of law that in any way affected the fabric of this essentially ecclesiological unit. For the purpose of law was to fashion life on this earth as a stage preparatory to the eternal goal: how was the layman to know what was conducive to this end? In every material respect he was subject to superior authority.

Within the ecclesiological unit no member had an inborn right to anything, this being perhaps the most extensive application of the idea of divine grace, or as St Paul had it: What I am, I am by the grace of God. The concept of grace in itself was a denial of any autonomous right: the whole existence of man was held to be a favour granted by God. Every prayer in one way or another clearly and convincingly conveyed this idea. If one wishes to understand the principles upon which this ecclesiological unit functioned from the ninth century onwards, one ought to keep this basic consideration in mind. And once this idea of grace is translated into law, the whole complexion of society and above all its hierarchical structure with its adjuncts of superiority and inferiority and the consequential duty of obedience becomes accessible to better understanding.

Here is the point concerning the application of the idea of rebirth to rulership itself. In a quite especial sense divinity had shown its favour towards, and bestowed its grace upon, the ruler: for he alone was what he was by the grace of God, and he also acknowledged this by the very title he adopted from the late eighth century onwards: *Rex Dei gratia*. Conversely he was not king as a result of any popular election or expression of popular will. Formally he was a creature of divinity and no longer responsible to the people or to the nobility. He formed an estate of his own (or what Maitland once most felicitously called a corporation sole), but it was not assuredly sufficient for the ruler to assert that he had received divine grace. This had to be visibly proved, hence the emergence of the unction which was performed by the higher ecclesiastics, who considered the anointing of the king a sacrament, and sacraments could be conferred only by the appropriate ecclesiastical officers. The bishops in a word had sandwiched themselves between divinity and the king by mediating the divine favour to him in the shape of chrism or other oil which proved that divine grace had in actual fact entered the body of the king.

Unction was modelled on the Old Testament, and it was here that the anointed king was shown to have changed his whole being and essence. This was a veritable rebirth. The relevant texts in fact concretely depicted the rebirth of the anointed king. This transformation of the king had far-reaching repercussions. Not only was he shown to have been distinguished by divinity, but his status was also hallowed in so far as he was now 'the

Lord's anointed' (the *christus Domini*), virtually inaccessible to ordinary mortals. He was inviolable and an offence committed against him was literally speaking *high* treason.

The ecclesiological character of the kingdom in actual fact demanded this divinely sanctioned headship. The king could now distribute favours downwards, so that the descending theme of government and law became reality. Obviously, the gulf between him and his subjects was too conspicuous to be overlooked, this naturally resulting in alienation. Indeed, he sat literally speaking as an isolated figure 'high' on the throne. Yet unction was one of the gateways through which the ecclesiastics, to wit, the bishops, advanced their position: it gave them a very powerful handle in so far as they could, as indeed they did, make the ruler an 'ecclesiastical person', but thereby the gulf between the king and his subjects, notably the barons, widened: it was as if the king had joined the ranks of clergy, and had left the lay princes and the laity out on a limb. On the other hand, the role of the bishops changed: they now assumed a determinative instead of a consultative role since, after all, it was not only they who had conferred divine grace on the king, but also they who knew best what was, and what was not, Christian and what should be legislated about by the king. It was indeed their monopoly of education and scholarship which gave them this enormous advantage in regard to knowledge. In a word, this governmental set-up, as evidenced from the ninth century onwards, was theocratic in character and ecclesiological in substance. The allocation of any constitutive role to the lay princes or the people at large would have contradicted the very essence of this ecclesiological unit. For since it was divinity that had entrusted the kingdom (or the people) to the ruler, precisely because he was viewed as the tutor of the kingdom and the kingdom as a ward or minor under age, how should a minor be credited with the faculty of 'electing' his own tutor?[16] Hence, juristically there was no means of calling 'the Lord's anointed' to account.

Indeed, in an ecclesiological society ordinary humanity was not only not qualified to play a part in the creation of the ruler: it could not play a part in the creation of law either, because its lack of the appropriate qualifications precluded it from occupying positions of authority. And the required qualifications were relative, that is, related to the ecclesiological principles. Above all law reflects the bases, the assumptions, the aspirations, the articulate and inarticulate maxims of a society, its programme and ethos: law distils broad ideological presuppositions into crisp language, and therefore of necessity involves knowledge and mastery of society's cosmological foundations. And within this ecclesiological unit it was the

---

16 For this tutorial function of kingship and the 'minority' of the kingdom, see *CR* pp. 172ff. and *CL*, ch. VIII.

professionals, the ecclesiastics, who claimed this specific knowledge and laid down the principles which should be enshrined in the law to be given by the rulers. After all, this society was entrusted to the ruler's care by divinity and hence had to be provided with laws that reflected the divine plan and corresponded to it. Leaving ideological considerations apart, the exclusion of the populace from decision making clearly had historical as well as educational reasons: in view of paucity of communications and widespread illiteracy, it would have been impossible to expect adequate knowledge among large segments of the populace. In short, once the social renaissance was set on course by government the dominant role of the (educated) clergy becomes easily explicable.

The vital and indispensable part played by government in implementing this renaissance in an ecclesiological sense has not yet been fully acknowledged. In the circumstances of the late eighth and ninth centuries only the government was capable of initiating this process. It is indeed at this juncture that the importance of the means by which this social renaissance was put into practice comes into full view. One of the chief instruments by which Christian cosmology was to be translated into reality was the law issued by the rulers themselves. Hence the unparalleled spate of legislation during the Carolingian period between the late eighth and the late ninth centuries. It was the 'kings by the grace of God' who directed their subjects in consonance with ecclesiological principles. The law was thoroughly suffused with the very essence of religious doctrines and ecclesiological provenance. The law breathed the spirit of the ecclesiastics who had evidently acted as royal advisers. Not until our own age had Europe experienced the concrete application of an ideology by means of the law in so unmistakable a manner as in the period during and after the Carolingian renaissance. Law concerned the 'right living' in society, and this requirement of the function of the law cannot be spelt out in any absolute sense: it relates to the character of society. Here what was called the *norma recte vivendi* (a term coined by Isidore of Seville in the early seventh century) could be determined only by reference to Christian cosmology, and hence the law to be issued differed materially from that applicable in an unregenerated, natural society. The very quantity, quality, contents and character of the law in the ninth century (as well as afterwards) shows what changes society had undergone within two generations.

Further incontrovertible proof of this transformation of society is furnished by the very active part played by the ecclesiastical assemblies, convoked as they were from the late eighth century onwards by the rulers themselves for the purpose of giving religious, disciplinary and educational guidelines to the people. In these synods the basic ingredients of a Christian law were discussed at length, formulated and enacted in the synodal decrees which constituted a further embodiment of the 'norm of right living' in the new society. And a great many of these decrees – in fact the socially important ones – were re-issued as capitularies by the kings themselves. The idea of unification, not to mention universality, was potently fostered in this legislation, because it did not discriminate between different regions and provinces. The obliteration of regional features in conjunction with the principle of unipolarity and totality was a hallmark of this legislation, in which, for evident reasons, the laity could not play any part.

A marked feature which in the present context deserves special attention concerns the consultation of ancient Christian literature by those whose duty (and right) it was to govern and legislate in an ecclesiological sense. Since on the one hand the Christian religion was not a 'natural', intuitive religion, but a highly sophisticated system, and on the other hand the law was merely the distillation of Christian cosmology, the necessity was soon felt to find out what Christian doctrine had propounded, what the Cyprians, the Tertullians, the Ambroses, Jeromes, Augustines, and so on, had had to say on precisely the points which required close study, quite apart from the statements made by the papacy and the relevant decrees issued by the great ecumenical councils of Christian antiquity. In a word, the consultation of literature in the widest possible meaning grew out of the need to obtain authoritative guidance, to find out what the great and renowned teachers and writers and ecclesiastics and popes had to say on the items to be the subject of legislation, items, that is, which were essential for the building of the 'new', 'regenerated' society. It was the search for the right norm which explains this consultation – and it was to be the same feature which we shall meet once more in the later renaissance when another set of authors was consulted for exactly the same purpose, though with a different slant and emphasis. Hence the rapidly increasing number of manuscripts of patristic writers from the ninth century onwards, which persuasively testifies to the increasing demand for them. For it was in the ancient Christian writers that the fundamental expositions of the Bible were to be found: it was from them that the Carolingians in the most literal sense wished to learn for their own purposes. And this learning process concerned such concrete governmental matters as the standing of the secular ruler in a Christian society, the principle of division of labour, the limits of obedience to superior orders, and dozens of related items. These were purely doctrines in the ancient writers and popes and councils, but the men of the high Middle Ages moulded them into the crisp language of the law. The basic point to bear in mind is that the consultation of books, sermons, letters, conciliar decrees, in short this rapidly escalating search for early Christian literature and its eager study, was a means to an end, and certainly not an end in itself.

A necessary by-product of this search and study of old authors was the spread of education to an extent not hitherto experienced in Western Europe. Admittedly, this education was overwhelmingly vocational – the idea of a liberal education did not exist – but it was on a far larger scale than it had been a generation earlier, say, in the middle of the eighth century. The proliferation of manuscripts – to count only the surviving copies – shows what great demand there must have been for them. For instance, in the early years of the ninth century, the archbishop of Lyons, Leidrad, commissioned copies of numerous volumes; similarly the archbishop of Salzburg ordered more than 150 volumes.[17] Further, this educational process included also pagan ancient writers, such as Virgil, Cicero, Suetonius, Seneca, though here it was not the substance but the manner of writing and linguistic expression which attracted attention.[18] For one could hardly expect that the way of living portrayed by pagan, 'unregenerated' authors could serve as a model from which an ecclesiological society could learn useful lessons. The overall result of this consultation of ancient authors was the full-scale Latinization of the Western outlook: Romanization of the fallow Western soil was one of the permanent bequests of this consultative process. And hand in hand with it went the identification of *Romanitas* and *Christianitas* which began its triumphant career from the Carolingian age onwards.

One of the most potent instruments in this process of Romanization (i.e. Latinization) was the Vulgate, that is, the Latin translation of the Bible. At no time in European history had the Bible been copied so often as in the Carolingian period. The proliferation of Bible manuscripts in virtually all parts of Western Europe shows how busy the *scriptoria* (the scribes' departments) in the various establishments, mainly monastic, must have been. Here in the Bible the basic religious issues and axioms were found: it was the very text upon which Christian cosmology rested. Obviously, both baptismal and social rebirth demanded the availability of the basic text – and this was written in Latin. The divine word was accessible only in the Latin language: God had spoken and acted through the Latin medium. It is impossible to exaggerate the impact which the Vulgate made upon so many subsequent generations. This process of Bible production exactly coincided in time with the government's launching of its programme. Again, the Bible was not studied for its own sake, but as a means to an end: to discover what divinity had pronounced on this or that item, so as to mould the respective decree or law correspondingly.

In the present context there are two main results which are directly

17 See *MGH Epp.* IV, 542–4 (Leidrad to Charlemagne in 813); *MGH SS.* IX, 770, n. 54: Arn 'plus quam 150 volumina iussit hic scribi.' Arn died in 821.
18 See the perceptive observations by F. Brunhölzl, *op. cit.* (above, n. 14), p. 319.

linked with the instruments of the social renaissance in the ecclesiological sense and which warrant a few observations. First, a momentum, so to speak, was generated which resulted in the production of a certain kind of literature: the monographic literature was in a broad sense religious, but focused specifically on particular topics, such as government, rulership, duties of the king, the laity, and so on. This kind of literature began in the ninth century and reached its high water mark in the eleventh. The very genre of the now exuberantly produced *Specula regum* ('Guides for Kings') proves how keenly aware contemporaries were of the functions of the king in this 'regenerated' society. Indeed the social renaissance called for this sort of books, since rulership in an ecclesiological society was as little 'natural' or 'intuitive' as Christianity itself was: it had to be explained and set forth. That is why from the ninth century onwards the *Specula regum* became so plentiful – there was no need and no demand for guidebooks in a natural, 'unregenerated' society. These books were first-rate scholarly tracts with profuse citations from the ancient Christian authors (notably St Augustine), who were thereby launched on a career which gained an ever-increasing momentum, that has till this very day not spent itself.

Side by side with these monographic productions there were works that copied ancient, mainly anonymous, tracts, such as the *Call of All Nations*,[19] or even translated Greek texts into Latin, such as the works of Pseudo-Denys, whose influence on the ecclesiological setting cannot be exaggerated:[20] it was he who coined the term 'hierarchy' and set forth the hierarchical–descending theme in its classical form and purity. This was also the time when, in order to boost their value, works were foisted upon St Augustine or another ancient Christian authority. Even pagan authors were dressed up – not indeed with their proper names – in a Christian garb. Here at least a passing reference should be made to the emergence of a specific medieval poetry which reflected the ecclesiological spirit: while this poetry rejected the poetic forms of the past, it wholly adopted the ecclesiastical rhythm of the hymns, that is, the iambic verse or trochaic metre.[21] Literature in the widest sense was harnessed to the religious programme which itself was the basic concern to the renaissance of society. This literature was a means to an end. Its study was not an end in itself.

Secondly, in close proximity to the literary productions stood the *Florilegia* which were the precursors of the modern collections of sources:

19 The author of this work (mid fifth century) (*De vocatione omnium gentium*) was probably Prosper of Aquitaine. Edition in *PL* 51; ET by P. De Letter in *ACW* 14(1952). Cf. also *PG* pp. 76f.
20 For editions, see p. 8, n. 24.
21 M. Manitius, *Geschichte der lateinischen Literatur des Mittelalters* I (reprinted Munich, 1973), p. 255.

they contained snippets from the Fathers, chiefly for quick reference and for teaching purposes. And an essential feature of the social renaissance was the accelerated pace of so-called canonical collections of the law: these were the legal counterpart to the purely literary genre and had the same function – to serve as models for the kind of right living in a Christian society. These collections derived from a great variety of sources the 'canons', decrees and laws which appeared as patterns suitable to be emulated by a 'regenerated' society. Of course, royal capitularies too were collected, but it was above all the canon law that began to take shape principally in the form of Pseudo-Isidore (845–853) which was to set the ecclesiological seal upon society for a very long time to come. That the decrees in Pseudo-Isidore were largely forged is of lesser concern than that the influence they exercised on subsequent generations firmly imprinted an ecclesiological complexion upon a society characterized by the descending theme of government and the hierarchical ordering of all groups within society. The deeper significance of Pseudo-Isidore is however that it constituted the exact legal parallel to the *Specula regum*: it was *au fond* conceived as a guide book that 'mirrored' the 'proper' way of living in a fully regenerated society. For this reason it had 'recourse' to the ancient papal (and conciliar) decrees – no matter how many were forged or falsified – and it was these decrees of the 'ancients' which it was the purpose of the collection to make available to ninth century contemporaries. The consultation of the ancient 'records' produced the 'law' here 'recorded' in these hundreds of fatiguing pages: it was to indicate how the ancients had regulated matters and how contemporary society should adopt the law portrayed in the collection as a guide for regulating Christian life. A work such as this is unthinkable without the idea of a renaissance. It attempted to supply contemporaries with the ancient and proper 'canon' of right living: this indeed is what the compilers themselves announced as their object in the preface.[22]

All these products initiated and engendered by the social renaissance exhibited the characteristic ecclesiological triad of unipolarity of the Christian life, universality of its norms which disregarded tribal and regional developments, and the totality of the Christian norms which demanded the whole, and not merely a segment, of the Christian. It is hardly necessary to point out the educational, cultural and social benefits which this development brought forth and imparted to an intellectually fallow ground. Above all, law is at all times a great educator, no matter whether it is made by expressing consent or by merely receiving it from 'superior' authority: law was a social regulator and showed the norm of

---

22   Ed. P. Hinschius, *Decretales Pseudo-Isidorianae* (reprinted Aalen, 1956), p. 17. For an assessment cf. *PG* pp. 177f. and *LP* pp. 128–31.

right living in this 'regenerated', reborn society. The accent lies on the 'right living' for which no absolute rule exists: it depends on the contents of the cosmology upon which a society is built. This was supposed to rest on exclusively Christian premisses, and hence the consultation of ancient Christian writers as well as of the Bible and the law was a very real necessity if the 'right' patterns for living were to be discovered.

There can be no legitimate doubt that the ecclesiological rebirth of society and rulership, modelled as each was on baptismal rebirth, marked a great advance in all public and social respects. The idea of a social rebirth was a grandiose concept which unquestionably was chiefly responsible for the birth of Latin Europe – no longer a mere geographical name, but an ideological entity with its own physiognomy that came into being in the ninth century. It was this idea of renaissance which also provided the bridge between the sophisticated late Roman–ecclesiastical thought patterns and the raw Germanic world.

It cannot be stressed strongly enough that the initiative in the direction of this social renaissance came from the rulers themselves. They alone were responsible: they embraced this idea spontaneously and voluntarily. But upon closer analysis one can speak here in more than one respect of a stunted rebirth, that is, of one that was not complete, because in the event the original, natural, unregenerate elements had not been subdued to the extent expected. The unregenerate condition was by no means eradicated: the regeneration or rebirth was only partially achieved. There emerged numerous points of friction that gave rise to tensions, because of the irreconcilability of basic standpoints. By wholeheartedly embracing the ecclesiological theme of rebirth, the king had to all intents and purposes delivered himself into the hands of those who 'knew the canon' of right living, those, in a word, who had the adequate knowledge of what was, and what was not, Christian. The very adoption of divine grace as the corner stone of rulership brought the ecclesiastics into the sphere of action, because from time immemorial they had claimed that matters of grace were their own particular province.

The inevitable conclusion was that the ecclesiological rebirth and the ecclesiastics were interlocked and indissolubly linked. The more effective the rebirth appeared to be, the more the ecclesiastics were able to point to its imperfections, and their reasoning was, on their own ecclesiological premisses, perfectly valid. That the rebirth was stunted, that it was imperfect, was easily demonstrable by reference to the efficacy of natural, unregenerate forces. Just to take one or two instances: there was the proprietary church system which, resting as it did on ownership of land, could hardly be fitted into an ecclesiological framework. How and why should mere ownership of a piece of land confer the right to appoint, control and judge ecclesiastical officers, the men whose prime *raison d'être* was the administration of divine grace? The king averred that the grace of God was the source of his rulership – yet the conferment of grace on the ruler lay entirely in the hands of the ecclesiastics who (beginning with Hincmar) from the ninth down to the eleventh century expressed in the royal inauguration rites the purely ministerial function of the king. He was 'elected' formally by the ecclesiastics[25] and received the divine grace through the pouring of chrism on his head. No autonomy could be attached to this kind of rulership, even leaving aside all the coronation promises and the oath.

Indeed, the very idea of rebirth generated problems of its own, derived as they were from the core of all rebirth, which concerned regeneration, here the neutralization of natural forces by divine grace. Or, as it has also been expressed, the charisma of blood was replaced by the charisma of grace. To be sure this was a theological problem which, in the present context, was transposed to the realm of society and government where it gave rise to numerous frictions and tensions, precisely because the rebirth was stunted or imperfect, because of the incomplete elimination of nature by grace, because of the unregenerate natural remnants which had not, as postulated, lost their force.[24] Evidently, only the alert contemporary in the eleventh and twelfth centuries was capable of grasping the full effects of this severe dilemma posed by the attempt at full implementation of the ecclesiological rebirth. And it was the alert contemporary who was to point the way out of this excruciatingly difficult situation by the operation of another rebirth which in the event constituted a partial reversal of the social and regal rebirths derived as they were from the baptismal model. This intellectually and historically important restorative process began with rulership and ended with the individual – exactly the reverse of the first renaissance process which began with the individual's baptism and proceeded to society and rulership. The correct understanding of this restorative process explains why and how there was a renaissance humanism at all. This humanist renaissance was contingent upon the ecclesiological configuration in the Middle Ages. Without it, the European phenomenon of a renaissance humanism would have been inexplicable.

---

23   Cf. *CR* pp. 81ff. and *PGP* pp. 145ff.
24   As indeed St Paul envisaged: 1 Cor. 5:7.

II

The Secularization of Government

Although government and society were complementary in the high Middle Ages, it was the government that set its seal upon society and directed its path. The government was – so the argument ran – set above the people or kingdom by divinity itself: eventually the people or kingdom were the property of God and were only temporarily committed to a particular ruler who had the duty to take care of the people's interests by acting as its tutor. Both origin and purpose of royal government made the king the sole organ who could take the initiative and effect any change in the structure of the kingdom or in its direction. An excellent example is the Carolingian renaissance by which a whole society was transformed into 'the people of God' and structured ecclesiologically. This renaissance was 'directed from above' quite in keeping with the descending theme of government. Yet, there was a paradox: the consistent application of the theocratic–ecclesiological principles harboured grave dangers for the rulers themselves, because the structure of their rulership manifested flaws that could hardly be squared with the fundamental ecclesiological premises which they professedly upheld.

It is undubitably true that, stripped of all paraphernalia, the Investiture Contest in the second half of the eleventh century concerned *au fond* the standing of the king in Christian society. It would be an unwarranted over-simplification to say that the king epitomized the laity, just as it would be only partly correct to say that the pope epitomized the clerical side – after all, quite a few of the bishops and archbishops were firm followers of the king and in conflict with the pope. That in the Investiture Conflict the German king was the prime target is easily explicable by the strong historically conditioned ties which his government had had with Italy since the mid-eighth century. No other European ruler was so intimately involved in peninsular affairs as the German king, although the issues of the Conflict were latent as well as patent in all Western kingdoms.

Paradoxically enough, the detachment from the people which the theocratic ruler had achieved by proclaiming that his power was the effluence of divine grace (and not of the popular will expressed in an election) was in the long run to prove a liability rather than an asset for him. That he formed an estate of his own which he did not, and could not, share with anyone else certainly was highly advantageous in some respects, but it could also become, as indeed it did, a most serious drawback, since he in his isolated exalted position was destined to face his foes alone. No doubt, the king stood outside and above the people which, because inarticulate and helpless, was entrusted to his care by God. The high status of the king was perhaps best expressed by his personal sovereignty: he was the 'King of the Saxons' or 'of the Franks', in other words personal ties between his 'Majestas' and the 'subjects' had been forged. Moreover, he sat on his throne high above the people to symbolize his superiority (sovereignty) having alone received the divine grace of rulership. He handed part of his grace on to his subjects, who thus enjoyed the king's grace, which they could also lose, thereby falling into royal disgrace. He enjoyed an unsurpassably great protection by being the Lord's anointed, because thereby the crime of *lèse majesté* was turned into a religious offence in that it concerned God's own protégé on earth.

On the other hand, this governmental structure had absorbed a great many strains of Germanic rulership which formed, so to speak, an amalgam with the religious–ecclesiological substance. This amalgam was not the result of any rational reflection derived from, or based on, any articulated doctrine, but had grown 'naturally', and had gradually evolved throughout the antecedent period. The belief was universal that Christian and Germanic elements were not only reconcilable, but had to all intents and purposes been harmoniously fused. Yet, as indicated, on closer analysis this governmental system and structure suffered from some grave inner contradictions, such as the already mentioned proprietary church system. It resulted in contradictions which were bound to give rise to serious questioning. Was it *right* – given the ecclesiological premises so loudly protested by the rulers themselves – that the king (or count or any other lay lord) should confer the ecclesiastical benefice as well as the office? Was, in other words, this proprietary church system, which had indeed become an essential structural element of rulership, reconcilable with fundamental Christian axioms? A contemporary chronicler writes 'so far no bishop is made by election, but only by the gift on the part of the king'.[1] Did the state of affairs illustrated in this quotation conform to a properly understood Christian ordering of society? Within the ecclesiological framework was it justifiable for a church to be 'inherited' by several

1 When the see of Liège became vacant after the death of Baldric in 1018, Henry II appointed Wolbod: 'Adhuc enim non electione, sed dono regis episcopus fiebat', according to Rupert of Deutz, *Chronicon s. Laurentii Leodiensis*, cap. 15, edition in *MGH SS* VIII, 267, lines 39f.

generations of the same family, as was the case with the so-called lower churches? That ecclesiastical offices could be freely bought and sold? Was there any justification for the king's granting to collegiate churches the 'privilege' to elect their superiors? To go a step further, was the assertion of the king's personal sovereignty a viable proposition within this fully-fledged ecclesiological framework? In a modern setting these inner contradictions might perhaps be compared to those of a communist society in which a free banking system, the stock exchange, foreign capital investments, and the like, operated, or to those of a capitalist society in which the acquisition of private property, the use of landed interests and the free disposal of the means of production were rendered nugatory by legislation.

It was all very well for a ruler in the late eleventh century to appeal to tradition, custom and the generally accepted practices which incontrovertibly prevailed everywhere,[2] but when once critically viewed and examined in the light of a mature Christian doctrinal background, tradition, practices and custom rapidly begin to melt away and vanish into thin air. They were to be seen as indefensible irrelevancies when measured by the yardstick of a rationally formulated and fixed programme. All rulers, and quite especially the most powerful of them, the German king, saw as their chief function the preservation of the *status quo* which had evolved out of custom. Indeed, before the late eleventh century there was no tract, no monograph, no writing which had rationally and constructively set forth a positive royal programme or had portrayed its structure, aims and details. When once old and deep-rooted tradition is exposed to a merciless, ruthless rationalism, the tradition and the institution supported by it disintegrate and eventually collapse. Customary practices can prosper, flourish and even display excellent and beneficial effects, so long as their inner contradictions are not shown up, and when this stage is reached, they cave in, because when tradition is confronted with rational argument, the former is bound to be the eventual loser. For it is no rational argument to maintain that a certain practice has always been followed. The question was not what had been done, or even why, or to what purpose, but rather whether in the light of a rationally conceived programme governmental measures conformed to the alleged Christian maxims as seen through the eyes of a rich and mature cosmology set forth in numerous tracts, manifestos, letters, decrees, and so on.

Indeed, this theocratic ruler was something of an amphibious creature – half cleric, half lay – and in governmental practice these were incompletely fused. That the natural Germanic unregenerated side was absorbed by, or

2   In parenthesis it may be pointed out that there is even an isolated papal reference to, though by no means an explicit endorsement of, the 'ancient custom' (*prisca consuetudo*) according to which the king ordered the consecration of the bishop appointed by him: John X in March 921, in *PL* 132.806f.

completely integrated into, the ecclesiological regenerated counterpart, is an unwarranted assumption. The government of the Salians in the earlier part of the eleventh century clearly showed the inner contradictions in practice. The measures taken by Henry III at Sutri in December 1046 manifested in concentrated form the workings of this governmental system. He deposed two popes, sent a third into exile, and appointed a new pope. He transferred bishops to Rome to have them made popes. All this, and much besides, was entirely in conformity with traditional practice.[3] And the more this system was practised, the more obtrusive the just-mentioned questions became. The crux of these questions was whether the king – or emperor – possessed the necessary qualifications for the control of a Christian society, which in actual fact meant the control of the high ecclesiastical officers, such as bishops, metropolitans and popes. Here indeed the dilemma facing any medieval king was most serious: no king in the eleventh century could govern his kingdom (which was nothing but a part of a universal ecclesiological unit) without the active participation of the higher clergy, notably the bishops in his kingdom.

The king's royal rebirth on the occasion of his receiving unction (and thereby the title-deed of his government by the grace of God) was only apt to bring the tension and inner contradictions of the theocratic king into a clearer relief. His royal rebirth was modelled on the individual's baptismal rebirth. Nature was here represented by the Germanic-natural mode of governing, and grace by his 'bearing the name and office of Christ', by his becoming 'the type of Christ', by his assuming the role of the *Athleta Christi*. Of all the mortals in his kingdom he was distinguished by divinity who had made him 'a co-regent of Christ'.[4] There could never be any doubt about the very real regeneration or rebirth of the king – the prayer texts and the formulae make this abundantly clear. Yet, there was not much evidence that this royal rebirth had in practice worked as it was intended to. The king was neither the one nor the other – no longer a mere natural governor who took governmental measures as his natural insight and assessment of a situation prompted, nor yet a full co-regent or athlete of Christ, as the coronation rituals had proclaimed.

Gregory VII never charged Henry IV with an aberration from faith or any deviation from Christian principles, but based his measures against him squarely on his violation of his duties as a Christian king. Gregory mercilessly exposed the contradictions of the kind of rulership represented by Henry who himself unwittingly and in no unmistakable manner strengthened his opponent's case by exclaiming: 'Me, the Lord's anointed,

---

3 Cf. *SHP* pp. 127ff.
4 These are the expressions as they occur in all medieval coronation rituals. They were composed in the ninth century and were essentially identical in structure and tenor throughout the Western kingdoms.

you have dared to touch.' Precisely – he was the Lord's anointed, but only through the mediation of the appropriate ecclesiastical officers, who anointed him and thus conferred divine grace on him, for a very specifically defined purpose (defined in the coronation orders), to govern the kingdom entrusted by God to him in the manner of a co-regent of Christ and of an *Athleta Christi*. It was this action which made the king what he was: a 'King by the grace of God'. By virtue of his having under-gone his regnal rebirth – so that as the source, the Old Testament, had it he became another man[5] – the king had clearly accepted the obligation contingent upon this status, that is the acceptance of the canonical rulings as to what was, and what was not, Christian in a Christian society.[6] In a word, he was not autonomous in his governorship. All this was – it hardly needs further pointing out – implicit in the very posture which the kings since the ninth century had freely assumed.

What was furthermore implicit was the isolation and alienation of the reborn king from the lay princes. There were actually far stronger ties between him and the ecclesiastical princes, for without them it was, as indicated, impossible to carry on with governmental business: the king knew them and they knew him and his plans. They were either his close relatives or had been members of his chancery. To lose control over them – the only literate and educated section in the kingdom – would have been tantamount to a modern government's losing control over its army or its public revenue. The acceptance of the Gregorian challenge was a govern-mental necessity and Henry's reported statement that he did not know why the pope so fiercely attacked him, since he did nothing but what his forbears had done (in which assertion he was perfectly correct), only gave Gregory a further handle against the king, for the Lord had not said that He was custom or tradition, but the truth. For, from the papacy's stand-point, tradition and truth certainly were not in harmony. Yet no contem-porary ruler had any other defence than recourse to tradition and custom, notoriously weak bases when confronted with closely argued, mature doctrinal systems.

What is of special interest in the present context is that the papacy invoked the law as the means to drive home its attack. The law invoked by the ecclesiastical side was law based on a sophisticated exposition of the Bible by scholars in the preceding centuries, beginning with Cyprian and Tertullian, above all the writings provided by Jerome, Ambrose, Augustine and the numerous decrees and statements of popes, councils and so on,

5 See, for instance, 1 Kgs. 10:6 and 9, 10, 11, 14; 2 Kgs. 7:14, etc. For details cf. *CR* pp. 71ff.

6 In sharply accentuated form this is what Gregory VII meant by his statement that the lowest exorcist was superior to any emperor: *Reg.* VIII. 21 (ed. E. Caspar, reprinted 1955, p. 555). For details see *PG* pp. 268ff., 344ff.

down to the late eleventh century. Against this highly rationalized system the royal side had nothing to set except the law based on unreflective practices and on tradition. Above all, the royal law did not mirror any cosmology or ideology, but was conditioned by time and space. On the other hand, there was no ecclesiastical law which did not reflect the characteristic features of unipolarity, universality and totality. That this law was considered the 'right law' for a Christian society, went without saying: ever since Isidore of Seville coined the phrase, the ecclesiastical law had always been viewed as the 'norm of right living' (*norma recte vivendi*) in a Christian society: it was called canon law. And herein lay its strength and the weakness of the royal law that had no such distinguished ancestry and rested upon mere custom, a somewhat mundane base in comparison with the 'celestial' origins of the canon law.

Once exposed, the weakness of the royal law revealed itself quite dramatically, because at the time there could hardly be a reply to such questions as whether custom and tradition, longevity and practice could turn a wrong into a right. However ancient a custom was, this in itself did not mean that it was also right. Evidently, since Christianity itself was not a natural religion, its precepts, maxims and principles could only be determined by a process of rational argumentation and intellectualized reasoning. The fixation of norms applicable to a Christian society therefore presupposed specific knowledge of the maxims underlying Christianity. In this appeal to the 'right law' lies the profound significance of the Investiture Contest. The supreme Christian authority, the papacy, had declared that in a Christian context the traditional royal law was a travesty of the law. Ancient standing and customary practices could not turn illegality into legality. It can readily be seen that this choice of means by the papacy – the law – was indeed a frontal attack on the institution of all rulership in any shape or form, because in matters affecting the essential fabric of society, here its Christian matrix, the ruler was not free to govern as he pleased: he lacked the essential ingredient of all rulership – autonomy. He lacked sharp contours and profile. Above all he lacked the means to parry the attack launched by the papacy – and that was the historic meaning of Canossa. Canossa showed the utter brittleness of the traditional theocratic rulership in the face of a determined, ruthless and well-aimed assault by the papacy on the most vulnerable part of the contemporary royal system – the absence of a body of law that was independent of any Roman–ecclesiastical parentage. What the recent development had amply demonstrated was that the theocratic ruler had, so to speak, become the victim of the very ideology which he had of his own accord been advocating ever since the ninth century. The ruler was caught, as it were, in the network of the system which he and his predecessors had striven to build up. The system itself devoured him. How, then, was the ruler to effect a release from the ecclesiological embrace and yet function as a Christian ruler? After Canossa that indeed was the acute problem. The severity of the dilemma needs no comment.

A further observation seems apposite here. The function of government in the early and high Middle Ages was to lead and to guide the population and the kingdom. Constructive leadership, and not just management, administration, and manipulation, was what was expected from government. The exercise of this function quite evidently flavoured the complexion of public life and set its imprint upon all sections, groups and classes of the population. It is not difficult to understand the, literally speaking, overriding importance of government in the Middle Ages. There was only a tiny fraction of the population that was capable of reading and writing; extremely few had anything approaching adequate knowledge of what was required in the public interest and in that of the kingdom, a feature which severely narrowed the circle of those capable of understanding, let alone of taking part in, public government. As already indicated, the kingdom, moreover, was conceived to be on the same level – juristically – as a minor under age who, by definition, needed a guiding hand. The Investiture Contest had, however, shown that in his function as a tutor of his kingdom the ruler was to be under severe restraint in precisely those matters which vitally affected the substance of the kingdom entrusted to him by divinity. Canossa made a change of the foundations of government imperative, if the ruler was to effect a release from his ecclesiological encumbrances and to fufil his function as leader. This was an inescapable conclusion demanding measures of an appropriate kind.

Paradoxically the solution of the dilemma which confronted the ruler was to a considerable extent facilitated by the Gregorian papacy itself. It understood itself as the institution which programmatically applied ancient (and not so ancient) Christian law. It was the papacy's constant reiteration that what it aimed at was merely the establishment of a state of affairs which was appropriate to a Christian society and for which the ancient laws, decrees, statutes, and statements had made ample provision. Indeed, the papacy had a most respectable reservoir of the very decrees to which Gregory had alluded – though not all of them were genuine. These exhibited a full-blooded cosmology in the language of the law. Yet the constant appeal by the Gregorian papacy to the law was in the end counterproductive. It potently stimulated royal (or imperial) interest in the law and it was actually instrumental in achieving the exact opposite of what was intended. On the royal side it provoked the search for the very law that the king had lacked: and the search was to produce the kind of law which was to set in motion the secularization of government, and of society, and eventually lead to humanism. In a word, the effect of the appeal to the law was not the full-scale implementation of the ecclesiologically based law embracing all relevant issues of concern to society, but the utilization of a secular law that was to be the foundation of the government and to give its ruler sharp contours and a well-defined profile. That the law was the strongest weapon in the hands of the papacy explains the need and search for a royal law that was capable of confronting the papal law on equal terms. Paradoxically, the one appeal to the law produced another appeal of the same kind, with consequences the dimensions of which have hitherto been barely realized.

Seen from a wider perspective, the renaissance of the fifteenth century casts its shadows back to the turn of the eleventh and twelfth centuries, that is, to the period after the calamitous and inglorious collapse of theocratic rulership at Canossa. For now the process that had begun in the Frankish age of the eighth and ninth centuries was put into reverse, though initially only within the orbit of government. But the important point to bear in mind is that the full effects of the rebirth or renaissance which had changed the complexion and foundations of society and its government in the eighth and ninth centuries and which had led to the exposure of the government to ecclesiastical attacks in the latter part of the eleventh century, were to be rendered nugatory by a partial reversal of the ruler's rebirth process, a reversal in which the law played a major role. In several basic respects, the picture that emerged in the course of the twelfth century was not at all unlike that which was witnessed in the eighth and ninth centuries: here as there the initiative belonged to the government, and in both instances it was the government which first experienced the effects of the renaissance – in the Frankish age the government was reborn in the ecclesiological sense, in the twelfth century it was reborn in the secular sense. And in both instances this change of the foundations of the government entailed a fundamental change in the outlook and complexion of society itself.

The appropriation of Roman law for governmental purposes during and after the Investiture Contest has rightly been considered one of the epochal events in the medieval period. Roman law began its triumphant European career as an indispensable instrument of government and, what is even more important, in the present context, was one of the vital means with which the ruler could effectively elude the grip of the papacy or the ecclesiastical hierarchy. It above all enabled the ruler to throw off the control exercised or attempted to be exercised over his government by the papacy and the ecclesiastics: they had claimed the control precisely because of the ecclesiological base upon which the ruler's government had rested. What, in short, Roman law, its study, and its application in the public field did was to set in motion the process of secularization on the governmental level. It was this secularization of governmental foundations and, therefore, of powers, which eventually conditioned the numerous

other features related to the so-called humanist renaissance: their emergence and development was contingent upon the secularization of public
government. Thereby the ruler was able to withdraw himself from the
highly exposed position which his ecclesiological foundations entailed and
to assume a function approximating autonomy. But the fate of the ruler
qua ruler is in the present context of only limited interest: for what is of
immediate and overriding interest is the utilization of Roman law for
governmental purposes which was an indispensable precondition, on the
historical level, for the subsequent humanist development. And once more
the initiating role of the government in the twelfth century should be
emphasized. In a word it was the ecclesiologically conditioned situation
which virtually forced the royal government to seek a base that was not
exposed to ecclesiastical surveillance. Seen from this angle, the ensuing
secularization and its sequel, humanism, were re-actions to the full-scale
attempt to implement ecclesiologically conditioned principles in public life.

The concrete beginnings of Roman law influence can be traced to the
Ravenna jurist, Petrus Crassus, who about 1084 wrote a tract entitled 'In
defence of King Henry'.[7] It was the first book that employed Roman law
in a professional manner and in the service of public government. The
tract was well written: its author knew the whole Roman law (the Digest
as well as the Code of Justinian) thoroughly and used it intelligently and
pungently to represent the papal measures against the king as basically
unjust, unlawful and indefensible. The tract was in fact the reply to
Gregory's attack on the absence of the right law on the royal side: the
appeal of Gregory was beginning to backfire. For however little concrete
knowledge man had of Roman law in the preceding ages, nobody ever
denied that it represented the acme of jurisprudential achievement. It was
a law that was rationally conceived and, by any standards, was technically
well-nigh perfect. The invocation of Roman law in defence of the king
was, therefore, in reality an appeal from the law (as postulated by the
papacy) to the law of the Romans, the distinction and ancientness of which
nobody could or did dispute: it in fact preceded any ecclesiastical law which
the papacy would have been able to invoke.

But the deeper significance of this employment of Roman law for
governmental purposes was that it was law made primarily by laymen for
laymen, and in any case as far as the Code was concerned, by laymen whose
Christianity could never be the subject of doubt. Further, many parts of
the Roman law were created entirely independently of Christianity, of the
papacy or the ecclesiastical hierarchy. The law in this most Roman of all
Roman creations was fixed, formulated and presented in a manner which
was to serve as a model for the jurisprudential science now beginning:

7   For some details cf. *PPI*, ch. II.

conciseness, immediate intelligibility, unambiguity, subtlety, elegance of diction, precision of expression and a specifically natural, human way of stating and solving juristic problems. The Code in particular dealt with matters which fell into the compartment of government.

Whether the harnessing of Roman law to the exigencies of a royal government in the late eleventh century was right or appropriate may well be open to doubt: Roman law knew nothing of the proprietary church system, nothing of a king by the grace of God, nothing of a Lord's anointed, nothing of a medieval ruler or a German king, nothing of an oath or a solemn royal coronation promise, and the numerous other adjuncts of theocratic and ecclesiologically conditioned rulership. But the very invocation of Roman law is in itself of profound significance. For this was the first time that an ancient Roman source was invoked as a model or as a pattern for non-ecclesiological purposes. The search for an answer to the charges raised by the papacy against contemporary kings led to the most easily available system – the Roman law – which admittedly needed adjustment and accommodation to contemporary conditions if it was to be usefully employed for governmental purposes, but, and this really is the point, it could, as indeed it did, serve as a model for governments and as such merits the full attention in the present context which is assuredly its due. The search for an answer to the papal charges produced a model in the shape of Roman law, knowledge of which in any case had never died out in Italy, and especially in Lombardy, or in Southern and other parts of France, all of which were educationally and intellectually far in advance of any other European region. As will be presently seen, the Roman law became a secular model for government that, because based on it, was able to escape ecclesiastical control. Roman law had assumed the function of a pattern, and that is especially significant in the present context. For, as the following chapters will show, the search for models or patterns constituted one of the most conspicuous features of renaissance humanism. And the invocation of Roman law in the late eleventh century initiates the subsequent long line of searches for distinguished ancient models. The regress or recourse to ancient models – the striking humanist renaissance trait – makes its first appearance as a consequence of the papal challenge in the Investiture Contest.

Intellectually Ravenna appears to have been a particularly lively place, as it could boast of a law school which in all relevant respects was a precursor of Bologna. The anti-pope Clement III was archbishop of Ravenna and educationally and culturally far superior to his famous opponent. At Ravenna there were 'Doctors of Laws' (*Legum Doctores*), a designation which indicates professionalism in law and in its study. They did not take long to realize what a useful contribution Roman law could make to a government that could face the papacy on its own terms – on the

terms of the law. And they began to examine the practical application of
Roman law to the issues of the day. The study of, and the penetration into,
Roman law received a mighty impulse from the contemporary conflicts,
perplexities and consequential questions. And among these the position
of the layman within Christian society stood very much in the foreground.
The Doctors at Ravenna were laymen, just as Petrus Crassus was.

It is essential to bear in mind that this study and exposition of Roman
law was a purely private effort, in no wise sponsored by, or even connected
with, any government, and of course this also applies to Bologna which
rapidly became the citadel of anything associated with the law. Indeed,
this spontaneous interest in, if not dedication to, Roman jurisprudential
topics is convincing proof of how much an alert, educated and receptive
laity considered itself affected by the prospect of a full-scale implementation of ecclesiological premises, notably of the law that was inspired,
conceived and controlled by ecclesiastics. But from its inception in the
early years of the twelfth century, Bologna university was entirely staffed
by laymen who trained laymen in Roman jurisprudence, and the law
glossed by, and lectured on by, laymen was the ancient Roman law which –
let this be repeated – was a law and a legal system made by laymen for
laymen. It would seem impossible to exaggerate the significance of this
feature. Indeed, the rapid rise of Bologna (and partly also of Modena in
Lombardy)[8] can only be explained effortlessly by the realization of scholars
that Roman jurisprudence was a most useful instrument by which contemporary needs could be met. At all times educational institutions and the
contents of education are directly linked with the ethos, the aims and
aspirations of contemporary society: studies, orientation and needs of
academic establishments cannot be considered in a vacuum, but are
faithful reflections of the contemporary outlook and background. This new
jurisprudential scholarship introduced new intellectual dimensions into all
spheres of higher education: Bologna was the first European university,
because no similar institution existed in antiquity. And the only subject
studied there during the first vital decades of its existence was Roman law,
and this was studied in answer to contemporary exigencies which concerned government and society. Roman law had become literally speaking
the classical model for governmental purposes. But it was only the first of
many such classical models. The influence of Roman law in the Middle
Ages opens up new perspectives in the history of renaissance humanism.

The conciseness of Roman law, its crisp terminology and conceptual
clarity, put into the shade all traditional forms of governmental thought,

8   See *LP* pp. 83ff.; further, J. Fried, *Die Entstehung des Juristenstandes im 12. Jahr-
    hundert: zur sozialen Stellung und politischen Bedeutung gelehrter Juristen in Bologna
    und Modena* (Cologne and Vienna, 1974).

which in any case were only inchoate and inarticulate. The study of Roman law opened up a system of law and government of a maturity the like of which had never been envisaged before. It showed a world in which the law reigned supreme, and that world was secular, precisely because ancient Rome had no connection with Christianity, with the papacy or the other ecclesiological factors. The ancient Roman law was contained in the Digest composed of the sayings of the classical Roman jurists of the first to the third centuries A.D. And it was in the Digest that the basic juris-prudential principles were to be found – precisely those of which governments had been wholly unaware. The Code contained the legal enactments of the emperors of late Roman antiquity. These incorporated a great many issues of concern to Christianity from the fourth to the sixth centuries, but were exclusively enactments by laymen. The Roman law received by men of the twelfth century was by no means opposed to any religious or ecclesiastical laws, but differed from them in tenor, aim and aspiration. Roman law was not concerned with a future life, was indifferent to ecclesiological maxims (precisely those which had so profusely developed in the antecedent ages) and was secular in outlook and conception. There was no room in the Digest (or for that matter in the Code) for the conception of earthly life as a mere transitory stage. Roman law was of this world, mundane and secular. Classical Roman law was human law *par excellence*.

There is a further consideration which explains the readiness of the early twelfth century for the absorption of Roman law and of its principles. For centuries, literate men, and to some extent others, had been familiar with the Bible in the shape of the Vulgate. This Latin translation contained a very great deal of Roman law terminology and expressions and ideas which were to convey the frequently very legalistic meaning of the Bible, and especially of the Old Testament. Through studying the Bible, man unconsciously absorbed a great deal of Roman law. The Bible in the shape of the Vulgate literally speaking prepared the ground for the reception of the 'real' Roman law. Man's consequent familiarity with Roman law powerfully assisted its professional study and the application of principles based upon it. And familiarity with a certain terminology is of inestimable value in launching a new system of thought. The Vulgate was one of the decisive preparatory agencies which paved the way for the easy and quick application of Roman law to problems of government.

The Investiture Contest had thrown up basic problems of government which stimulated the study of Roman law. The Vulgate facilitated the reception of Roman law as a basis of scholarly study and to no lesser extent its subsequent practical application. What, however, made Roman law an instrument by which the process of secularization of government and of its foundations was so successfully set in motion? Here some specific topics of pure Roman parentage are conspicuous, although they have hitherto received little attention in modern historiography.

From the governmental point of view the general jurisprudential principles were set forth in the Digest and the specific enactments in the Code. Taken together they exhibited monarchic government in its purest form. The enactments in the Code exhibited in unadulterated manner the descending theme of government with all its attendant adjuncts, and the Digest supplied the juristic bases for this monarchic government. According to the Digest there was the so-called *lex regia* (the 'royal law'). This stated that the Roman people had transferred all its own powers to the prince, that is, the emperor, who thereby became pre-eminently the monarchic ruler whose will alone counted.[9] The material ingredient of all law and in fact of all governmental measures in Roman law was the will of the prince (the *voluntas principis*), against whose authority there was no possibility of appeal. Autonomous rulership was established by a very simple device and without any recourse to the grace of God or the ruler's rebirth or to any of the numerous Christian tenets which had grown superabundantly in the medieval period. The theme of Roman imperial monarchy and the theme of religious monotheism showed a certain kinship and could easily be amalgamated, as indeed they were, in the late Roman empire from the fourth to the sixth centuries.

This unique monarchic position of the late Roman emperor manifested itself primarily in his legislative capacity: he was the sole legislator and in this role he had exclusive control over all laws, which included also the public law. The famous Roman jurist of the late second century A.D., Ulpian, has left us the classic definition of the Roman public law. The Digest reports that according to him public law generally related to the Roman common weal and specifically referred to sacred things, to the priests as administrators of sacred matters, and to the civil service.[10] Ulpian knew nothing of Christianity and his definition obviously reflected the state of things in the ancient Roman world.

Evidently, in the hands of the late Roman emperor this public law proved itself a most useful handle for the exercising of his legislative omnipotence.

9   The relevant text is in the Digest, I.4.1. For the *lex regia* see *LP* pp. 56ff., and for detailed discussion see T. Mommsen, *Römisches Staatsrecht*, 3rd edition (Leipzig, 1908), II.2.840ff., especially 876, note; further, *Fontes iuris Romani anteiustiniani*, ed. S. Riccobono (Milan, 1941), p. 155. For the spectacular 'discovery' of the actual text by Cola di Rienzo, see p. 138.

10 See Ulpian in Dig. I.1.1(2): ... publicum ius in sacris, sacerdotibus et in magistratibus consistit.' For some details about the application of this see *LP* pp. 37, 59ff. and 'The constitutional significance of Constantine the Great's settlement' in *JEH*, 27(1976), 1–16. For the Ulpian passage in particular see M. Kaser, 'Zur Methodologie der römischen Rechtsquellenforschung' in *SB Vienna*, 227(1972), at p. 44, n. 75, and p. 56.

It was virtually tailored to embrace all ecclesiastical matters, since the sacred things and the priests formed a vital part of this law. It was indeed on the basis of the Roman public law that the emperors convoked the general councils of Christian antiquity, that they appointed, transferred and dismissed the highest ecclesiastical officers, that they could fix, enlarge and modify diocesan boundaries, that they could pronounce judgments in ecclesiastical matters, in short, as far as organized Christianity (the Church) was concerned the Roman public law – of ancient republican parentage – enabled the full deployment of imperial monarchic powers. Indeed, *Romanitas* and *Christianitas* fused, because the former absorbed the latter through the medium of the all-embracing public law. It was this amalgamation of 'Romanity' and Christianity which made it possible to transfer the ancient Roman characterization of the law as sacred or divine – the *lex divalis* or the *leges sacratae* or *sacratissimae* – to the laws issued by the Christian emperors: it was on the same grounds that Justinian could say in the sixth century that his legal enactments 'emanate from our divine mouth', and so on. The legislative omnipotence was perhaps best summed up in the Justinianean adoption of the Hellenistic view that the emperor was the personification of the law: he was the *lex animata*. All this was achieved with a minimum of intellectual effort. The Roman emperor as depicted in the Roman law was autonomous. He was not only independent of any control exercised by an ecclesiastical body, but above all he was, by virtue of his monarchic functions, the sole controlling organ of all essential ecclesiastical matters.

It certainly does not need much historical imagination to visualize the attraction of Roman law for a government that was as hard pressed as the German government was. Roman law was in many fundamental respects a most effective answer to the Gregorian challenges – it was precisely the kind of law that largely prevented intervention by the papacy on juristic grounds. None of the ecclesiological presuppositions existed; the ruler had a profiled countenance with clean-cut features that sharply contrasted with the somewhat amorphous physiognomy of the traditional theocratic ruler who was 'King by the grace of God'. Above all, within this Roman law, hallowed as it was by its ancientness, its unsurpassed maturity and ideological opulence in regard to governmental matters, the exercise of government was shown to be the basic issue of public law. And public law was the instrument that enabled the late Roman emperors to harness the ecclesiastical organism to their governmental designs. In exactly the same way the Roman public law enabled twelfth-century rulers to bypass the proprietary church system, which was indeed indefensible from the ecclesiological standpoint. Admittedly, the proprietary church system had become public law that rested on practice and custom, but what a poor relation this public law was in comparison with Ulpian's. Here was ancient Roman legal wisdom written down by a classical Roman jurist and far removed from the myopic, self-centred, earthen view of the importance of a piece of land. By relying on the secular Roman law the rulers stood on far more solid ground than they had done by operating within the ecclesiological system which left them widely exposed to ecclesiastical intervention. By utilizing Roman law and especially its public law, rulers were able to throw off ecclesiological fetters and they returned, so to speak, to the secular position from which they had originally set out, and yet they remained Christian in outlook and complexion. This process of secularization was set in motion by the German government during the first half of the twelfth century.

It is quite clearly no coincidence that one of the most influential scholars, perhaps even the intellectual fountain-head of Bologna, was also the most trusted confidant and counsellor of Henry V. Irnerius found himself excommunicated together with his imperial master. At Bologna, however, he can without exaggeration be designated the initiator of the new scholarship of Roman law.[11] What is of immediate concern is that Henry V (we shall probably never know whether Irnerius advised him in this matter) was the first medieval king who programmatically and consistently called himself 'King of the Romans' (*Rex Romanorum*). Henceforth this designation was constantly used down to the fifteenth century, if not beyond. Nothing in this title indicated to an outsider that its bearer was a German king. From the moment of election every German king now became a 'King of the Romans'. In this capacity he had (so it was claimed on his behalf) everything that pertained to the 'emperor of the Romans'. After all, the Eastern emperor in Constantinople was officially the *Basileus ton Romaion* of which in fact the *Rex Romanorum* was the exact Latin equivalent. Differently expressed, the emperor of the Romans crowned by the pope – and for historical and ideological reasons only the pope could perform this coronation in the West – was simply a formalized or solemnized king of the Romans. And as such he evidently had need of the appropriate law, which could obviously be none other than the Roman law. No Germanic law, no customary law, no ecclesiologically conditioned law could fulfil this requirement. The fully-fledged Roman law was the only law that a king or emperor of the Romans could rightly call his own.

Just as the Gregorian appeal to the law was counter-productive, in the same way the very creation and idea of a Roman emperor also proved in the end counter-productive for the papacy. Originally in the ninth century created as an instrument against Constantinople and conceived as the extended protecting arm of the papacy on a universal scale, he now assumed a role that was in basic respects not all that different from that of

11   Cf. *LP*, pp. 84f. with literature.

the Eastern emperor. Thus by assuming the function of the 'King of the Romans' the German king claimed to have a right to become emperor of the Romans at the hands of the pope and had every reason to call the Roman law his own law. The profound significance is that his government had changed its foundations – an ecclesiologically conditioned government now took on a secular complexion. It was the restoration of the very kind of government that the rebirth of the ruler was supposed to have supplanted. In a word, the secularization of the government's foundations signified the return to the status of the king before he had experienced a rebirth through unction and the receipt of divine grace. In order to be a king of the Romans it was indeed not necessary to be in receipt of divine grace, for he had no celestial parentage. Divine grace merely supplemented his status, but did not create it. He was and claimed to be an autonomous ruler. And this indeed was Staufen ideology as classically expressed from Frederick I onwards.

The process of secularization that stretched, of course, over several decades, eventually saw the emergence of a government which had strongly marked 'romanizing' features. One has but to look at the early Staufen rulers[12] and examine their language in the products of their chancery to see what a great and indeed profound change had been wrought in the structure and outlook of their government when compared with, say, that of the Salian government some two generations earlier. The language used in the documents is particularly revealing: it is the self-confident, firm, assertive terminology of the autonomous ruler who has thrown off all pretexts of humility and all protestations of unworthiness and speaks in the somewhat bombastic language of the late Roman imperial chancery. The conspicuous model was Justinian whose output both as a codifier and legislator was now fully available. And the laws of the (Staufen) emperors came to be inserted into the body of the Code (of Roman law), so that an enactment by Diocletian or Marcian was followed by one issued by Frederick I or Frederick II. Since they were Roman rulers, their laws supplemented the Roman law, in which their legislative measures found a legitimate place. The consequence of this change of the structure and basis of the German government (and of its offspring) is not yet fully realized: the ruler was secularized and restored to the status of an unregenerated ruler. But as far as the romanizing process went, it too had far-reaching consequences which are of no interest in this context. It must suffice to mention that it exercised influence in all spheres of law and jurisprudence in continental Europe and eventually led to the phenomenon known as the Reception of Roman law.

---

12 For details see R. M. Herkenrath, 'Regnum und imperium in der frühstaufischen Kanzlei' in *SB Vienna* 224(1969), fasc. 5.

To a very marked degree the Staufen government in Germany from the mid-twelfth century onwards began to show unmistakable manifestations of its secular character. The communications between Frederick I and the papacy show defiant self-assurance, intrepid rejection of ecclesiologically conditioned demands and a radiating self-confidence which sharply contrasted with the attitudes of earlier governments. It is not necessary to go into details now, but a few outstanding signposts should indicate the secularist trend. Since Roman law had become the emperor's own law, its special protection by him was self-evident – hence the decree by which students and masters of the university of Bologna were to enjoy special imperial protection. This decree, *Habita*, was by order of the emperor inserted into the Code of Justinian and was called, quite in conformity with ancient Roman practice, a *lex sacra*, just as the Roman laws themselves were designated in this decree as *leges sacrae*.[13] At the same time the empire over which Frederick presided became the *sacrum imperium*, a novel and yet ancient appellation which on the one hand revived the sacrality of Roman governmental institutions, and yet on the other hand drew a sharp dividing line between the *sacrum imperium* and the *sancta Romana ecclesia*. In more than one sense can the description be seen as a renaissance of the ancient, secular Roman empire. The appellation was to remain in force until 1806. Even the residence of the ruler now became 'our sacred palace'. And, as already indicated, the language in the official documents revealed the change: the richness and sonority of the vocabulary, the tone, tenor and formulation of governmental aims, the unambiguous forthrightness – all these mirrored the new awareness of the fundamental strength the government derived from its newly acquired foundations. Secularization of rulership in this context meant the de-sacralization of the ruler in the contemporary ecclesiological sense and his 'sacralization' in the Roman law sense, which yielded a mundane, secular and natural ruler.

These and many other expressions, as well as the actual measures taken, compellingly direct our gaze to the Roman public law, which dealt with the *ius in sacris et sacerdotibus*, that is, the law relating to sacral matters and to the priesthood. There is no margin of doubt that the Staufen government manipulated the Roman public law exceedingly well. It was perhaps the firmest constitutional foundation for the transaction of governmental business – it provided a handle for controlling the ecclesiastics, yet avoided any strictures that arose from operating with the proprietary church system. Nevertheless, it was nothing new: it was very ancient Roman law, and what stronger base could any government have than this body of law? And the actual situation to all intents and purposes asked for the concrete

---

13   Details in *LP*, pp. 93f., where further literature and sources will be found.

application of the powers comprehended in public law. There had been a double election in Rome resulting in schism and the threat of a divided Christendom. It was a contingency in which Frederick had played no part, but as successor of the Roman emperors and as a Christian it was his duty to remove this threat, and the pattern was in actual fact provided by the late Roman empire in which there were also threats to Christian unity that were removed by the actions of the emperors. The instrument was the general council. All the four great ecumenical councils of Christian antiquity were convoked solely by the emperors as the custodians of the public weal for which the Roman public law had made provision, for the sacral matters and their administrators, the priests, were essential parts of this public law. Thus, the Staufen government too convoked a general council to decide who was the rightful pope. It was to be attended by the representatives of Western kingdoms. Not only the convocation but also the actual proceedings were modelled on the Roman pattern, notably on Constantine. The speech which Frederick made in opening the Council of Pavia in February 1160 was in its essential parts a copy of the speech made by Constantine at the Council of Nicaea in 325. Even the manner of arriving at a verdict was the same as that observed in Nicaea: the emperor did not take part in the voting.[14] Moreover, the way in which the Staufen government enforced its policy and dealt with recalcitrant bishops and abbots proved how much more effective, elegant and speedy was the exercise of monarchic powers based on the Roman public law than of those resting on the (old) proprietary church system.[15]

Since Roman law had become a vital instrument in the secularization of government, it also restored the ruler's sovereignty, the hallmark of rulership. The process of the secularization of government and its foundations explains the gradual receding into the background of the theocratic elements of rulership as the twelfth and thirteenth centuries advanced. Less and less notice was taken of the ruler as 'the Lord's anointed' and of the other attributes of theocratic rulership, though when it appeared advantageous they could still be paraded and re-employed, with diminishing returns. The readiness of the government to absorb Roman law principles also explains the popularity of Roman law studies in the twelfth and thirteenth centuries. Nobody would have gone to Bologna or to the

---

14 For the implications see *PPI*, ch. II.

15 The oftentimes invoked 'feudalization of the imperial church' is hardly sufficient to explain fully the stern control exercised by Frederick I over the ecclesiastics. On this 'feudalization' see again P. Classen, 'Das Wormser Konkordat in der deutschen Verfassungsgeschichte' in *Vorträge und Forschungen*, 17(1973), 411ff., especially 425ff. Apart from the narrow issue embraced in the Concordat of Worms, the structural change of the government's foundations and the consequential control of the public law by the ruler must be added to make the actual practice of government comprehensible.

other famous sees of jurisprudential learning if Roman law had not provided an answer to contemporary needs or proved itself useful. No educational institution and no pursuit of special branches of learning can be understood in a vacuum; they are closely related to society and government. It is mere romanticism to hold that people studied Roman law for its own sake.

Although the process of secularization of government was for historical, geographical and ideological reasons first set in motion by the German government, it would be quite mistaken to think that other governments were not also affected by this same process. It is true that the development was not so spectacular elsewhere, but the underlying motivation – release from ecclesiological constrictions – was the same, and the German example was no doubt carefully noted by other governments.[16] Moreover, the veritably 'international' composition of the student body at Bologna and other law universities persuasively shows how attractive the study of Roman law had become in the course of the twelfth and thirteenth centuries. Attention should be drawn to two specific instances which, because originating in Roman law, were convincing manifestations of the secularist orientation of governments.

It may be recalled that in conformity with the king's rebirth the so-called regnal years of the ruler had hitherto been reckoned from the day of his coronation, or more precisely from the moment of his receiving unction which conferred the divine grace of rulership on him. Now, however, according to Roman law the so-called *dies ortus*, that is, the day upon which the ruler began to reign, was that of his actual accession. This law[17] was issued on 3 August 389 – hence long before any coronation or feudal inauguration. The German king Philip of Swabia appears to have been one of the first Western rulers to adopt this Roman rule: he dated his documents from the moment of his accession, which was the day on which he was elected (8 March 1198), and not from the day of his unction and coronation (8 September 1198).[18] The English and French kings followed suit. Henry III was king for 57 years, so the introduction of the new dating was delayed until Edward I, whose regnal years began on the day of his father's funeral (20 November 1272); he was not anointed and crowned until nearly two years later (19 August 1274). The situation in France was very similar: Louis IX was king for four-and-a-half decades, so here too the new dating mechanics were not adopted until Philip III's accession. The significance of this device is clearly the relegation of the

---

16 Especially by the English king, Henry II, whose constitutional and legislative measures as well as his conflict with Becket should long have been seen in this context.
17 Codex III.12.7(5). For details see *PPI*, ch. VI.
18 *MGH Const.* II.no.1, p. 2; no.15, p. 18.

unction (and coronation) to a secondary place. The king's rebirth as an 'Athlete of Christ' or 'The Lord's Anointed' was no longer considered essential. He was restored to his former regally unregenerated status, in a word, he re-assumed his secular status. Divine grace was no longer seen to be the constitutive element of the ruler's powers. The theocratic kind of rulership was withering away, although the title 'King by the grace of God' was kept – and in some countries is still used to this day.

The other instance is well known, although it too has not attracted attention in the present context, to which it evidently belongs. The formula first used in thirteenth-century France (and later also in other kingdoms) of the *Rex in regno suo imperator*[19] – the king in his kingdom as an emperor – receives its significance only in relation to the Roman law based secularized rulership. The formula did not mean that the French king (or for that matter other kings) had any imperial aspirations or pursued in any way universalist aims. Far from it. Nor was it identical in meaning, nor had indeed it any link, with the statement which Innocent III had made in regard to the French king who would not recognize a superior in temporal matters. The profound significance of the formula was that whatever Roman law said about the constitutional position of the emperor now applied to the king in his kingdom. That is to say, the king who assumed the position of an emperor in his realm attributed to himself the full monarchic functions which the Roman law had accorded to the emperor, and among these none was more important and relevant to government (as the German government had shown) than the handling of the Roman public law, by which the monarchic power could most effectively be displayed. This indeed provided the instrument which enabled the ruler to exercise control over the clergy in his kingdom, since they were embraced in the public law now handled and guarded by the king. This function presupposed the de-sacralization of the ruler and heralded the first and unmistakable glimmerings of Gallicanism and of an embryonic national church.

In brief, the significance of the formula was that the secular ancient Roman law had become an integral part of the governmental system and machinery of a national king. Can one wonder that the French kings in the last decades of the thirteenth century attracted ever increasing numbers of the *légistes* to the service of their chancery? It was the able graduates of Roman law from Orléans, Montpellier and Toulouse who were now to staff the royal chancery, for at Paris the study of Roman law had been prohibited since 1219 by Pope Honorius III; but it flourished with all the

19 For modern literature on this see *LP*, pp. 182, n. 5, 222, n. 2, and for a view with wider perspectives see Franco Simone, 'Il Petrarca e la cultura francese del suo tempo' in *Studi Francesi*, 41(1970), 200ff., especially 203–10 and 403–5, although the Innocentian passage is not strictly relevant – cf. text.

greater vigour in the other French sees of learning, including above all Toulouse, which was a papally founded university. That the king functioned as an emperor in his kingdom is perhaps the most eloquent testimony of the influence of Roman law upon the constitution of the rapidly rising national states. The control of the clergy by the king was thus based on ancient Roman law principles enshrined as they were in the Roman public law. Who else but the king should look after the interests of the body public which was the very core of the public law of Rome? No other system of law could have achieved this effect with so little effort. This control was unquestionably an issue of public law, of which the secularized ruler was indubitably the trustee, guardian and administrator. It was this standpoint which explained the measures enacted by the English Henry VIII in 1534. And the true and formidable extent of this new (and yet so old) regal function emerges only when it is considered in conjunction with the simultaneous development of territorial sovereignty and nationalism which will presently engage us.

It is worth while in the present context to invite attention to a feature which has hardly been noticed and yet is immediately relevant. Whereas the formula of the *Rex in regno imperator* expressed in secular language the supreme power of the (territorial) king, there is an exact parallel in the form of the *Princeps in ecclesia* which expresses precisely the same thought in the traditional ecclesiological language. The 'Ruler in the Church', however – and this really is the deeper significance of the formula – turns the time-honoured Ambrosian point of view upside down. It may be recalled that in his fiery speech against Auxentius Ambrose coined the memorable phrase 'Imperator *intra ecclesiam*, non supra ecclesiam est' ('The emperor is within the Church, not above it'). The unambiguous meaning is that the (Christian) emperor is a member of the Church, with the consequence that he has to accept its teachings and rulings relative to the well-being of all the members of the Church. Now, however, 'the Ruler in the Church' came to mean the exact opposite: because he had the right to apply the public law and because the Church indubitably concerned the public interest, he was credited with the right to deal with ecclesiastical matters, hence was 'in the Church'. Seen from another angle, this was the late medieval expression of what more than a millenium earlier Constantine the Great had declared to be the proper state of affairs, that is, that as emperor he was 'the overseer of the external matters of the Church'.[20]

The role played by Roman law should now be clearly discernible. It

---

20 For Ambrose, see his speech (cap. 36) in *PL* 16.1061; for Constantine's role see J. Straub, *Regeneratio imperii* (Darmstadt, 1972), pp. 119ff., and W. Ullmann, *art. cit.* (above, n. 10), at pp. 11ff.

released the ruler from ecclesiological encumbrances by secularizing his government's foundations. As already observed, the ruler depicted in Roman law served as a model for the rebirth, the restoration, the resuscitation of the ruler who, though a Christian, based his government on classical Roman law. In particular adopting the Roman public law as his own law, his theocratic foundations recovered their original secular character: the ruler had been, so to speak, 'humanized', reborn (to use baptismal language) into an unregenerated status. But this reborn 'human' ruler did not merely imitate; he developed and adjusted the late Roman emperor's functions to the exigencies of his kingdom. The regress to Roman law as a model for governments is indeed one of the earliest manifestations of renaissance humanism – provoked as it was by the application of logically greatly extended ecclesiological premisses. The king was, as it were, challenged on the very ground which initially he himself had chosen freely and on his own initiative. The idea of the ruler's rebirth or renaissance on the occasion of his inauguration (unction and coronation) was neutralized by the re-emergence of the rebirth or renaissance of the former secular ruler. What better model was available than the hallowed Roman law?

Over and above this effect of Roman law upon government, its influence in another sphere was no less important and far-reaching. By establishing a link with ancient Rome, Roman law acted as a force that potently engendered a historical sense and promoted historical perspectives. This aspect needs only to be stated for it to be grasped in its full significance. From the first half of the twelfth century Roman law and its study was a mighty begetter of a historical–secular kind of outlook that was to be clearly reflected in precisely the quarter which had first experienced the impact of Roman law – the Staufen government, where Frederick I's uncle, Otto of Freising, was one of the earliest writers of history to be aware of the role of purely mundane–human–secular dimensions in the historical process. To this effect of Roman law far too little attention has been paid.[21] Roman law provided perhaps the strongest and most genuine linkage with ancient Rome, and thus could not but help acting as a potent stimulant to historical pursuits. Can one be surprised that it was jurists who were among the earliest humanists to combine jurisprudence with history?[22]

Yet there is no warrant for saying that the secularization of government

---

21 Although approaching the problem from a different angle, D. R. Kelley makes some very important observations on this topic in his 'Clio and the lawyers: Forms of historical consciousness in medieval jurisprudence' in *Medievalia et Humanistica*, n.s.5(1974), 25ff., especially 30ff.

22 See below pp. 132, 163.

had weakened the strength of the royally pursued descending theme of government. On the contrary, it remained the operational basis of government. After all, the model, the late Roman emperor, had given the lead in this respect too.[23] It was as a preconditioning factor, and a vital one, that governmental secularization assumed its proper place among the forces that were to lead to renaissance humanism. But government cannot be viewed in a vacuum, because it is by definition correlated to society. And it is to a survey of secularism in society that we now must turn.

23   In this context attention should be drawn to the standpoint of Frederick II in his conflict with the papacy. He asserted that, while the pope was to govern in accordance with the ascending theme of government and therefore remain responsible to the members of the Church, the emperor's government was to be based on the descending theme. For details see W. Ullmann, 'Some reflections on the opposition of Frederick II to the papacy' in *Archivio storico Pugliese*, 13(1960), 3–26.

III

Secularism in Society

All governmental measures must be viewed in relation to society at large. Unless seen against the social background, the secularization of government does not assume its full historic significance. It is therefore necessary to draw attention to features in contemporary society which were highly responsive to, and in actual fact complemented and supplemented, the governmentally inspired process of secularization. These features were of varied and variegated provenance: they had extremely little, if anything, in common with each other; they were as often as not spontaneous and independent of each other and moved on a level that was partly historically conditioned and partly linked with specific economic, intellectual and cultural developments as they emerged in the course of the twelfth and thirteenth centuries. None of the features to which we will presently turn were in any way governmentally conditioned or in any shape or form dependent on the (central) government. What was significant was the simultaneous emergence of secular features in government as well as in society at large, where they unquestionably reflected a natural growth. And it was this combination of secular phenomena on the governmental and social levels which potently prepared the soil for renaissance humanism understood in a historical sense.

A greater participation of the laity in matters involving the public weal and the social ordering was perhaps the most conspicuous characteristic in the twelfth century. The emergence of the laity in virtually all walks of life was to a large extent conditioned by the very issues of the Investiture Contest, and was a reaction to it. The rise of the universities was one such response. They were primarily institutions concerned with jurisprudence and attendant questions directly relevant to government. The fructifying effect of the universities in the twelfth and thirteenth centuries is still not fully appreciated. The study above all of Roman law opened up perspectives of intellectual dimensions which earlier generations had been incapable of envisaging. Hitherto not only had suitable educational attainments been lacking, but also the immediate interest which was aroused as a result of the bitter conflict, touching as it did so many realms of social and governmental activity. Academic jurisprudence was of vital assistance in the process which restored man's full humanity and effected his rebirth as 'mere man'. Contemporaries were able to see through the, as it were, visual filter of Roman law a society that was built on secular foundations.

At the same time an expansive papacy unwittingly provided a platform for the deployment of the laity. The crusading idea, and particularly its execution, was entirely dependent on the active participation of the laity, from the commanders in the field down to the lowliest villein. It was the crusaders who had to do the fighting, not the ecclesiastics. No governmental theme is capable of execution unless the governors and governed are actively involved. This truism is conspicuous in the crusading movement and it paradoxically enough appeared like a flash of lightning on the horizon in Gregory VII's reign when he appealed to the lay masses to boycott the divine services of simonists, concubinists, etc. The proclamation of a lay strike by the papacy was a symptom that highlighted the inner contradictions of the very theme militantly propounded by the papacy which allocated to the laity a merely executive role. But it was the crusades – major military undertakings of 'global' dimensions directed against the East, not to mention minor military campaigns in other parts of Europe – which contributed a very great deal to the 'emancipation' of an alert and responsive laity. At least passing mention should here be made concerning the military orders, closely linked as they were with the crusades, which in actual fact gave birth to them (the Hospitallers; the Templars; the Teutonic Knights). Their prosperity, their excellent organization and above all the detailed knowledge of far-away regions which their members had (notably of the Near East, Russia, Prussia, etc.) not only made them an influential organ in contemporary Europe but also enormously expanded the intellectual horizon of the individual members.

In this context a piquant paradox deserves a passing remark. Ecclesiastical assemblies from the early thirteenth century onwards unwittingly introduced secularist features into their own composition, and this in connection with the very idea of a crusade. None of the ecclesiastical councils before the Fourth Lateran in 1215 contained any lay element. They were exclusively the preserve of the ecclesiastics. Indeed, the polarization of laity and clergy was given practical expression by Charlemagne's immediate successor, Louis I.[1] But to the Fourth Lateran Council Innocent III invited for the first time in the medieval period the representatives of lay rulers, so as to make the council a universal assembly. Thereby a pronouncedly secularist feature was given some recognition, albeit not in any determinative way, for the lay representatives had no right to vote and

1   Cf. *PG*, p. 143, also 124ff.

attended exclusively as a result of papal invitation.[2] Nevertheless, this was a special feature of all subsequent medieval universal councils, down to the Fifth Lateran Council (1512), which reverted to an exclusively clerical composition. It cannot reasonably be disputed that this recognition was potentially of great importance for the concomitant social development, and was indeed an unmistakable symptom.

It is of course not without significance that this Fourth Lateran Council was concerned with the launching of a crusade. Certainly, the crusader or the member of a military order or the missionary became acquainted with a culture, with social customs, with social orders and living conditions of a kind entirely different from anything with which he had hitherto been familiar. Evidently, by virtue of a 'natural' process, in the field or during the actual campaign the links with a superior authority were loosened; the horizon of the layman widened; the limited vision of the lowly cleric increased and broadened into a worldly view in the literal sense. Trade with distant regions and in hitherto unknown products emerged for the first time in Europe. The gaze of the western and central European widened far beyond the parish pump and parochial concerns. The effects were a sharpening of man's perception with a consequent deepening of observational powers and the awareness of the 'otherness' of regions not his own. These effects could be felt in both town and country, but more immediately in the former, where commerce, stimulated by the new trades and ancillary industries, assumed hitherto unknown proportions. Where formerly there had been natural economy on a large scale, money economy came gradually to replace it. The profit motive too, with the concomitant human secular appetite, was soon to yield the first manifestations of capitalism, especially when in the thirteenth century gold came to be valued as an article of exchange as well as of the mint. It was the city which was particularly suited to the concentration of industry and manufacture of goods as well as of trade: witness Venice, Genoa, the Champagne, and notably the Flemish woollen industries. In the cities the fairs were held; not only did artistic skill have more outlet in the cities, but they also provided a constant reservoir of apprentices and skilled manual craftsmen; in the cities the educational facilities were incomparably greater than in the countryside; it was in the cities that the universities flourished; in the cities religious life had indubitably a complexion that was different from the open country. The monastic establishments, old and new, were almost by definition located in the country, usually far away from towns. In brief, the lay element which overwhelmingly constituted the urban population had rapidly come to the fore and become the dominant part of the town in the shape of the wealthy merchants and the rising bourgeoisie, an em-

2 See *SHP*, pp. 221f., 240.

bryonic segment of the third estate and equalling its agrarian counterpart in importance. That this development was not exactly the same in all parts of Europe is self-evident. Once more, the Northern Italian townships and regions were in the forefront, closely followed by those French regions which were always intellectually and socially ahead of other parts of Europe.

With the growth of the town populations clearly it became necessary to make regulations concerning socially relevant matters. There was not much sophistication and theorizing, to respond to the basic actual needs of town life and to enact legislative measures, which could be taken only by those who had knowledge, ability, and experience in the very matters which demanded measures, that is to say by the townsmen themselves, because they best knew the needs of the town. Statutes issued by certain townships – once more with Italy in the lead – were law made by the people itself. The machinery also evolved quite 'naturally': the public assembly or union was an association of purely secular character and became the obvious platform for the discussion of matters directly relevant to the well-being of the town. The result was circumspect creation of the law by representative assemblies which revealed undoubted maturity and aware-ness of social exigencies. All this was the practical and unreflective appli-cation of the ascending theme of government and law in relation to the civic life of the community, which had a predominantly secularist com-plexion. Hence the preponderance of the laity. And it was here and in this context that the idea of representation found its natural habitat, and without the antecedent cultivation of the soil humanism would hardly have made the great and quick strides that it was to make. Physically the representative 'parliaments' assembled in the big churches, a practice which the Second Council of Lyons in 1274 ordered to cease forthwith.[3]

Not the least interesting facet of this development was that to the administrative and judicial needs of the towns very great care was devoted. The appointment of judges – the podestà – their qualifications, their responsibility and accountability, the scope and tenure of their office, the recruitment of the notariate, and many attendant topics, received detailed treatment in the municipal statutes of the late twelfth and thirteenth centuries down to the sixteenth in the North, and later also in the South, Italian townships. This personnel was exclusively lay and trained in the law at one of the great sees of jurisprudence. Its members came from the strata of their own society, and no charisma was attached to them. What they had in common with the ecclesiastics was special knowledge. The latter claimed to have it in matters divine, and therefore

---

3 In *VI:* III.23.2. The *glossa ordinaria* remarked here that this decree was especially directed against Italian communes which held their 'parlamenta' in their churches. St Paul's, Frankfurt, had distinguished models.

claimed to be specially qualified to govern an ecclesiological society because it was of divine origin; the former had special knowledge in matters relative to their own secular society and this knowledge was vocational and related to a secular kind of community. They above all had a healthy sense of reality. And since by virtue of their training they were thoroughly familiar with Roman jurisprudence, their judicial or administrative decisions rested on Roman law, the classic prototype of law that was issued by laymen for laymen.

What the towns also showed and what apparently was a 'natural' response to social needs was the formation of numerous associations, fraternities, gilds, corporations of merchants, and so on, in a word, the thirteenth century showed the corporative spirit everywhere in Europe very much alive and striking deep roots. And these corporations were partly vocational, partly religious, partly charitable, partly recreational, and were to all intents and purposes voluntary and autonomous bodies, demonstrating as they did the manifestation of the natural desire to form a corporate union for the better pursuit of specific aims. Additionally significant in the present context is that these natural–secular corporations had a very learned and elaborate prototypical structure in Roman law which thereby proved itself partly seminal, and partly confirmative, for nothing was more characteristic of Roman law (and the Romans) than the institution of a corporation (or as it was called in the law books a *universitas*). Academic jurisprudence and practical exigencies formed a natural alliance of secular orientation and direction.

Corresponding features were to be found in the villages, where one witnessed exactly the same natural mode of treating 'public business' as in the towns, with the qualification that everything was in a minor key and of restricted scope. Practical demands dictated measures to be taken to protect the village community and especially grass-land, fields, meadows, woods, quarries, etc. Hence also the need for policing and protecting the harvest from the depredations of animals and human encroachments by taking appropriate 'legislative' measures. Of equal concern was the provision of water supply, fire-fighting services, and the supervision of correct weights and measures in the milling, baking, brick-making and similar trades. The villagers elected their 'officers' in the shape of the watchmen, public criers, and so on. The picture in the countryside showed communities governing themselves by 'natural' insight and judgment uncontaminated by doctrine. In the rural as in the urban scene 'natural man' had been accorded his 'natural' place within mundane environs.

It was precisely in the rural context that the feudal contract obtained its all-pervading influence. For land constituted the basis of the feudal contract from times immemorial. The accent lies on the contractual nature of feudalism which had evolved quite 'naturally' and had its own very distinct physiognomy and catered for mundane, practical contingencies. Despite the great variety of forms which feudalism assumed in medieval Europe, it everywhere had one element in common, and that was its contractual bond between lord and vassal. However secular in origin and mundane in operation, the feudal contract was affirmed by an oath which solemnized the contractual agreement, but did not create it. The oath strengthened the mutual obligations, which were reinforced by the appeal to divinity. This feudal arrangement affected all parts of the populace, and nowhere more so than in England which was covered by a finely spun web of feudal ties, so that everyone held land from everyone else. The arrangement potently promoted the idea of teamwork, because neither of the two contracting parties could do without the other. Although it was the laity which was most closely involved, the clergy was by no means omitted.[4]

Medieval kingship was amphibious. The king was both a theocratic ruler and a feudal lord, and the two functions were sometimes difficult to reconcile. For reasons irrelevant in this context, it was the feudal component part of kingship which prevailed in England from the early thirteenth century, whereas in France (and other kingdoms) it was the theocratic part. It must be pointed out that no other system had taken such firm roots in the native soil of a country as the feudal system, which operated in practice as a team consisting of the king and his tenants-in-chief, the barons. The system was wholly this-worldly, wholly secular and mundane. The creation of law within this framework was a joint effort between king and barons: it was all very human, practical, unsophisticated. Law was made jointly, and not given by the superior to an inferior within the feudal framework. The operative element was consent, and the law thus created was common to king and barons. There are three interests vital to man: life, liberty and property, and it was these three human interests which in Europe were first protected by a law common to king and baron. In Magna Carta, article 39, it was precisely these three fundamental matters which formed the topic of a specific clause arrived at by the consent of king and baronage.[5] Just as the interests were this-worldly, so was this law: wholly unsophisticated and pragmatic. The embryonic beginnings of what later came to be known as the common law can here be seen. The law of the land was the law common to king and barons and this law protected most effectively life, liberty and property. And since the law was a joint effort by king and barons, and embodied consent, its change, abolition or suspension needed mutual agreement – the doctrine of Bracton largely followed in practice. The king was under the law.

---

4 Some teasing problems arose in this connection, since some bishops claimed to have a double status. For some examples and details cf. *PPI*, ch. IX, at n. 107.

5 Some details in *IS*, pp. 71ff., supplemented in GT, pp. 53ff., and in IT, pp. 60ff.

Feudal kingship was given its constitutional habitat, and despite some strenuous efforts by successive English kings to wriggle out of this constitutional framework, it remained the basic structure of rulership which eventually was to lead to constitutional monarchy.

What the observer is here confronted with is the institutionalization of feudal government, which is indeed the exact parallel to the institutionalization of the Roman law based rulership elsewhere. Both are humanly devised; both have a secular, if not also historically conditioned, basis; both have a secular, mundane outlook. Both were the result of accepting the challenge that lay in theocratic rulership. What distinguished them was their origin: the one was native and restricted the scope of rulership in vital matters; the other was based on, and adapted to, a system that was alien to medieval government itself and was above all intended to be sternly monarchic.

Feudal law and rulership powerfully, yet unobtrusively, contributed to the harmonization of the various social strata. The principle of team-work inherent in all feudal arrangements linked the relevant parts of the populace together and brought about social cohesiveness. It also produced a healthy integration of the active parts of society into one organic whole and made for flexibility, adjustability and compromise. Thereby the abrasiveness of a closely argued rational–ideological system came to be avoided, for the simple reason that feudal arrangements were pragmatic, if not averse to any ideological, systematic speculation. Their 'naturalness' made them resilient and resistant, if not immune, to any conceptualized thought-pattern. And feudal society also showed that a co-existence could come about between it and the ecclesiologically conceived society. The operation of feudal kingship by no means abolished the theocratic component part of kingship, but modified its exercise. It was the flexibility of the feudal system which made this co-existence possible. And on the distant horizon the faint contours of bipolarity can be discerned. Differently expressed, practical, humanly comprehended exigencies and possibly the example of earlier judicial decisions shaped the law – in somewhat sharp contrast to the monarchically conceived systems (such as the Roman or canon law) which set out from a general rule in the 'authoritative' texts and deduced therefrom the individual law. One might indeed here see the inductive and deductive methods applied within law and jurisprudence: the latter set out from a universal 'authoritative' principle and squeezed the last ounce out of it for particular cases, whereas the former started from a mass of individual contingencies and cases and constructed therefrom a general rule. This assuredly was the juristic equivalent of the contemporaneously, but wholly independently, emerging inductive method that was to characterize the natural sciences.

One of the indubitable effects of a fully operational feudal system, such as prevailed in thirteenth-century England, was the liberalization of those sections of society which were partners of the feudal contract: they had to take part in public matters which were their own concern, such as the creation of the law, its application and its administration. Laymen were to a large extent occupied in the Hundred Courts, County Courts, Shire Courts, and other venues of the judicial machinery which dispensed justice. Admittedly, they were not 'learned' in the law, they were not *iurisperiti*, and they applied an idea of justice which was, one may safely assume, uncontaminated by any dogmatic views. The gentry, that is, the members of the feudal organism, operated in their capacity as judicial officers on the basis of a 'natural' insight and assessment and evaluation of a situation. However unburdened by learning, they were resourceful enough in finding 'commonsense' solutions to tricky and otherwise intractable legal and constitutional problems, as the records of the thirteenth century amply prove Neither the idea of consent nor that of representation could find a legitimate habitat within the ecclesiological system. The verdict of the judicial officers however was the verdict of 'the country'. They acted in behalf of the country and 'represented' it. Similarly, consent became an integral element in the law creative process, for the simple reason that both parts of the feudal contract had to be active. Hence the feudal ordering fostered social consciousness and responsibility and presupposed maturity and a sense of independence in proposing or arriving at measures relevant to the well-being of society.

The situation as it developed in the course of the thirteenth century shows how gradual and slow, and sometimes also how painful, the evolution was. The characteristic feature of this purely pragmatic outlook was that it had all the appurtenances of a mundane, this-worldly existence. Nevertheless, it would be wholly erroneous to think that this outlook harboured any opposition to the accepted, traditional and official Christianity. Nothing would be further from the truth. But, by virtue of their own inherent developmental force, such situations tend to grow into something entirely new, which in the end detaches itself from the base upon which it has originally grown. The men in thirteenth-century England acted as 'natural' men when they worked the feudal contract, and had not the remotest intention of opposing any ecclesiological axioms, of which in all likelihood they had only a bare glimmer. They were hardly capable of realizing that there might be some difficulties in reconciling the two standpoints. These men – whether barons, merchants or knights in the shires – acted as nature had ordained. It was a natural social urge that manifested itself in the men of the thirteenth century in England as in France or Germany.

Pursuit of knowledge that exclusively concerns the past, that illumines, opens up and uncovers bygone ages for the benefit of contemporaries, that

explains the actions of men living in distant periods, has always been a
sign of intellectual reflection and curiosity. When one turns to medieval
historiography, one notices once more that in the course of the twelfth
century some not inconsiderable changes in perspective were taking place.
To a large extent historiography in the earlier Middle Ages down to the
twelfth century was an extended biblical exegesis, the core of which was
that everything happened 'by the determinate counsel and foreknowledge
of God' (Acts 2: 23) and that events took place which demonstrated God's
plan. Actuality was seen as the unfolding of a divinely designed programme
and the purpose of writing history was to show how well or how badly this
plan was executed. Seen from a different angle it was the salvific prospect
– salvation – which gave meaning to the events in the past. This standpoint
makes clear why the 'universal histories' almost always started with the
interpretation of the Book of Genesis to proceed chronologically down to
the chronicler's own time. One could indeed here speak of a *Geschichts-
theologie*,[6] a history that was conceived from an essentially theological
angle. Christ was seen as the centre of things and therefore as the saviour
in the literal meaning of the term: the development that had taken place
since Christ's birth was seen in a light different from that which had gone
before. The very concept of the *annus salutis* – 'the year of grace' – or the
computation of time by 'B.C.' or 'A.D.' are obvious pointers to this notion
of history. In a word, divinity was alleged to have revealed itself in the
deeds of men. The chronicler, annalist, etc., merely recorded, he did not
explain: his 'record' was an account of what had happened (or was said to
have happened). This perspective goes some way toward explaining the
'objectivity' in medieval historiography which has often enough been
noticed. As a rule little, if any, attention was paid to individual features,
motivations, aims, characteristics, to group or individual personalities, the
effects of certain intellectual, economic or cultural movements upon the
course of events, and so on. The very title of Guibert of Nogent's work,
'Gesta Dei *per* Francos', brings this kind of historiographical conception
into clear relief. No less indicative are the *Gesta Normannorum* by William
of Jumièges of a little earlier date (late eleventh century), dedicated to
William the Conqueror who became king of the English through God's
will – or in less exalted language was the legitimate ruler of England.[7] A
highly characteristic example is the *Historia scholastica* by Petrus Comestor,

---

6 E. Meuthen in W. Lammers (ed.), *Geschichtsdenken und Geschichtsbild im M.A.*
(Darmstadt, 1965), p. 237. Good observations in A. Gransden, *Historical Writing in
England c. 550 to c. 1307* (London, 1974), pp. 154–5. For the patristic background see
E. P. Meijering, *God Being History* (Amsterdam and Oxford, 1975), especially pp.
52ff. and 81ff.
7 Ed. J. Marx, *Guillaume de Jumièges: Gesta Normannorum Ducum* (Paris, 1914), pp. 2f.
This dedicatory letter significantly refers to William's ancestry and the baptismal
rebirth of Rollo: 'Tandem ad sanctam *infantiam* saluberrimo fonte *renati*.'

written in the twelfth century, which was one of the most popular 'historical' works.[8]

Since history was a record of the deeds of men seen as instruments of
divinity, which most conspicuously focused attention on the rulers, the
yardstick of assessment was the type of Christian ruler seen on the basis
of what was held to be the traditional Christian pattern of rulership. And
this pattern followed the norms of the *novitas vitae* as could be read from
the ninth century in the numerous *Specula regum*. It is incontrovertible
that the king's own rebirth as 'King by the Grace of God' and therefore as
'The Lord's Anointed' had here particular significance. A specific set of
norms was applicable to him alone. He stood on a lonely pedestal or sat on
the throne high above his subjects, thus forming an estate of his own that
he could not, and did not, share with anyone else. Hence the very idea of
the king's rebirth postulated different criteria of judgment applicable to
him alone: they referred to the 'type of Christian ruler'. This typological
aspect of medieval kingship must be kept in mind when one attempts to
understand earlier medieval historiography. This type was in fact enshrined in the royal coronation orders from the ninth century onwards,
which literally refer to the king as *Typus Christi*. It was the type of
Christian ruler that was the object of historiography. Obviously it was
clerics who wrote the chronicles etc. down to the twelfth century: it was
understandable that they should apply ecclesiological axioms to the past.
This kind of historiography was wholly embedded in the thought-pattern
provided by unipolarity. Salvation in the future life was the one aim
towards which every Christian and quite specifically every Christian ruler
was to aspire by directing the subjects whom God had committed to his
care. That was the meaning of the terminology used a thousandfold –
regnum nobis commissum or 'the people entrusted to us' – which implicitly
presupposed the idea of the king's rebirth. It was the idea of rebirth which
reverberated throughout historiography down to the twelfth century, and
to some considerable extent also beyond.

The typological orientation also explains the very large quantity of
hagiographic writings. In the earlier Middle Ages especially they assumed
proportions and dimensions which stand in no relation whatsoever to their
worth as historical sources. What the numerous saints' *Lives* intended to
show was the type of man (or woman) who in a pronounced degree fulfilled the norms of the 'new life'. Applied to the field of government, the
saints' lives were intended to be practical demonstrations of what a
Christian ruler 'really' was and what the *Specula regum* set forth in a

---

8   On the function of history in this context cf. the instructive observations by H.
Wolter, 'Geschichtliche Bildung im Rahmen der artes liberales' in *Artes liberales*, ed.
J. Koch (Leiden and Cologne, 1959), pp. 50–83, especially John of Salisbury, pp. 54ff.;
Hugh of St Victor and Thierry of Chartres, pp. 60ff.

scholarly and doctrinal manner by detailing the duties of Christian king-ship. The saints – and there were quite a few who were invented to demonstrate a particular type of conformity – represented easily under-standable models for others. Therein lay the true significance of these *Vitae*: they showed an objective type of man or ruler and it was this that mattered, that is, the deeds of the man, the miracles he worked, the changes he wrought by his works of charity, and so on. At the same time there was virtually nothing that resembled what is commonly understood to be biography or autobiography. Of the latter there is not even a worth-while exception to the rule, while for the former there are some, such as Einhard's *Vita Karoli*, Asser's *Life of King Alfred*, or Wipo's biographical sketch of Conrad II or the anonymous *Vita Heinrici IV*, but these are partly modelled on (Roman) prototypes or give so fragmentary or de-hydrated a picture that they hardly provide an adequate biography. Is it not significant that in his preface Wipo apologetically says that to compose this historical account is not forbidden by religion?[9] Yet it would be wholly erroneous to say that chroniclers etc. lacked the ability to describe individual features. On the contrary, some of them had excellent observ-ational powers. One has but to mention Liutprand of Cremona's portrayal of Byzantine scenes, or Lambert of Hersfeld's concealed (and dangerously misleading) 'objective' record of Henry IV, or Orderic Vitalis' sketchy portraits of some of his Norman personalities, to realize that the talent was quite obviously there. But it was encapsuled in the *Gesta*, in the objective record, and was not employed to explain historically relevant motivations or lines of communication or cause and effect.

The change in the twelfth century comes gradually and almost imper-ceptibly. This change was largely due to the severe jolts which the Investi-ture Contest had administered to alert contemporaries. The attempt to explain an evolving situation by reference to humanly conceived and understandable effects is the result of an awareness of factors which had hitherto been neglected or not recognized in their causal efficacy. A 'causal' historiography must needs put the actors into the foreground: it involved the comprehension of motives, aims, and aspirations from a merely human perspective. This attempt to explain cause and effect in humanly comprehensible terms made it necessary that greater and greater attention should be paid to the natural forces propelling the individual, since he it was who was beginning to be held to have initiated the actions to be explained to humans in humanly understandable terms. Hence the widening of the intellectual horizon and perception that accompanies this new trend. No longer circumscribed by the rigid framework of biblical

9 'Illa igitur est causa scribendi, quod nulla vetat religio et commendat intentio et proderit patriae', Wipo, *Vita Chuonradi*, edition in *MGH SS*, XI.255, lines 41f.

exegesis and a fixed divine design, the chronicler, or interpreter, or indeed historian, begins to look at the mundane causes and effects observable by man with his own natural gifts. And the evaluation adopted secular or human criteria rather than the one assumed to be pre-designed by the ecclesiological or religious or biblical theme. No longer is it the 'monobasic' kind of description or accounting of events, but the multiformity, the plurality and complexity of motivations, variegated interests and pursuits of the acting rulers and lesser mortals which concerns the historian. Herewith, however, the theme of totality suffered quite serious inroads. Previously it was by no means uncommon to call a general historical work simply *Ecclesiastical History* – good examples are Bede or Orderic Vitalis.[10] In the course of the twelfth century this kind of 'totalitarian' ecclesiastical history begins to give way to atomizing historiography, in which the ecclesiologically conceived theme of totality – the Church embracing the totality of life – is no longer predominant.

A new historiographical orientation with firm contours and concrete horizon is presented by Otto of Freising. It is clearly no coincidence that Otto of Freising began to tread new paths. His education, his high ecclesiastical offices (he was successively abbot of Morimund and bishop of Freising), and above all his intimate and very close relations with his nephew, Frederick I, and his participation in the crusading enterprise at the side of his step-brother Conrad III in the Near East (1147–1150), engendered an outlook that, in some respects at least, quite radically differed from the customary approach to historical writings. And, as already indicated, the Roman law opened up vistas which were peculiarly apt to promote the secular dimensions of historical studies. And the impact of Roman law was felt in precisely the reign of Otto's nephew, the Staufen Frederick Barbarossa. Although Otto's *Chronica* are still greatly influenced by traditional modes of thought, such as the emphasis on the nothingness and purely transitory character of terrestrial life, nonetheless a closer analysis shows an underlying philosophy of history that constitutes a rather marked departure from accepted ways of thinking about the past. To him change was the constantly occurring and observable element in history, change, that is, that affected society no less than its government. This standpoint reveals not only well-developed observational powers but also deep reflection and an extraordinary knowledge of ancient literature.

---

10   It is perhaps noteworthy that Orderic's first book begins with a 'Life of Christ', supposedly biographical: it may be that Orderic tried to separate the historical from the theological Christ: *Hist. Eccles.*, I.1–15, in *PL* 188.17–60. A similar trend is observable in Eadmer. Biographical accounts of Christ above all seem to become fashionable, cf. Alexander Neckam's 'Life and Suffering of Christ' which in Latin metric form (aaaa; bbbb; etc.) portrays for didactic and edifying purposes a 'life' of Christ at the end of the twelfth century: Ms. in ULC: Ee 6.29, fol. 45r–54v.

Rerum cognoscere causas constituted for him the substance and object of historical investigation.[11]

Otto was one of the first to harness medical knowledge to the explanation of historical developments: for him the kaleidoscopic pattern of the past was contingent upon the physiological composition of man himself. It was in this context that he spoke of the '*humana* potentia', of purely human power which was the real kernel of all history. The deployment of human power by ordinary mortals was what made history.[12] The characteristic feature of (what he most significantly called) the '*mundialis* dignitas' was its changeability, unpredictability and restlessness. Indeed, the concepts of the 'mundane' and of the 'human' become operational instruments in Otto's thought-pattern. For him it is man himself who is and becomes the dynamic organ, is himself responsible, because he initiates developments. And there is very little suggestion that it is reborn man who is at the centre of the stage, but man as such and his *human* potential. Man's *humanitas* enters the historic stage and it is composed of many strains and elements: 'humanity is the inner core of man's real being and consists of many parts.'[13] And indeed most significantly part of this *humanitas* is his *animalitas*.[14] The role allocated to the individual is that of a moving organ that changes the course of mundane events. This is a standpoint that accords well with the process of secularization observable in contemporary government. However much this basic conception of *humanitas* depends on Gilbert de la Porrée[15] the important point here is that the individual, man himself, precisely because he has an *individua substantia*, becomes the bearer of historical developments. He is one whole and approaches the level of autonomy. The *individua substantia*, Otto says, is by itself a unit.[16] Man carries the individuality in himself and follows his own *animalitas* as well as his *rationalitas*.[17] Or seen from yet another angle Otto views man as a *persona mundialis*, that is, as a person who belongs to this world and is

---

11   *Gesta Friderici*, edition in *MGH SSRRGG*, 3rd edition (1912), p. 16. Cf. Virgil, *Georgics*, II. 490 (Loeb, p. 150) ('Fortunate he is who has been able to discover the causes of things'). Cf. also Cicero, *De natura deorum*, I. 48 (Loeb, p. 114) ('Mysteries when rationally interpreted prove to have more to do with the nature of things than with that of the gods'); *id.*, *De officiis*, I. 4 (Loeb, p. 12).

12   Cf., e.g., *Chronica* (edition in *MGH SSRRGG* (1912), II.51, p. 129; I Prol., p. 8; also V Prol., p. 227. Cf. J. Koch (in Lammers, above, n. 6), pp. 321ff.

13   *Gesta*, p. 18: 'Humanitas quae est integrum *esse hominis* et ex multis formis composita.'

14   Rightly pointed out by J. Koch, *loc. cit.*, p. 341. Cf. also M.-D. Chenu, *Nature, Man and Society in the 12th Century* (Chicago, 1969), pp. 194f. See now G. Wolf, 'Das 12. Jahrhundert als Geburtsstunde der Moderne und die Frage nach der Krise der Geschichtswissenschaft' in *Misc. Medievalia*, 9(1974), 80ff., who rightly sees in Otto of Freising an instance of the new historical thinking.

15   See on this J. Koch, *loc. cit.*, p. 342 (also on Boethius).

16   *Gesta*, p. 79: 'est per se una.'

17   I.5, p. 18. Also I.55, pp. 77f.

subjected to all the laws of the world, as he declares in his dedicatory letter to Frederick Barbarossa. To this concept of the *persona mundialis* special attention must be drawn. It designates man as a creature of this world who is credited with the power to set into motion historically relevant actions. 'By rational insight' (*intuitu rationis*), Otto tells us, he wishes to portray the past,[18] which is a standpoint that reveals a development of considerable dimensions. The monopoly of religiously orientated and ecclesiologically determined aims and motivations is broken.

Otto of Freising is an early example of the new thought-patterns which see no conflict between the ecclesiological and the secular points of view. On the contrary, they are said to be in harmony with each other. One of the purposes of his writing *The Two Cities* was precisely to emphasize the permanence and immutability of the community in the *civitas Dei*,[19] which stands in sharp contradistinction to the never ending change that occurred in the *civitas terrena*. Or seen from yet another angle the naturalness of this world necessarily involves change – as testified by medical science and the insight it allows into the natural (or physical) composition of man, and change means evolution, growth and decay as well as recovery. The historical process therefore followed the natural line, and hence, after a very long lapse of time, the personality (*personalitas*) of man once more becomes the object of examination, analysis and evaluation. It is the *human* personality which partakes in the natural process of change and is thereby clearly distinguished from the baptismally conditioned new creature. Otto's terminology throws into clear relief the secularized ways of thinking which began to characterize the age. To use his own words once again, the *persona mundialis* and its concomitant *personalitas*, man's *humanitas* and its component part, his *animalitas*, reveal themselves in the historical process. The observer here witnesses in Otto of Freising a cosmology that is in no wise opposed to the purely transcendental, religious or ecclesiologically orientated cosmology. On the contrary, both supplement each other.

There is a remarkable similarity between Otto of Freising and his contemporary William of Malmesbury, in regard to both the rational, cognitive and critical method and to the weight ascribed to secular–mundane features. The strongly marked interest in the manifestations of mundane life, mundane history and the mundane dimensions of government is certainly a feature that is highly significant. It convincingly shows that, entirely independently, two such eminent writers ascribed to the mundane–secular perspectives greater attention than they had hitherto

18   For this see J. Koch, p. 346.
19   Prol. I *Chron.*, p. 6. For excellent observations see J. Spörl in *Geschichtsdenken* (above, n. 6), pp. 298ff.

received. We have just seen what form this heightened mundane interest took in Otto of Freising. This same concern emerged in William of Malmesbury, who divided the subject of history into its two component parts, epitomized by secular–mundane royal history on the one hand, and ecclesiastical–religious history on the other. To the former corresponded his *Gesta Regum* (the deeds of the kings) and to the latter his *Gesta Pontificum* (the deeds of the bishops). This division implicitly questioned the totality point of view. The contemporaneity of these points of view expressed by Otto and William makes a comparison between these two masters of historical writing a fascinating object of analysis.

Indeed, a 'mundanized' or 'humanized' historiography was the exact complement of the secularized basis of government. Both government and historiography were manifestations of the same secular spirit that for entirely different reasons had come to prevail in the urban, rural and feudal communities. The close proximity between government and historiography is not difficult to understand, since the chief organs in the antecedent and the new historiographical orientation were the governments, or rather the rulers themselves. But the meaning and function of this focal point began to change, since it was no longer the hallowed typology of Christian rulership that reigned supreme in historical writings, but, to use Otto of Freising's terminology, the *individua substantia* made concrete in the ruler himself as a *persona mundialis*. Here it must once more be stressed what a powerful stimulus the secularization of government had provided. This process could well be seen as an initiating impulse and pre-condition for the 'mundanization' or 'humanization' of historiography. Moreover, the educational advances in the towns reflected by the growth of established universities and the foundations of new ones, better schooling, and in the early thirteenth century the spread of learning by the Friars, very persuasively mirrored this liberalization of intellectual forces.[20]

For this liberalization of intellectual forces the twelfth-century jurist, diplomat and translator Burgundio of Pisa (died 1193) might well serve

---

20 Here Gerald of Wales must be mentioned: his works are distinguished by his extremely well developed and acute sense of observation, knowledge of men, and descriptive powers, which allow him to portray men, scenes and situations vividly. He was one of the first who might be called a social historian. His attention is riveted on nature itself, on the hills and rivers no less than on the comic side in social relations, especially in the higher circles. Less than a generation afterwards the Franciscan Salimbene of Parma was to compose his *Chronica*, which testifies to a highly developed sense of realism. The work is a social and cultural history of thirteenth-century Italy: it is full of details which so far had never been observed or, if observed, had been considered too mundane, and therefore too trivial, to be recorded: after all, they were 'merely' human details, such as eating and drinking habits, jokes, the all-too-human deficiencies of the monastic brethren, the intrigues among the high and low, not to mention his lively character portraits (*Chronica*, edition in *MGH SS* XXXII. 1–652; GT (1914); IT (1925)).

as an example. As he wrote in the second half of the century, he merits a few remarks in the present context. He was not only thoroughly versed in Greek, but he also translated a very great number of Greek works into Latin and had a European reputation as a many-sided scholar, for which John of Salisbury may be cited as a witness.[21] Apart from some Homilies by Chrysostom on the Matthean and Johannine gospels, he translated an astonishingly large number of medical writings by Galenus, the great compiler of medical writings in the second century A.D. This interest in medicine by so versatile a scholar as Burgundio assumes its special significance when it is linked with the translation of the work by Nemesius of Emesa, a Syrian bishop of the fourth century who wrote a book on the nature of man. The recipient of Burgundio's translation, *De natura hominis*, was none other than Frederick Barbarossa, whom the translator addressed in the dedicatory letter in these words: 'Since I had noticed in our conversations that Your Majesty would wish to know the nature of things' – *rerum naturam cognoscere*: the same classical terminology, it will be noted, as Otto of Freising used – 'as well as their causes, I have resolved to translate this book for Your Majesty's benefit . . .'[22] The contents of this Epistle prove in fact how well versed Burgundio was in problems of Greek natural science. In fact, the tract is really an anthropological–medical dissertation on man within a Christian setting. Man is simply a species of the genus 'animal': and man is constantly referred to as an animal and his capabilities are 'animales virtutes'.[23] The distance between this kind of approach and the one adopted, say, two generations earlier, is so obvious that no further comment is necessary, except to remark that the fertility of the soil for this sort of production is proved by the very great number of still surviving manuscripts.

It was precisely in pursuit of historical enquiries on a mundane–human level that the new genre of biography began to replace hagiographic

---

21 John of Salisbury, *Metalogicus*, IV.7. For details see P. Classen, *Burgundio of Pisa, Richter, Gesandter, Übersetzer* (= *SB* Heidelberg, 1974, fasc. 4).

22 New edition with FT by G. Verbeke and J. R. Moncho, *Némésius d'Émèse* (= *Corpus Latinum commentariorum in Aristotelem Graecorum*; suppl. I, Leiden, 1975). ET in *LCC* IV(1955). For the beginning of the revival of patristic knowledge in the twelfth century, especially in regard to the philosophical view of man, see E. Garin, 'La dignitas hominis e la letteratura patristica' in *Rin*, 1(1938), 102ff., especially 112ff. on Nemesius. Cf. also below, p. 105, n. 36.

23 Cf. *ed. cit.*, Cap. 4, p. 69: the body exists 'simul cum animalibus virtutibus'. The tract summed up Greek natural and medical thought, including Aristotle, Galenus, Hippocrates, etc. The author treats of the function of the heart, pulsation ('vitalis spiritus ab hoc (corde) per arterias ad totum corpus disseminatur', Cap. 23, p. 107), respiration, digestion, metabolism, kidneys, teeth, tongue, etc. But this was only one of the Greek works current which must have softened up the soil for the reception of Greek 'political' thought.

literature.[24] The hagiographical work – or legend – depicted a typical portrait quite in conformity with the prevailing typology, but the biographical work focuses its attention on the reality of the human personality and its characteristic and individual traits. Some English works clearly point to the future, such as the Life of Anselm by Eadmer, or the tentative biographies of Thomas Becket by Herbert of Bosham and by Alan of Tewkesbury, or Gerald of Wales' biographical sketches of Hugh of Lincoln or Geoffrey of York, where a portrayal of personal features was attempted. There is no doubt that a keen eye for the physiognomy and the individual bearing of historical personages characterized a good deal of twelfth-century writing, such as that already mentioned of William of Malmesbury, or Ailred of Rievaulx, or Ralph Diceto, which clearly point to Suetonius as a model. As indicated, Gerald of Wales revealed quite extraordinary powers of observation in the description of the Welsh and Irish customs as well as of the regional animalic world.[25]

Throughout the thirteenth century the biographical genre makes steady progress and gains in depth and width. The observational powers of some thirteenth-century biographers would seem extremely keen, witness, for instance, the biographical sketch of Frederick II by one of his teachers, depicting the youth as he 'really' was in 1207.[26] What marked this new literature was the intention of the author, which was to present not a type to be emulated, but a real personality in its individual uniqueness. The first biography of Thomas Aquinas gives us vivid personal glimpses of the man walking up and down in the garden of the priory obviously searching for an adequate answer to specific sets of problems or the best formulation of a train of thought, or talking shop at meals – and forgetting matters of a more mundane kind. The significance of the new biographical literary productions lies in the concentration on man himself, on his natural, personal characteristics, on his *humanitas* and, as Otto of Freising would have added, also on his *animalitas*, which commanded increasing attention.

But no less significant in this context is the first tentative appearance of autobiography – an entirely new literary species. If we exempt the autobiographical sketch by the Jewish convert Hermann of Cologne, who was later an abbot (about 1130–1140),[27] Gerald of Wales, once more, seems one of the earliest who collected material with a view to writing a work

---

24 For a masterly survey see M. Manitius, *Geschichte der lateinischen Literatur des M.A.* III, (reprinted Munich, 1973), p. 566ff. Cf. also H. Wellmer, *Persönliches Memento im deutschen M.A.* (Stuttgart, 1973).
25 Cf. above, n. 20, and especially A. Gransden, 'Realistic observation in twelfth-century England' in *Speculum*, 47(1972), 29ff., with some excellent illustrations from Gerald's *Topographia Hibernica*.
26 See K. Hampe, 'Kaiser Friedrich II.' in *HZ*, 83(1899), 1–42, at pp. 8ff.
27 Cf. M. Manitius, *op. cit.*, III.592f.

entitled *De rebus a se gestis* (about 1205):[28] Gerald was perceptive enough
to be capable of self-criticism. Another notable autobiographical work is
that by Philippe of Novare[29] who is at once mature, observant, and self-
critical in his self-portrait, which allows later generations more than a
glimpse of a Frenchman engaged in high public office and seen through
his own eyes. Dante's *Vita nuova* is clearly outstanding in conception,
style and dexterity of presentation. Both biography and autobiography
prove how much natural man, his personality and humanity, had attracted
general attention in the course of the thirteenth century. The age of
typology was giving way to one which recognized man's natural complexity.

In proximity to the topic of biography and autobiography stands that of
vernacular literature. The cultivation of vernacular language as a literary
medium became a clearly perceptible feature observable in England,
France and Germany from the latter part of the twelfth century onwards,
so much so that even legal works – notoriously the most conservative
intellectual products – came to be written in the vernacular. The significance of the vernacular as a legitimate means of literary exposition lies not
in the relegation of Latin to a secondary place, but in the indisputable
demand by wide sections of the populace for literary productions which
satisfied them on their own level. Hence the great variety of legends,
visionary stories, allegorical explanations of the Bible, and not least the
demand for translations from the Bible into a vernacular idiom. Versified
hagiographical *Lives* written in the vernacular for perusal by the laity
make their début in the thirteenth century, for which Matthew Paris can
serve as an illustration. It is nevertheless worthy of remark that there was a
paucity and poverty of religious songs in the vernacular during the
twelfth and thirteenth centuries. To a veritable plethora of Latin hymns
there corresponded only a few vernacular hymns. Latin assuredly maintained its monopoly in the strictly ecclesiastical and religious precincts. It
was clearly understood to belong to a world different from that populated
by ordinary mankind. Latin was, so to speak, the medium of communication with divinity which expressed the mediatory function of the priesthood within a linguistic framework. But in spheres of purely human,

28 Ed. and ET by E. H. Butler (1937), *The Autobiography of Giraldus Cambrensis*. See
especially the introduction, pp. 22ff. For Gerald see also A. Gransden, *op. cit.* (above,
n. 6), p. 242. In the brief autobiographical sketch by Orderic Vitalis which is a
thanksgiving prayer he refers to his own baptism through which 'by water and the
Holy Ghost you have reborn me' ('me regenerasti').

29 *Philippe de Novare: Memoires (1218–1243)*, edition in *Les classiques français du moyen
âge*, ed. Mario Roques, X(1913). An earlier instance was Guibert of Nogent's *De
vita sua*, about which see J. F. Benton in the introduction to the ET in his *Self and
Society in Medieval France: The Memoirs of Abbot Guibert of Nogent* (New York,
1970).

secular concern the vernacular idiom gradually expanded and even came to include philosophical enquiries.[30]

Indeed, could the subtler feelings, reactions, shades of meaning, nuances of affection, enchantment and disappointment, emotions of love, passion, envy, and so on, be expressed with the same facility and felicity in Latin as in the vernacular? Latin had been a dead language since the sixth century – except in the lecture halls and in disputations and examinations in the universities – and ordinary mortals including rulers, scholars, and ecclesiastics thought and conversed and felt and sensed in their own tongue. The acceleration of vernacular literature furnishes incontrovertible proof of the efficacy of the laws of demand and supply. Latin was accessible to only a tiny part of the population, but the vernacular idiom found a ready response. Whereas in the earlier part of the twelfth century Orderic Vitalis had begun his *Ecclesiastical History* with an 'account' of the life of Christ[31] and a little later Petrus Comestor dealt with the same topic within the frame of his *Historia scholastica*,[32] a generation afterwards (around 1187) a Bavarian priest, Wernher, was to write three poems in the vernacular to portray the life of the Virgin. Since the New Testament gave no details, the 'facts' are worthless, but this defect fades into the background when due weight is given to the intention of composing a life of the Virgin.[33]

Talent for vernacular compositions was abundantly in evidence. In this context at least a passing mention must be made of the *Nibelungenlied* in German-speaking regions which received its eventual fixation and formulation at the turn of the twelfth and thirteenth centuries, when the

---

30 For the beginnings of vernacular literature cf. the classic exposition by E. Curtius, *European Literature in the Latin M.A.* (New York, 1953), pp. 383ff.: 'Latin culture and poetry precede, French follows.' Cf. also p. 387. For obvious reasons I omit Anglo-Saxon and Irish vernacular products. What deserves at least a passing remark is that in the Eastern empire the so-called vernacular literature also began to flourish in the twelfth century, though essentially it was a common form of Greek which as 'Attic Greek' underscored the continuity with classical antiquity. For details, see H.-G. Beck, *Geschichte der byzantinischen Volksliteratur* (Munich, 1971), pp. 4ff. In the West there was a sharp dividing line between the vernacular and the Latin. Here is a wide field of comparative research with large social, literary, intellectual and linguistic implications. For some remarks on this topic cf. W. Ullmann, *The Future of Medieval History* (Cambridge, 1973), pp. 26f.

31 See above, p. 64, n. 10.

32 He called this part *Historia evangelica* (*PL* 198, at col. 1537ff.). For Alexander Neckam's biography see also above, n. 10. Yet it should also be pointed out that Ludolph of Saxony's *Vita Jesu Christi e quatuor evangeliis concinnata*, written in the thirteenth century, enjoyed no fewer than eighty-eight editions and translations into numerous languages. See M. I. Bodenstedt, *The Vita Christi of Ludolph the Carthusian* (Washington, 1944).

33 For this see A. Hauck, *Kirchengeschichte Deutschlands*, IV, 8th edition (reprinted 1965), p. 531.

numerous ancestral strands were drawn together. Its underlying tone and message is lay, secular, mundane and yet it is suffused with a severe philosophical (and moral) tenor – the problem of human guilt, the explanation of evil, the intelligibility of the ever present suffering caused by vicissitudes. No less significant here is the stress on the autonomy of the human will, which shows how ancient mythological themes could be harnessed to the service of 'moral' problems and treated in the vernacular. The literary device of the vernacular epic that presents a problem which besets all mankind at all times and places was particularly impressive and evocative. That in the twelfth century the French vernacular (as instanced by Chrétien de Troyes) became especially important within literary domains is understandable in view of the vast expanse of Norman and Angevin rule, and the strong influence which French culture had on the other end of Europe, that is the South of Italy and Sicily where, under William II, the last legitimate Norman king of Hauteville had married the youngest daughter of Henry II (Joan). This two-pronged French influence was to set its seal upon vernacular literature in large areas of Europe from the twelfth century onwards. For French literature exercised a conspicuous influence on German vernacular poetry in the early thirteenth century, which 'was to prove the most brilliant in the history of medieval German literature',[34] evidenced by, say, Hartmann von Aue, Gottfried von Strasbourg or Wolfram von Eschenbach, whose epic is suffused with a naturalism that is indeed refreshing.

The increased demand for vernacular literature as the thirteenth century progressed made 'bilingualism' a virtual necessity for a time. What the observer witnesses is the hitherto not fully appreciated feature of men writing in both tongues – in Latin as well as in the vernacular. The turn of the thirteenth century shows two excellent examples and both are Italians:[35] Dante and Cino da Pistoia. The former, himself an advocate of the vernacular, wrote not only the most beautiful and superb Italian prose and poetry, but also equally well-composed Latin tracts with the same felicity of expression and the same facility of style as was at his disposal in the vernacular. Dante's friend Cino was one of the really great jurists at the time: his juristic commentaries are models of clarity and simplicity, whereas his Italian poems show the same man in the realm of poetic licence. The significance of this indubitably unique feature – not confined

---

34　See J. G. Robertson, *A History of German Literature*, 6th edition (London, 1970), p. 71. At the same time there can be witnessed 'political poetry' concerned as it was with the double election in 1198, for which see now E. Thurnher, 'Die deutsche Hofpoesie um Friedrich II.' in *Deutsches Archiv*, 31(1975), 215ff., at pp. 218f.; later Walther von der Vogelweide and Reinmar of Zweten became 'court poets' (pp. 225ff.).

35　For a competent survey cf. B. Pullan, *A History of the Early Renaissance in Italy* (London, 1973), pp. 175ff.

to Italy – is that one and the same individual as a man of the universal order wrote in Latin, the traditional medium for broadcasting universal themes and which, as indicated, so powerfully assisted ecclesiological universalism, whereas as a member of his ethnic or national or linguistic group he employed the vernacular. In the former capacity he pursued the universal line, disregarding natural boundaries, hence was literally supranatural, whereas in the latter capacity he moved on a narrower, natural, plane. This bilingual literary capacity was highly characteristic of this age of transition. Man was still both a *homo universalis* and a member of his nation; he was universal and particular; he partook linguistically in the natural as well as in the supranatural concerns, by composing in the vernacular as well as in the Latin idiom; he was both (to use the ecclesiologically traditional terminology) an unregenerated and a regenerated creature. In these bilingual precincts the theme of bipolarity is symptomatically expressed.

At least a passing remark should be made about two specimens of another genre which are illuminating from a different standpoint. The oldest of the *Chansons de geste* – the *Chanson de Roland* – was translated into the German vernacular by Conrad of Regensburg about 1140.[36] Although it does not attain the poetic vigour of the original French,[37] it nevertheless assumes significance in our context, because it is a good example of how powerful national animosities had been even at this incipient stage. Conrad excised all French elements and substituted for them a strongly religious theme. Charlemagne thus became the legendary Christian missionary who brought to the infidels with fire and sword the true religion which, needless to say, they at once embraced. The other vernacular specimen comes largely from the same Conrad written about 1152–4: it is in fact the oldest historical work composed in the German vernacular. The *Kaiserchronik* is less important as regards its main theme – a very great deal belongs to the realm of lively imagination – than for the less exalted activities of lowly-placed mortals. The work tells us much about knights, burgesses and peasants as well as about the way townships began to treat their municipal business in the council room in which matters of concern to all were discussed. The determinative part of the towns consisted of the merchants, and the author had a sharp eye for the socio-economic differences that divided rich from poor, a feature that was apparently far more conspicuous in the town than in the country.[38] The *Kaiserchronik* also mirrors the impact which the laity was beginning to

---

36 *Rolandslied*, ed. C. Wesle (Bonn, 1928).
37 Cf. R. Fawtier, *La chanson de Roland: étude historique* (Paris, 1933).
38 Edition in *MGH Deutsche Chroniken*, I(1892). See especially verses 1585, 2130, 8112, 10680ff., 14555, etc. For details cf. now C. Gellinck, *Die deutsche Kaiserchronik: Erzähltechnik und Kritik* (Frankfurt, 1971).

make. The work is a remarkable mixture of uncritically reproduced legends and some hard and well-observed facts. It was to be eclipsed by the highly advanced Italian urban histories by, say, Dino Compagni or Ricardo Malaspina in the thirteenth century.

But the *Kaiserchronik* was by no means the only historical work of the twelfth century that was composed in the vernacular. In the second half of this same twelfth century came also to be written the historiographically important *Geste des Normans* by Wace, who in actual fact was in the service of Henry II and commissioned by him. The work was probably written in England but in French.[39] This kind of historical literature in the form of poetry was continued by another *amicus curiae* of Henry II, Benoit de Saint-Maure, who was also commissioned by the king: he wrote the *Chronique des ducs de Normandie* which – like Wace before him – he did not finish. In 1174 Henry entrusted somebody else (whose name has not been transmitted) to bring the work to a successful conclusion.[40]

In the latter half of the twelfth century the strict enforcement of ecclesiastical governmental principles in all spheres of religious, social and cultural life provoked increasing resistance in many quarters throughout Europe. This enforcement stimulated an enquiry into the Bible, universally held to be the foundation of all ecclesiastical and hence also governmental axioms. Now, resistance and criticism had not been entirely unknown features in previous ages but what has hardly been properly assessed in its historical context is that they had not taken the form which they now took. For in combination they whetted the appetite for Bible reading, so that the members of the resistance or opposition groups could form their own opinions. In other words, they wished to know more about the text of the Bible, but this could not be achieved until and unless it was available in translation. This explains the appearance of biblical translations in the beginning of the thirteenth century.[41] The geographical distribution of these vernacular translations was sporadic and uneven, but the very evident need and demand for translations is symptomatic, not only because it shows the awakening of a critical and searching spirit that could be satisfied only by a text readily understandable, but also because it proves a detachment on the part of the laity from the concept of the official hierarchy as the sole interpreters and expositors of the Bible. Latin

---

39 Ed. H. Andresen, *Maistre Wace's roman de Rou et les ducs de Normandie* (Heilbronn, 1877–9). Excellent critical introduction by the editor, especially pp. LXVIIIff. and XCIIIff.

40 Details in P. A. Becker, *Zur romanischen Literaturgeschichte* (Munich, 1967), pp. 466–95.

41 For details see H. Grundmann, *Religiöse Bewegungen im M.A.*, new edition (Darmstadt, 1961), pp. 447ff. The first French and German translations followed in quick succession. There were frequent decrees prohibiting vernacular translations which were primarily intended for use by preachers.

was the prerogative of the educated elite – it is certainly of some interest to note that governments, despite all their secularist protestations, did not encourage biblical translations – and Latin was held to be the language of divinity, as was daily shown in the services and rites. One may go as far as to say that down to the late fourteenth century there was an in-built resistance to turning the Latin text of the Bible (or for that matter of prayers, etc. in the services) into a vernacular idiom. And when the Bible was translated, the popular response was by no means as overwhelming as one would have expected it to be. But in the present context the relevance of a vernacular Bible text is plain: it was a touchstone of increasing interest on the part of the laity and of a critical attitude towards deductions drawn from a book the contents of which were, by virtue of a language barrier, hidden from the large mass of the population. Among the forces which engendered renaissance humanism biblical translations indubitably demand attention.

Translation from one language into another, together with vernacular compositions, could not but help to sharpen the awareness of differences in society, customs, habits, outlook (however much conditioned by history, geography or natural forces) of neighbouring peoples, in a word, of national differences. The emergence of vernacular literature was evidence of the articulation of groups which by virtue of linguistic, ethnic, biological or other natural factors were to assume nationhood. The nation was a natural unit, and as such had evidently great affinities with natural, unregenerated, man: the nation was natural man writ large. And it was assuredly no coincidence that the idea of nationhood began to make its entry onto the historical stage at the same time as the vernacular began its triumphant career. The differences between the French, the Germans and the Southerners were clearly in evidence in the late twelfth century, however much they may have shared common ecclesiological or religious premises.

Seen from a wider historical angle, however, the emergence of the nation was little more than the rebirth or restoration, the renaissance, of the old tribal groups under a different name. The Lombards, the Bur-gundians, the Franks, the Frisians, the Saxons, etc., had all been absorbed by the ecclesiological universal unit, and ceased to exist as independent entities. The parallelism with the individual is too striking to be overlooked. Just as natural man was absorbed into the universal Church, and ceased to be an autonomous being precisely because of this absorption, in the same way the tribal groups as natural unregenerated entities were 'regenerated' and vanished as independent units, because they were submerged in the ecclesiological universal unit. Within the ecclesiological unit there was no room for an independent, autonomous nation.

It is indeed astonishing to witness the progress of the idea of nationhood in the thirteenth century. A few examples should illustrate this trend. The historian and later cardinal James of Vitry (died 1254) tells us that in academic circles at Paris university in the beginning of the century the French were known as high-spirited, gentle and effeminate; the Germans as raving, boisterous and inclined to obscenities in social and convivial functions; the Lombards as avaricious, malicious and faint-hearted; the Romans as seditious, violent and light with their fingers; the Sicilians as tyrannous and cruel.[42] Or, to go into a different field, the Poitevins in the 20s and 30s of the thirteenth century were considered 'foreigners' by the 'native' English barons. In the universities it was the 'nations' which formed the constituent component parts of the academic community. In the ecclesiastical councils, which were universal councils, the principle of voting by 'nations' was also accepted in the thirteenth century. In a word, the nation as a homogeneous group had most decidedly emerged as a unit and as an influential factor which it certainly had not previously been. The essential point is that the nation was seen as a perfectly natural union that was soon to acquire legal, corporate personality. Its autonomy that came to be expressed in territorial sovereignty, potently prepared as this was by the change of the *Rex Francorum* into a *Rex Franciae* (or the *Rex Anglorum* into the *Rex Angliae*) and the like, corresponded to the autonomy of those who were its members. The nation was, indeed, natural man writ large.

In the 80s of the thirteenth century the canon of Cologne, Alexander of Roes, wrote a number of works which reveal not only how keenly observant, perceptive and alert men were in regard to the differences in the characteristics of the nations in Europe, but also the extent of their ability to harness these differences to a constructive integrating programme, in itself barely a figleaf to hide the disintegrating effects of the national units. What is especially noteworthy is that Alexander was not in the least touched by the new cosmologies as they were broadcast in all academic circles: he was blissfully unaware of the new Aristotelian ideas which just then were the topic of widely differing scholarly expositions. He neatly categorized what he considered the traits of the three 'principal' nations – the French, the German and the Italians (their inclusion is certainly remarkable at this time) – and utilized these to construct a programme that would still fit the traditional ecclesiological pattern. The triad consisting of the clergy, the empire and scholarship (*sacerdotium, imperium, studium*) should form the pillars of the universal entity because by these three the basic virtues of soul, body and intellect 'the holy catholic church' was

---

42 See James of Vitry, *Historia occidentalis*, ed. J. F. Hinnebusch (Fribourg, 1972), ch. 7, p. 92, lines 1–21. Cf. the editor at p. 12: 'Jacques is certainly one of the most clear-sighted observers of church life in his day . . . an informed and profound judge of local conditions.'

sustained.[43] According to him the Trinity (God the Father, the Son and the Holy Ghost) had disposed that these three parts of Europe should constitute the Church.[44] The three were symbolized by Rome (the Church), Paris (scholarship) and the four sees in which imperial power was at one time located (Aachen, Arles, Milan and Rome). The innate, natural faculties of the members of the nations should be harnessed to the service of an all-embracing ecclesiological unit, the Church,[45] in order to stem the fragmentation of the universal body of Christians. Indeed, it was the fusion of this still largely embryonic nationalism in the thirteenth century with the emerging concept of the State as a natural unit which was to yield the national State. This combination of nationalism and etatism was to seal the demise of medieval universality, totality and unipolarity, and to provide the scaffolding of the modern European structure.

How receptive in fact the soil was for the new Aristotelian cosmology can be further shown by the same Alexander, who seems to have been one of the earliest writers to portray a sociological classification in his enumeration of three orders which constituted the German, French and Italian nations. These were the common people, the military, and the clergy. And the special qualities of each nation were represented by the relevant order – thus in Italy it was the common people who dominated the public scene; in Germany this role belonged to the nobility, that is the military caste, and in France to the clergy. Each nation received its imprint from the predominant order or class or group. Not the least noteworthy thesis of Alexander was that the nation was prior to the social order.[46] A point of view such as this goes a long way toward explaining how and why Aristotelian theses were so effortlessly absorbed. Aristotle's view that the whole was prior to the part and the State prior to the citizen had assuredly been anticipated in an un-Aristotelian manner by Alexander of Roes who was quite uncontaminated by any contact with 'The Philosopher'. Yet in another way he foreshadowed Dante by saying that the law to be created

---

43 Alexander, *Memoriale*, ed. H. Grundmann and H. Heimpel (Weimar, 1949), p. 48. See also his *Notitia saeculi*, ed. *ibid.*, cc. 12f., pp. 84ff.

44 *Notitia*, cap. 12, p. 84. The theme here touched upon is that of the so-called *translatio studii* (from Athens to Paris), a well-known medieval topic. For this see A. G. Jonkers, 'Translatio studii' in *Misc. medievalia in memoriam Jan Frederik Niermeyer* (Groningen, 1967), pp. 41–51; Franco Simone in *Studi Francesi*, 42(1970), 407–10, and *id.* in *Renaissance, Maniérisme, Baroque* (Paris, 1972), pp. 17–37; G. Mombello in *Culture et politique en France à l'époque de l'humanisme et de la renaissance*, ed. Franco Simone (Turin, 1974), pp. 43ff., at pp. 94–6.

45 For these qualities (which he divided into good and bad ones) of the French, Germans and Italians, see cap. 13, p. 84. Very similar characterizations were to be made in the humanist age by, say, Salutati, cf. his *Epistolario* I.141, and in other places, occasioned as they were by the calamitous effects of the Great Schism.

46 *Notitia*, cap. 15, p. 86f.: 'naturaliter precedit ordinem.'

and applied in each particular realm must take proper cognisance of the diverse needs of time, place and person. In a word, different nations demand different laws. It is here the relativity of law which now is made a focal point, and the universal absoluteness of the law is on the way out.[47] The significance of such views is that they reveal the adoption of relative theses in the place of absolute principles. There was diversity and differentiation where previously there was uniformity. As he in fact stresses, what one man approves may be an abomination to another.[48]

For an assessment of the forces which prepared the ground for renaissance humanism and its doctrinal preliminary, the Aristotelian absorption, mention should be made of the reports which were presented by ambassadors, whether they were official or unofficial, permanent or temporary. These served to widen the imagination and vision of Western man. Assuredly, if not a new planet, certainly the unknown social customs and practices of hitherto remote peoples, now swam 'into his ken'. In any event, contact with infidels on a commercial basis had rapidly increased since the twelfth century: Christian and Saracen (or infidel) met, exchanged goods and learned to respect and trust each other. Economic considerations obviously outweighed religious views: the reborn man apparently found it quite 'natural' to deal with the infidel supplier of goods for marketing or manufacturing purposes in the West. And the establishment of the feudal kingdom in Jerusalem furnished the concrete base for constant reporting and trading.[49] The crusades greatly sharpened the observational powers of the participants, and some descriptions, for instance, of the third crusade vividly testify to the impact which the negroes in the Sultan's army had made upon the crusaders.[50] Since missionary enterprises needed careful preparation, detailed knowledge of the countries to be christianized was necessary. It is in this context that the reports from distant lands became essential. For instance, Giovanni di Piano's report of his journey – lasting some two years – to Innocent IV is a fascinating first-hand account: he was the pope's 'roving' ambassador to the Grand Khan of the Tartars. Louis IX emulated Innocent and sent William of Rubruk, one of his

---

47 *Ibid.*, cap. 16, pp. 88ff.: 'Licet iura principum omnes constringant, tamen pro diversitate temporum, locorum et personarum temperanda sunt iura.' Here he also operates with the triad of *decet*, *libet* and *licet* which originated in St Bernard, cf. for details *PG* p. 427, n. 1. For Dante, see below, p. 129.

48 *Notitia*, p. 88, lines 27f.: 'Quod ab uno homine sustinetur, in alio abominabile reputatur.' For Pierre Dubois's similar view see below, p. 124.

49 See J. Riley-Smith, *The Feudal Nobility and the Kingdom of Jerusalem* (*1174–1277*) (London, 1973) with full relevant bibliographical details, pp. 322–6. Further accounts in regard to the Arabs in Sicily in D. Abulafia, *The Two Italies* (Cambridge, 1976).

50 Cf. A. Gransden, *Historical Writing* (above, n. 6), p. 239: the negroes were 'of enormous height and terrible ferocity, wore red turbans instead of helmets and brandished their clubs with iron teeth, the blows of which neither helmet nor shield could withstand' (from the early thirteenth century *Itinerarium peregrinorum*).

Franciscans, to the same ruler. Even Mongolia came within the purview of papal missionary efforts: six Minorites constituted the embassy. And there was Marco Polo who travelled to China in the 70s of the thirteenth century.[51] The formal reports of the ambassadors and the diary of Marco Polo are excellent witnesses of the acute perception and observation of virtually everything of interest to an alert and intelligent man: climatic conditions, flora and fauna, wild and tamed animals, the customs of rich and poor, their manners, their idiosyncracies, methods of trading, manufacturing and marketing, social and economic relations, and so on. What mattered was unadorned existence, the real and natural manifestations of civic, social, cultural and economic life, divested of any regard for religious, let alone conventional Christian, principles. Life as it really was, as nature had evolved, was what was reported. It was the purely mundane, exclusively secular aspect of these reports which attracted attention. Yet, this mundane point of view was in no wise perceived to constitute a contrast to the accepted, sophisticated religious or ecclesiastical standpoint: the reporters were commissioned by authorities of the highest rank, including the papacy, and were themselves clerics, sometimes of no mean standing. To be sure, baptismal rebirth and its ecclesiological effects did not stand in the forefront of these unvarnished reports.

Indeed, there is every justification for saying that from the mid twelfth century onwards 'something began to stir in the art of Western Europe: a fresh sense of the immediacies of concrete experience, a new attachment to physical actualities.'[52] These were rightly called 'the first symptoms of the coming naturalism.' That even within the philosophical and theological framework[53] observation of natural phenomena came to be attractive can only cause surprise if Arab influences are disregarded. And it was Arab influence from the twelfth century onwards which found clear expression in the works of a number of writers, among whom special mention should be made of a pupil of Alexander Neckam,[54] Alfred of Sareshel, more commonly known as Alfredus Anglicus. The very title of his tract *De motu cordis* ('On the movement of the heart') indicates the naturalist–scientific trend, however much it was embedded in a theological framework. Alfred

51 Cf. M. Komroff, *Contemporaries of Marco Polo: Travel Records of William of Rubruk, John Pian di Carpini and Friar Oderic* (London, 1929).
52 See the admirable study by Lynn White, 'Natural science and naturalistic art in the M.A.' in *AHR*, 52(1947), 421ff.; the quotations are at p. 425. See also the fundamental work by Lynn Thorndyke on experimental science and his brilliant intervention 'On the originality of the Renaissance' in *JHI*, 4(1943), at pp. 72ff.
53 For the philosophical and theological views on nature, see M.-D. Chenu, *op. cit.* (above, n. 14), pp. 4–48, in regard to reason and faith, the secular (profane) and the sacred, which were 'diverse, but not adverse' (Alan of Lille).
54 The manuscript mentioned above, n. 10, is a miscellaneous codex which contains a number of essays on topics concerning natural science (fol. 1–11vo.). They may well be ascribed to Alexander Neckam.

still more than Alexander (to whom the work is dedicated, showing that it was written in the very early thirteenth century) has an adequate grounding in Aristotelian doctrines which he employs with good effect in the explanation of certain physiological and also psychological features such as procreative processes, conception and pregnancy, the formation of the embryo and its becoming an 'animal', the thesis of movement as a natural process, the concept of nervous energy, and so on. These are the heraldings of a new orientation – and Alfred himself translated a pseudo-Aristotelian tract from Arabic into Latin – in which philosophy, medicine and natural science are still plainly undifferentiated branches of scholarship. In his Preface Alfred claimed that the human heart had not yet been made a focal point of examination,[55] although it provided the link between the soul and the body: the echo of Aristotle's biology and natural philosophy seems unmistakable. Not the brain, but the heart was the seat of the soul which 'animates' the body.[56] The essence of life includes both animalic and vegetable existence before physical death.[57] Hence his recognition of the function of the arteries, the veins, pulsation, lungs in relation to the heart, the activity of muscles, digestion, etc. But the invisible driving force is the soul, situated in the heart, where the intellect resides, and this explains his attention to the cerebral functions. Consequently, the soul sets natural operations in motion.[58] In Alfred's most important operational concept of the *animalitas* the functions of both the 'anima' (soul) and the 'animal' are included. There is no need to stress the crucial consequences this (double) meaning of *animalitas* was to have when the basic Pauline concept of *homo animalis*[59] is recalled. Familiarity with a terminology always greatly facilitates the acceptance of a new doctrine or theory that employs familiar terms, however different their significance in the new context may be. Alfred may well be called a bridge-builder between the (traditional) Platonic and the (new) Aristotelian philosophy and psychology.

Another Englishman, Bartholomaeus Anglicus, an exact contemporary of Alexander Neckam and Alfred of Sareshel, is worthy of remark, since his encyclopedic *De proprietatibus rerum*[60] ('On the properties of things')

---

55   It was the organ 'nostris adhuc ignotum intemptatumque phisicis' (ed. C. Baeumker in *Beiträge zur Geschichte der Philosophie des M.A.*, XXIII (1923), preface, cap. 3, p. 4).
56   *Ibid.*, cap. 8, p. 33, line 18: 'Cor igitur animae domicilium, hic enim anima primum pulsat.'
57   *Ibid.*, cap. 5 and lib. II., pp. 9ff.; also III. 4, p. 14 and VIII. 6, p. 33.
58   *Ibid.*, XI. 23, p. 55, adopting the Aristotelian thesis: 'Naturae operationes in corpore semper animalis anima movet et disponit.'
59   1 Cor. 2:14: 'natural man' (originally: *anthropos psychikos*).
60   There were numerous editions. A very useful survey in C. Langlois, *La connaissance de la nature et du monde au M.A.* (Paris, 1911), pp. 114ff., at 128ff. Some excerpts in ET in E. Grant (ed.), *A Source Book of Medieval Science* (Cambridge, Mass., 1974), pp. 383f. (on light); cf. also p. 813.

contains a compilation of similar anatomical–philosophical and biological statements and views, yet is firmly encapsuled in the traditional Platonic–Augustinian cosmology. The influence of this work – the author was at Oxford (*c.* 1220) and taught as a Friar at Magdeburg – was felt right down to the sixteenth century and it was very often translated into the vernacular, including middle English (by John Trevisa in the fourteenth century[61]). The work has a strong leaning towards naturalist–medical analyses and in difficult questions tends to accept an eclectic explanation, which has always been a guarantee for widespread acceptance. What these few instances clearly show is that the ground was very well prepared for the reception of fully-fledged new cosmological themes, the focal point of which was the concept of nature in its human manifestation. It is comprehensible that perceptive minds began to feel somewhat apprehensive about this novel trend. An example is the subtle Alan of Lille who sarcastically addressed Nature by drily referring to 'the imbecility of your humanity and the darkness of your ignorance'.[62]

Seen against this background the emergence of what in the thirteenth century was called the *scientia naturalis,* a designation which is still valid, cannot cause much surprise. Adequate examination of natural phenomena presupposes the application of the inductive method of enquiry, as indeed was explicitly advocated at the time by the Oxford and other naturalist schools.[63] And the effects here were as revolutionary as they were to be in the counterpart of the natural sciences, that is to say, within the realm of politics. The concentration on natural science from the thirteenth century onwards is a predominant feature of the intellectual landscape. The Oxford school (Roger Bacon, for example[64]) has left its mark on many branches of natural science. Its motto that 'without experiments nothing

---

61   New critical edition in two volumes (Oxford, 1975).
62   See Alan's *Liber de planctu naturae,* in *PL* 210.431ff., at 454D: 'Tuae humanitatis imbecillitati compatior, ignorantiae tuae tenebras . . . teneor extirpare.' (ET cited above, p. 15, n. 3, p. 46). The work was contemporary with the writings mentioned in the text.
63   For some details, and for modern literature on natural science, cf. *IS,* pp. 113ff., to which should be added A. Maier, *Die Vorläufer Galileos im 14. Jahrhundert* (Rome, 1949). For some selected passages of the thirteenth century see *Source Book* (above, n. 60), on magnetism, pp. 367f.; botany and zoology, pp. 681–98; geology, pp. 624–9; motion, pp. 272–85; optics, pp. 376–441. Here Albert the Great is particularly outstanding, cf. the descriptions of animals, pp. 654–7; on comets, pp. 539–47, and so on. Only a few years hence the versatile Giles of Rome was to write one of the earliest tracts on human embryology. See for this the most perceptive work by M. A. Hewson, *Giles of Rome and the Medieval Theory of Conception* (London, 1975), who rightly points out (pp. vii, 50f.) the close connection between natural science as exemplified by Giles's tract *On The Formation of the Human Body in the Womb* (*De formatione corporis humani in utero*) and the incipient humanism.
64   For some passages see *Source Book* on the lens of the eye, p. 400; light, pp. 393–7; visual perception, pp. 407–10; refraction, pp. 423–30; etc.

can be known adequately' was a significant portent. The construction by John Buridan, a pupil of Ockham, of a theory of celestial mechanics[65] which in some fundamental respects was akin to that of Copernicus, was an outstanding achievement. Albert of Saxony too anticipated a number of Copernican theses.[66] There was no longer to be recourse to faith and belief as the basis of understanding – as expressed in St Anselm's philosophical axiom 'I believe in order to understand' ('credo ut intelligam') – but rather to rational demonstration and to humanly understandable processes to explain the phenomena of this visible and corporeal world. The attack on credulity[67] led to a veritably new cosmology in the literal meaning of the term as evidenced by the suggestion, made in 1271 by Robertus Anglicus, that time should be measured objectively. The hitherto commonly accepted 'timelessness' of life (possibly engendered if not postulated by the conjoining of the present and the future (eternal) life) was to give way to objective and exact measurements of time which were effected by the mechanical clock. It eventually counted twenty-four equal parts of the day from noon to noon. This is what recently has rightly been called 'the secularization of time'.[68]

Above all, however, it was medical science as the science concerned with the bodily well-being of natural man that made rapid advances from the late thirteenth century onwards.[69] Paris and Bologna were conspicuous in anatomy and surgery. At Oxford public academic lectures in surgery began about the middle of the fourteenth century. The incidence of the Black Death was most important. Just as the two world wars in our century resulted in an enormous expansion and advance of medical knowledge, in the same way the bubonic plague was the cause of greatly intensified interest in medical matters. The role of the Black Death as a contingency that urgently forced contemporaries to consider physical matters of humanity has not yet been properly assessed. The appalling mortality all over Europe, the cruel, sudden onset and the spread of the disease had the effects of a bloody revolution and of an earthquake com-

65   *Ibid.*, pp. 277–83, 621f., 500–3.
66   He was the first rector of the university of Vienna in 1365. For selected topics, *Source Book*, pp. 335–42 (on motion); p. 348 (on velocity).
67   For examples, see *PGP*, p. 257f.
68   See, on the manuscript of Robertus Anglicus, Lynn Thorndike, 'Invention of the mechanical clock about 1271 A.D.' in *Speculum*, 16(1941), 242–3. Further, J. Leclercq, 'Zeiterfahrung' in *Misc Medievalia*, 9(1974), 1ff.; the quotation at p. 16. A striking clock was first found at Westminster and Augsburg in 1365–6, *ibid.*, p. 13, and slightly earlier at Southwark and St Albans. Before the mechanical clock time was measured by the sundial and the water clock.
69   For introductory observations see M. Bataillon, 'Humanisme, médecine et politique' in *Culture* (above, n. 44), pp. 439–51 (with a useful bibliography).

bined. It powerfully stimulated medical science.[70] The explanations attempted show how much observation and consequential thought had been prompted by this disaster. Thus, in many tracts of the fourteenth century pollution of the air came within the purview of investigation, the transmission of the disease by putrid fumes of decaying matter was taken into account; stagnant water, rotting plants, unburied corpses, exhalation and so on, were considered as causative agents. Measures were suggested to prevent the incidence of disease, such as burning of houses, control of movements and the supervision of public sanitation. The papacy at Avignon took vigorous steps to discover the cause of the epidemic by encouraging and ordering numerous dissections.[71] The death toll among medical men within and without the universities was particularly heavy.[72] What is of immediate concern is that the Black Death greatly sharpened the observational powers and directed attention to the *physis* of humanity and the environs within which man lived and by which he was affected. For reflective thinkers, such as Petrarch, the Black Death prompted moralistic views and the desire to conquer physical death by transcending it philosophically.[73]

Artistic productions are at all times suitable means of representing abstract thought in concrete and easily understandable forms. It is therefore comprehensible why typology prevailed in the fine arts to a much more marked degree than in any other intellectual discipline. This is especially noticeable in illuminations of manuscripts, in glass and wall paintings, especially in churches, where the persons portrayed revealed few individual traits or features. This typological representation obviously has the same roots as the anonymity of artists, copyists and illuminators of manuscripts, architects, builders, etc., or as the ubiquitous symbolism intended to convey an idea in tangible form. In principle this typology was intimately linked with the hierarchical ordering of society in which everyone had his place or station or vocation fixed and therefore represented a 'type' that fulfilled a particular function.[74] To the 'type' in the realm of the visual arts corresponded the concept in the precincts of abstract thought. The typological aspect was unmistakable in illuminations, sculpture and the like, where the artist was especially concerned with the external symbols that portrayed not so much the person as his

---

70 See for all this A. M. Campbell, *The Black Death and Men of Learning* (New York, 1931), p. 109.
71 *Ibid.*, p. 120.
72 See *ibid.*, pp. 146ff.
73 Especially in his *Trionfi*, on which see R. N. Watkins, 'Petrarch and the Black Death: from fear to monuments' in *SR*, 19(1972), 196–223.
74 Cf. 1 Cor. 7:20 and Innocent III in his *Register* I.471 (ed. O. Hageneder *et al.*, Graz and Cologne, 1964), p. 693.

office or function and thus 'typified' him in an objective manner. Our earlier observations in regard to the typology of rulership are also applicable here, notably the ruler as the *Typus Christi*, as all medieval royal coronation rituals designated him.

But a critical analysis of some artistic productions from the late twelfth century onwards goes once more to show that there was an inconspicuous and yet noticeable shift of emphasis in certain kinds of artistic creative work. The development in the arts might be said to be 'From the future life to the present' or 'From deity to humanity'. Or, as has rightly been said, men now tried 'to bring God down to earth and to see and touch him. It was as though Europe had become populated with doubting Thomases eager to thrust their fingers into the very wounds of Christ.'[75] The type began to give way to the portrayal of real and natural people. The new Orders of Friars gave a great stimulus to the arts. For the directness of approach to religious topics advocated by them presupposed a knowledge of the Bible, and here especially of the New Testament. The stories had to be told in a realistic manner, shorn of all theological accessories.

This direct approach – evidenced also by the contemporaneous Bible translations – powerfully stimulated the pictorial representation of gospel stories, with the result that they came to be set in natural surroundings which actually meant the environs with which the artist himself was familiar: their setting was contemporaneous. Typology was replaced by the presentation of natural reality, hence also the slow emergence of landscape painting. As might be expected, every artist perceived a gospel story in a different light, and in this way his product represented the subjective impact which biblical events and situations had made upon him. It was the emergence of a sense of reality in all walks of life which characterized many human activities in the thirteenth century. And with this went the development of a keen sense of curiosity. The change was particularly noticeable in churches belonging to the Friars or built by them. They usually had large wall areas which served the purpose of realistically presenting consecutive gospel stories exceedingly well. 'Soon the sacred stories were to speak from the walls to the faithful.'[76] Gothic art reflected a fundamental change of attitude towards the natural environment.[77] Indeed, part of the secret of the Friars' success lay in their pungent explanation of the Bible, and here the visual arts proved themselves a most important vehicle in this fresh 'mission at home'. In fact, one could go further and say that the work of the Friars stimulated the concrete visual fixation of Christian themes for the benefit of the ordinary, illiterate

75   Lynn White, *art. cit.*, (above, n. 52), p. 429.
76   For this see W. Goetz, 'Die Entwicklung des Wirklichkeitssinnes vom 12. zum 14. Jahrhundert' in *AKG*, 27(1937), 33ff., at p. 64.
77   Lynn White, *art. cit.*, p. 428.

mortal. All this mirrors 'the new dramatic naturalism'.[78] There is no exaggeration in the claim that 'St Francis first taught Europe that nature was interesting and important in and of itself.'[79]

Very similar observations can be made about sculpture, such as the superb work by the Naumburg Master in the 1230s or in the contemporaneous cathedral of Strasbourg: here indeed the natural found a realistic, earth-bound representation: no longer was the aim of the unknown artists the sometimes stilted typology or symbolic figure of holiness, truth, beauty, etc., but the portrayal of the coarse peasant, the sly Judas or the suffering Christ. This new kind of artistic expression brought home the point of a parable or event or story told most memorably in the Bible. One might well be tempted to speak here of a transformation of sacral matters into their mundane–secular counterparts: they were brought down to earth. Or as has been said in a related context: 'Divine persons became people of flesh and blood.'[80] They were no longer removed from everyday reality and dwelling inaccessibly in other regions, but concretely, tangibly and realistically conveying the message that had hitherto usually been rendered in abstract words or letters. This was indeed one of the reasons why they could never make so deep an impact as their visual presentation. It was the attention to detail and realistic portraiture which the thirteenth century showed. This is not to say that earlier artists were incapable of perceiving individual traits: these features were not considered worthy of consideration.[81]

The variegated culture of Southern Italy and Sicily – Christian, Arabic, Jewish, Byzantine, Norman – was an amalgamation that of itself exercised an influence far beyond its own geographical precincts. It was the meeting place between East and West and as such fused the various cultural strands, which produced its own brand of naturalism. The collection of animals which Frederick II kept in his court and which went travelling around with him was perhaps the most conspicuous manifestation of the 'new' interest. It was indeed a whole menagerie that accompanied him to Ravenna in 1231 when hitherto unknown animals stared at the astonished onlookers: elephants, camels, panthers, lions, leopards, giraffes, owls and falcons.[82] This circus show was repeated several times in Italy – most of the wild animals were presents from the Sultan – and some animals made their way to Germany, for instance, monkeys, camels and leopards. When one links this extraordinary exhibition with the literary and scientific

78 *Ibid.*, p. 431.
79 *Ibid.*, p. 433.
80 See W. Goetz, *art. cit.* (above, n. 76), p. 68.
81 Cf. my observations in *IS* pp. 41ff., and K. Hampe, *art. cit.* (above, n. 26), p. 11.
82 Cf. C. H. Haskins, *Studies in the History of Medieval Science*, 3rd edition (London, 1960), pp. 254ff.

influence radiating from the same quarter, one can perhaps dimly gauge
how much intelligently observing contemporaries had become aware of the
differences which existed in the natural or animalic world. This indeed
would go a long way towards explaining the rapidly increasing concentration of interest that was focused on natural habits and on nature itself.
One can well understand how proudly the French artist Villard de
Honnecourt noted in his sketch book after having drawn a lion from life:
'Et bien sacies que cis lions fu contrefais al vif'.[83] To draw from life as it
was and as it was observed became something approaching a popular
fashion. Hand in hand with this went a sharpening of the observational
powers: the attempt at an exact portrayal of the wings of the bird as it rose
to attain its proper height or the masterly colouring of the various feathers
of the falcon are persuasive examples of the talent now awakened.[84] What
one witnesses everywhere in contemporary Europe is the discovery or
rediscovery of nature and of its phenomena which was unmistakably
reflected in contemporary art. Seen differently, the humility of microcosm
replaced the limitless design of macrocosm.

From the mid thirteenth century onwards sculptures and paintings of
ordinary human beings as stylized a-human types began to decline in all
parts of Europe. The natural appearance of men was shown, their natural
movements, natural gestures – in short, the artistic product mirrored
human anatomy and facial expressions which indicated joy, sorrow, grief,
alertness, expectancy, deviousness, and so on, with a suitable setting,
including flora and fauna, mountains, rocks and dales. The landscape as a
frame for the presentation of scenes forms background as well as fore-
ground. As the thirteenth century wears on, the change becomes striking:
Niccolo Pisano, Giotto and many others represent man's naturalness and
thus restore him literally to a position which had been submerged in the
previous mode of type presentation. Pisano's marble relief in the baptistry
at Pisa is a supreme example of this reborn natural man in his natural
surroundings, and the subject is Christ's birth in a Roman setting. The
figures move gracefully and yet are full of vitality and robustness, and the
vividness of the situation is greatly enhanced by the crumpled clothing
which clearly is intended as an integral feature. All the numerous details
evoke the impression in the observer that the figures are just about to
'step out' of the relief. This natural and realistically perceived and rendered
corporality is as captivating as it is fascinating.

Giotto's presentation of Joachim and the shepherds (at Padua), to choose
just another instance, breathes profound spirituality which is all the more
impressive as it is set against a natural background, in itself so tenderly

83   *Ibid.*
84   Details in W. Goetz, *art. cit.*, p. 66.

painted that one would be tempted to say it is merely alluded to. What the observer beholds is the naturally questioning, anxious, if not piercing, expression of one of the shepherds. The naturalness of the movements portrayed with utter simplicity is a feature that reveals Giotto's intense powers of observation. Very similar remarks can be made about Duccio, whose 'Crucifixion' is a masterpiece of contemporary painting: in its perspectives, in the details of realistic portraiture of human suffering and agony, it can have few parallels. But nothing would be more misleading than to think that Pisano, Giotto and their contemporaries were solely the products of the Italian genius. Exactly contemporaneously and assuredly independently of them, there were native English artists at work who in several artistic forms produced examples of the natural humanity of the physiognomy that can well stand comparison with the Italian masters. An observant visitor to Westminster Abbey will notice a number of corbels which are in every respect superb pieces of craftsmanship and artistic talent, such as the face of a master craftsman of the mid thirteenth century, or the face of Edward I as Lord Edward of the same period. From 1291 come the gilt-bronze effigies of Henry III and of Eleanore of Castile, both by William Torel: they show – notably Eleanore's effigy – a grasp of the natural facial expressions which allow considerable insight into individual character traits. 'The ability to produce outstanding and extremely naturalistic work' showed itself convincingly in these artistic reflections of well-observed features.[85] A sign of this naturalistic orientation of art was also the simultaneously emerging desire to preserve one's own glory and status for posterity by appropriate artistic means, mainly statues, busts, and the like – evidently a symptom of the aversion from typology.[86]

It is well-nigh indisputable that the thirteenth century witnessed a heightened awareness of nature or of what was believed to be natural. The sense of realism thereby engendered – frequently identified with naturalism – began to infiltrate into most of the relevant branches of intellectual, scholarly, and artistic disciplines, in short talent that had lain dormant for so many centuries came to be released and deployed in a creative and original way. And it had lain dormant because as a result of baptismal rebirth natural man had figuratively been washed away by baptismal

---

85 A. Tomlinson in the introduction to *The Medieval Face* (London, National Portrait Gallery, 1974). This naturalism is similarly observable in iconography and Passion plays, cf. C. Davidson, 'Civic concern and iconography in the York Passion' in *Annuale Mediaevale*, 15(1974), 125–49, who states that 'glass painting was revitalized by the civic spirit' in York windows and 'plays were civic endeavours' by the guilds for popular audiences (p. 129). Stress was laid on the '*human* reluctance' of Christ when led to the crucifixion (p. 131) (italics original).

86 Despite his opposition to the new trends Boniface VIII incurred paradoxically the opprobrium of idolatry because of the portraits and statues he had ordered. Cf. C. Sommer, *Die Anklage der Idolatrie gegen Papst Bonifaz VIII.* (Freiburg, 1920).

waters, so that no margin was left for any useful deployment of talent that concentrated on nature and the natural. The prevalent wholeness standpoint had absorbed the whole of man (and therefore of society), and what belonged to nature was not treated in a positive sense. But it should be stressed once more that all these activities which we have just now briefly sketched were entirely unconnected with each other. There was no mutual relationship or fructification between, say, feudal arrangements and artistic products, between the emergence of vernacular literature and an incipient historical criticism, between the crusader and new literary genres, such as biography or autobiography, and so on. These numerous and wholly unrelated new manifestations provide the indispensable historical background to the new Aristotelian cosmology, and constitute the backcloth of what with every justification can be called renaissance humanism.

The implicit significance of these manifold manifestations of secularism was that natural, mundane and human objects were accorded a value and purpose of their own, and not merely seen as instruments in the pursuit of other-worldly aims and aspirations. They were quite obviously perceived as existing in their own right and as functioning for their own sakes. In other words, the so-called *naturalia* or *humana* or *mundana* in the widest sense possessed innate, positive value and were therefore worth intensive study and attention. They revealed themselves in unmistakable clarity as the expressions and reflections of natural humanity. Nevertheless – and this is an essential point – they were not yet conceived as integral parts of a wider pattern but were seen only in their isolated, self-contained state, precisely because no relationship was established between them. They provided, however, perhaps the most fertile soil for the reception, adaptation and cultivation of Aristotelian philosophy, notably his theses relative to society and man in his function as a citizen. Secularization of government and secularism in society supplied a secure base for an historically understood renaissance humanism.

IV

Citizen-Centred Renaissance

Rarely can a social philosophy have fallen on a more responsive soil than Aristotle's in the mid thirteenth century. Once his works had become available in competent Latin translations, his views completely won the day. This was not necessarily the effect of their intrinsic merits. For the presupposition for an acceptance of new doctrines is that they fall on receptive ears and are tuned in to an appropriately prepared frame of mind. This truism has particular relevance in the present context. Aristotle's cosmology in the literal sense was exclusively this-worldly; it was a closely integrated system concerned with the physical world which served as a basis for the erection of a philosophical and ethical superstructure. The core was the concept of nature. It is in virtually every pertinent respect the very opposite of what the traditional Christian ecclesiological outlook had postulated. Hence the very progress and the very extent of the success of his themes in the thirteenth century convincingly proves the intellectual readiness for accepting his bases and their consequences and implications. Indeed, the response demonstrated that the pre-conditions were amply in evidence. Aristotle's theories can be seen as the articulated rationale of the theses and axioms and principles, in short of the inarticulate premises, that had found expression in the numerous variegated secular instances which we have just surveyed. His basic standpoint was understood as a *pièce justificative*: 'the philosopher' had said and taught long before there was any Christianity or ecclesiology, and he made known conceptually and abstractly what was practically and concretely applied, done and seen by thirteenth-century contemporaries.

Aristotle provided, in a word, a consistent theory and presented a closely-argued and well-knit system. What had appeared to be no more than merely isolated, unconnected or disconnected secular features, were now seen to fit into a well-ordered whole. Each and every one of the apparently unconnected secular expressions was now seen by alert contemporaries as merely a specific emanation of a system or a world outlook or a cosmology that rested on physical, that is natural, premises. Aristotle's system confirmed in theory what was abundantly conspicuous in practical reality. It was, literally, a useful theory which, entirely independent of contemporary circumstances and situations, furnished a philosophical confirmation in abstract terms of what was concretely in existence. The ease and speed with which his theses were accommodated and became operational in diverse schools of thought testifies to the fertility of the soil upon which they fell. One has but to envisage the state of things two or three generations earlier to realize how infertile the ground would have been for his theories: they would hardly have evoked a ripple. The extent, if not also the significance, of his success can be measured by the ease with which he was adapted to a cosmology that in some basic respects was alien to his fundamental outlook, for the traditional ecclesiology and naturalist Aristotelianism would have seemed to make strange bedfellows.

The absorption of Aristotelian themes yielded a cosmology at once old and new, at once revolutionary and restorative, at once generative and regenerative, at once looking forward and backward, at once progressive and retrogressive. It energized and mobilized by its very simplicity and 'naturalness' and conformity with 'natural' modes of thought intellectual forces that had hitherto lain dormant. Governmental structures had, we have seen, undergone a process of secularization, and secularism abounded in all walks of life and all departments of intellectual pursuits. As far as society was concerned, it was Aristotle's *Politics* that was immediately relevant, for it showed that there *was* conceptually what governments and others had so far vainly tried to find: a society that rested on natural foundations. The *Politics* was the social and political expression of a physically conceived world order. The Aristotelian concept of nature was a vital key to the understanding of the working of this (natural) society, a theory that by the mid thirteenth century was assured of immediate success in the realms of thought, if not yet also in practice.

To Aristotle nature had its own laws; it worked on its own principles and pursued its own end; it was the essence and very core of man himself. It was nature that 'implants the social instinct in men' (*Politics* 1.2.15, etc.); it constitutes man's dynamic force; it explains the animalic kernel of man, however much endowed with reason he may be; it shows why man takes his place among other natural creatures; it proves that plants and other animals were created for man's sake (1.8.12, etc.). Man is therefore by nature a political animal and of necessity by his natural instinct is part of, and takes part in, his own society which is the State. The State, for Aristotle, is as much a natural creation as man is. Here the already mentioned earlier translations from the Greek into Latin provided a not unimportant link with Greek philosophy and thought. Burgundio's translation of the Syrian Nemesius had not only familiarized late twelfth and early thirteenth century people with the nature of man (the very title of the book), but had also given the following rendering of Aristotle's definition of man as a 'civil animal' – the original Greek had *politikos*:

By nature man is made a gregarious and civil animal, for one alone is incapable of coping with all matters. It is therefore clear that states were set up for the sake of man's transactions and for keeping order.[1]

It is not difficult to see how many echoes these ideas must have evoked in thirteenth-century contemporaries. The very designation of man as a 'political' (or 'civil') 'animal' was sure to strike a resonance and yet at the same time introduced in the most economic way possible – with one word – a category of thought which belonged to an order hitherto but dimly, if at all, perceived: the political order to which man belonged distinguished him from all other animals, and it was in a specific function that man operated within this political order – and this was in the function as a citizen. Evidently, the Pauline *homo animalis* at once sprang to mind, but whereas for Paul and subsequent Christian doctrine the natural creature (the 'animalic man') was replaced by the 'new man' as a consequence of baptismal rebirth, in Aristotle's system this natural creature by virtue of its very naturalness assumed a pivotal role. The adoption, application and appropriation of this Aristotelian conception by thirteenth-century man – as we shall presently see – involved the restoration or resurrection or rebirth of this man of nature whom baptism had relegated to the background and neutralized if not wholly eliminated. And this Pauline 'animalic man' was the Aristotelian political animal. 'The force of Aristotle's impact lay in its essential naturalism and humanism . . . he thus generated an altogether novel approach to man, *homo ut homo*.'[2]

The re-emergence or rebirth or renaissance of natural man, or what Eugenio Garin in a different context most felicitously called 'the rehabilitation of man in his earthly environs',[3] did not necessarily entail a replacement of man reborn through grace, but only the loss of his monopoly: he had to share his place with the restored and reborn natural man. One could say that the renaissance of natural man implied, as far as the public or secular or mundane order went, a de-sacralization or a re-humanization

---

1 See Burgundio's translation (above, p. 68, n. 22), cap. 1, p. 14: 'Natura enim gregarium et civile animal factus est homo: unus enim nullus sufficiens est sibi ipsi ad universa. Manifestum igitur est quod civitates propter negotiationes et disciplinas constitutae sunt.' The Greek term for *civitas* here is *politeia*, also rendered by Burgundio as *civilitas* (cap. 36, p. 133). Man therefore was 'a rational animal'. For Aristotle's natural philosophy see G. A. Seeck (ed.), *Die Naturphilosophie des Aristoteles* (Darmstadt, 1975), especially J. H. Randall, pp. 238ff. On this topic see now also M. A. Hewson, *op. cit.* (above, p. 81, n. 63), pp. 39f., 188f., 241 (linking his *Politics* with his naturalism).
2 M. A. Hewson, *op. cit.*, p. 240.
3 E. Garin, *L'educazione* (above, p. 5, n. 17), p. 32f.

of the Pauline 'new creature'. Natural man – the *homo animalis* – experienced a rebirth and was accorded a standing that he had not hitherto as a matter of principle enjoyed, however much it was in tune with the practical manifestations of his humanity. Restored natural man now had a legitimate standing, and this exclusively on mundane, secular, natural premisses.

New cosmological dimensions came to be introduced. Whereas previously the relationship between grace and nature bristled with difficulties and was of a delicate and brittle character, it was now to become one of co-existence and accommodation. From the historical–mundane angle the essential point was that through baptism natural man had been, so to speak, blacked out, although, as experience proved throughout the ages, his neutralization or elimination or erasure was never as complete as dogma and the ecclesiologically inspired law had postulated. By way of paradoxical accentuation one might say that nature did not allow natural man to be wholly atrophied. Nature could not be rendered wholly ineffective. A natural core clearly remained that asserted itself in various ways, or in less exalted language some of 'the old Adam' was still left.[4] But by the renaissance of natural man baptismal rebirth had been, as it were, partially put into reverse. Natural man was restored to his full stature within the secular–mundane order, and he claimed his due attention as a man of flesh. From the mid thirteenth century therefore both carnal generation (natural man) and baptismal regeneration through grace (the Pauline 'new creature') had now legitimate standing in doctrine, the one by virtue of the operation of nature, the other by virtue of the operation of grace.

The restitution of man himself untouched by grace – *homo* – brought with it above all also the concentration on his own being and natural substance, his own '*human*itas'. This, as will be recalled, had come more and more to the fore since the twelfth century and had in any case had a secure habitat in pure theology, notably in patristic christology. The concept was familiar to every literate and educated man, and very likely also to many others. The point was not, however, merely the familiarity with the concept, but the position and function accorded to *humanitas* as such, for as a result of natural man's rebirth his humanity, his inner essence and being, became a central, if not a pivotal, item since it expressed the very substance of natural man. It is not therefore difficult to understand why there was a very close relationship between this renaissance of natural man and the pursuit of studies relative to man's *humanitas* – after centuries of hibernation it was now the essence of unadulterated natural man which was once more given a place in the cosmological order. In

---

4 Cf. below, p. 111. St Paul's exhortation (1 Cor. 5:7) springs to mind.

preceding ages there was little need or occasion to encourage an examination or analysis of man's natural *humanitas*. What mattered was the
baptismally reborn man who was said to have divested himself of his
naturalness, which had disappeared from vision and was not considered a
worthwhile object of investigation. It seems hardly surprising that man's
natural humanity should now take the centre of the stage, although this
rather obvious relationship has been accorded insufficient attention by
modern scholarship.

Very similar observations can be made about nature, which had found
its accommodation within legal precincts in the shape of natural law.
There had been a *ius naturale* in the ancient Roman law. There was also
the same concept, though with different connotations, in the work of
Gratian, whence it took on a new lease of life among both lawyers and
theologians. In a word, this concept was as familiar to contemporary
literate man as that of *humanitas*. It consequently very greatly facilitated
the adoption of naturalist modes of thinking. And it was above all the
jurists who were once more the pacemakers and suppliers of conceptual
instruments, though they were very closely followed by the theologians,
who effectively assisted in the accommodation of the new concept of
nature.[5] As we have remarked before, nothing is of greater assistance to the
acceptance of a new theory than familiarity with its terminology, however
greatly the intrinsic meanings of the terms may differ.

At this juncture it is advisable to point out that the significance of the
renaissance of natural man (and herewith of the richly flowing train of
thought that was now set in motion) can be adequately assessed only
against the ecclesiological background. It was precisely the effects of
baptismal rebirth which had determined the ecclesiological complexion of
society, of government, of law, of rulership, of constitutional development,
not to speak of learning and scholarship – in short, medieval society and
all its known manifestations were shaped in a decisive way, if not created,
by the conception of baptismally regenerated man, by the Christian, and
in consequence the attendant axioms of unipolarity, totality and also
universality became operational. There can be no doubt that the segment
in which the effects of baptismal rebirth were particularly pronounced and
incisive was that of the public field or the social or mundane order. It was
here in this secular realm that, precisely because the law was the vehicle
which translated into practice the idea of baptismal rebirth in a social and
governmental context, the renaissance of natural man was bound to

5 For the jurists see R. Weigand, *Die Naturrechtslehre der Legisten und Dekretisten von
   Irnerius bis Accursius und von Gratian bis Johannes Teutonicus* (Cologne and Vienna,
   1967); and for the theologians see O. Lottin, *Psychologie et morale aux xii*e *et xiii*e
   siècles (Louvain and Gembloux, 1948), II.72ff. (still the best survey). Much relevant
   material also in R. Javelet, (below, n. 36).

display its greatest impact. For on an Aristotelian basis a new mental category, that of the political order, came to be introduced, with the result that the ecclesiological monopoly was broken. The rebirth of natural man was to have its profoundest effects within political precincts. Hence there is every justification for saying that the renaissance of natural man was conditioned by the antecedent ecclesiology which had implemented baptismal rebirth. The monothematic characteristics of this baptismal rebirth had reverberated throughout all layers of society.

The fundamental Aristotelian point that ignited, so to speak, immediate interest in the thirteenth century was the conceptual separation of politics from ethics, presented as this separation succinctly was in the distinction between 'the good man' and 'the good citizen'. Morality was, as it were, brought down to earth and took its place next to politics. Both moved on a mundane, secular level and clearly had nothing to do with religion in conceptual respects. The significance of this separation is twofold. First, the totality standpoint was severely dented – reborn natural man was subjected to two sets of norms (and no longer to one only): to ethical norms as mere man as well as to political norms as a citizen, however much in an ideal world the two sets were said to be identical. But there can be no doubt that this was the beginning of the process of atomization, characterized by the fragmentation of the whole into religious, moral, political and further norms. And this distinction also signalled the emergence of the bipolarity point of view in the place of unipolarity. The individual as man and as citizen pursued this-worldly aims, whereas as a Christian his gaze was directed towards an end beyond this world.

Secondly, there is the emergence of the concept of the State as the collectivized citizen: the State as the aggregate of all citizens was the citizen writ large. And both the State and the citizen moved entirely on the natural–human level which, indeed, was the level that served as a platform for the various secular manifestations already surveyed. The significance of this can hardly be exaggerated. Citizenship was as indissolubly linked with the new category of politics as was ethics with the individual in his private capacity. Historically, it was the citizen and the State which first captured the imagination and the interest of scholars who concerned themselves with social and governmental matters. Both were new operational concepts – indeed, the citizen and the State were the theme of Aristotle's *Politics*. It is assuredly no coincidence that the most pronounced secular manifestations – prior to the Aristotelian absorption – were in the public, governmental, mundane, fields, that is, in fields in which baptismally reborn man had claimed his monopoly of function and demanded consequential governmental application (the descending theme of government, the concession principle, etc.). This field proved itself therefore a quite especially fruitful and well-prepared ground in all parts of Europe.

Here it is as well to draw attention once more to the importance of the process of secularization that was governmentally initiated. For this secularization radiated its influence through all strata of society. The incipient and intense interest in the citizen's humanity – his very essence: his '*human*itas' – from the second half of the thirteenth century on is easily understandable. Both he and his humanity were to all intents and purposes a *terra incognita*. The resultant humanism therefore concerned itself with a natural entity and as such had nothing to do with any supranatural matters, such as grace or other religious axioms. Humanism began its triumphant career as part of the enquiry into the reborn citizen who was an integral member of the natural State. What the observer is confronted with here is renaissance humanism in the literal meaning of the term: it is the rebirth of humanity.[6] Both the ideas of rebirth (renaissance) and of humanity were strongly rooted in the past, which explains their ready acceptance and assimilation by thirteenth-century contemporaries. This humanism was specifically related to the citizen and his State as creations of nature. The rebirth or re-humanization of the (Pauline) 'new creature' involved the scholarly discussion of man's *humanitas*. This scholarly focus on man's humanity gave rise to what can for brevity's sake be called renaissance humanism in its pristine shape. And it was indeed scholarship which brought to fruition the process of 'humanization' that was in practice begun by governments in the form of secularizing their found-ations, and accompanied by the many secular manifestations mentioned earlier.[7] Aristotle had supplied the tools.

The renaissance of natural man also involved the 'de-mundanization' of what had been called 'spiritual' elements, that is, those derived from, or based on, grace and concerned with supranatural matters. They came to be assigned to their proper a-secular, supranatural spheres and conse-quently were taken out of the secular orbit. The natural and the supra-natural concepts emerged in a collectivized or organized shape as the State and the Church, the former consisting of citizens who answered to natural, and the latter consisting of the faithful who answered to supranatural, criteria. And since the State was a product of nature, its jurisdiction did not extend to matters within the supranatural precincts, and conversely, ecclesiastical jurisdiction was not to concern itself with matters of this world. Obviously, the conceptualized dichotomy severely impugned, even

6 For the resultant new view of life and new branches of scholarship see E. Garin in his 'Kultur der Renaissance' (above, p. 5, n. 17), at p. 501.
7 For the conventional explanation of the Renaissance see B. Pullan, *op. cit.* (above, p. 72, n. 35), pp. 165ff., and the literature cited at p. 361.

if it did not altogether eliminate, the hitherto prevailing principle of uni-polarity and replaced it by that of bipolarity. That is to say, the natural and the supranatural were each credited with their own norms and premises and ends. And exactly the same observations applied to the members of the two bodies: this resultant bipolarity – a natural and a supranatural terminal – was the inescapable result of the rebirth of natural man, who was now accorded a status which, on its own premises, baptismal rebirth had denied him. Having been restored to the position which he was said to have lost through baptism, he now re-occupied in the natural sphere the position of which the faithful Christian had hitherto claimed a monopoly.

It will be readily seen that the underlying cosmology was radically different from the traditional. Yet it would be erroneous to say that the Aristotelian adherents in the thirteenth century and subsequent ages had in any way perceived this newly emerging world outlook to be opposed, let alone hostile, to Christianity. Once his works became available in a good Latin translation, they took the lecture-halls and studies by storm. This shows how ready the soil was for the Aristotelian reception. For instance, in describing the final scene of the Last Judgment the Cambridge Franciscan Walter Wimborne, teaching in the 60s of the thirteenth century, held that the Chair would lecture to the blessed on Aristotle's Nicomachean Ethics and hoped that his prayers to the Virgin would secure him a place in the audience.[8]

If one takes some of the best interpreters of Aristotle,[9] Thomas Aquinas and his followers, as illustrative examples, they show that through in-geniously synthesizing Aristotelian and traditional Christian principles they considered that the newly emerging cosmology was merely an accommodation of ancient Aristotelian philosophy harnessed to Christian doctrine for its own benefit. In fact, this adjustment was seen as a welcome enrichment and enlargement of the Christian outlook. The view that 'Thomas was but Aristotle sainted'[10] is understandable. One of the key axioms that made the synthesis possible was the thesis that divinity itself was the author of nature, or as Thomas Aquinas had it: God was the *auctor* or *conditor naturae*, because God was *summus regens*. Thomism created a symbiosis of Aristotelian–naturalist and Christian–supranatural themes.

8 See, for this not uncharacteristic enthusiasm for Aristotle, B. Smalley, *English Friars and Antiquity* (Oxford, 1960), pp. 50f.
9 See M. Grabmann, *Mittelalterliches Geistesleben* (Munich, 1926), I.308f. For the radical exponents of Aristotelian naturalism, such as Siger of Brabant and his school at Paris, see E. Gilson, *History of Christian Philosophy in the M.A.* (London, 1955), pp. 244f., and especially F. van Steenberghen, *La philosophie au xiiie siècle* (Louvain and Paris, 1966), pp. 393ff., 430ff.; further, W. Ullmann, in *JTS*, n.s.27(1976), 58ff., at 66–70.
10 Cf. H. Baker, *The Dignity of Man* (above, p. 3, n. 16), p. 194.

Natural man and the Christian, the naturally generated and the baptismally regenerated man, the (natural) State and the (supranatural) Church, nature and grace, were complementary to each other. Nevertheless, it is commonly overlooked that one of the famous Parisian masters, William of Auxerre, himself a notable commentator on some Aristotelian works and a member of the commission appointed to examine Aristotelian writings in the 30s of the thirteenth century, taught in an exclusively theological context that nature and grace stood in a mutual relation to each other and that 'grace perfects nature'.[11] The full significance of this thesis in regard to social and political matters emerged a generation later in the Thomist formula that 'grace does not do away with nature but perfects it.'[12] Not surprisingly, this Thomist thesis proved itself especially attractive to the early humanists.[13]

The citizen and his State, and the Christian and his Church, were independent entities, because their premisses and ends differed. Yet they complemented each other, and if the supranatural ends pursued by the Church were to be brought to bear upon the State, this could only be to the advantage of the latter; but for its proper functioning it did not need the supranatural Church. For, as the same Thomas declared, there was a *duplex ordo in rebus* (a double ordering in things), since each entity worked on different principles. Thus within the State there was growth, evolution, adjustment to emerging contingencies, dissimilarities in cultural attainments with consequential governmental, constitutional and social diversities, which were partly also caused by differing climatic or other physical circumstances, and there was evidently also decline and decay, whereas the supranatural Church as a specific foundation instituted by divinity possessed none of these variable features: its programme was given once and for all, and it merely needed to be applied and executed. And it was a divine pledge that this institution possessed sempiternity. Hence in the one realm the ascending theme of government operated, in the other it was the descending counterpart.

Accordingly, the Aristotelian–Thomist theses stressed the *instinctus naturae* which impelled social living and engendered harmony: it was this

11 See William of Auxerre, *Summa aurea* (above, p. 19, n. 14), II tract. 14, 2nda qu., fol. 69rb: 'Licet autem diversa sint secundum essentiam bonum nature et bonum gratie, tamen formaliter unum et idem sunt et etiam finaliter, quia unum est perfectio alterius. *Gratia enim naturam perficit . . .*' See also John of Salisbury in the twelfth century, who held that 'grace fertilizes nature' ('gratia naturam fecundat') in *Metalogicus*, I.1; but he drew no conclusion from it.

12 For details cf. L. Lachance, *L'humanisme politique de s. Thomas d'Aquin: individu et état* (Paris and Montreal, 1965); also *PGP* pp. 243ff. In his introduction to *Aquinas: Selected Political Writings* (Oxford, 1948), A. P. d'Entrèves, p. xiii, called the Thomist formula given in the text 'a stroke of genius and the reason for his success'.

13 See the complaint by Johannes Dominici, below, p. 144, n. 59.

instinct of nature which formed the essential fibre of the State, and was
clearly inapplicable to the Church which was not built on a natural
instinct, but on a divine promise. Because the social instinct was implanted
in humans, man's *humanitas* demanded, and now also received, accelerated
attention. The arrangements of social relations within the State were the
effluence of purely natural assessments of human contingencies, not
necessarily burdened by religious or theological or ecclesiological considerations. The creation of law was a purely human concern. Natural reason,
experience, and judgment were the cornerstones of this purely human
outlook. The renaissance or re-humanization of man, and hence the
rehabilitation of the citizen, necessarily postulated a human cosmology.
This renaissance necessitated the application of principles germane to
natural man's humanity, and here was the starting-point of a correctly
understood humanism. It was the mutability of human nature which
Thomas stressed and which distinguished it from the immutability of the
divine ordering. For the concept of immutability presupposes that it is
always the same everywhere: 'natura autem hominis est mutabilis.'[14] The
perception that man's nature was changeable clearly underlay the relativity
principle of the new cosmology and differentiated it from the absolute,
immutable norms prevalent in the traditional thesis. And in strongly
subscribing to the Aristotelian view expressed in the *Metaphysics* that 'by
nature every man desires to know things' Thomas elevated the natural
human urge and thirst for knowledge of which St Paul had evidently a
lower opinion.[15] Thomas's was a 'natural theology'.[16] Precisely because he
was a rational being, man had the natural urge to increase his knowledge
and to penetrate into the substance of things.

No longer was faith the material ingredient of the law. It was replaced by
consent, rationally arrived at by human discussion. But consent presupposed exchange of views, debate relative to means and ends, and
orderly examination by rational argument. And this is what Aristotle had
called *politeuein*, which the translator William of Moerbeke rendered by
the new term of *politizare*, that is, to politicize, which means to engage in
politics. It is perhaps worthy of remark that Cicero, the mediator of Greek

14 Thomas, *Summa theologiae*, II-iiae, qu. 57, art. 2, ad I: 'Natura autem hominis est
    mutabilis, et ideo quod naturale est homini, potest aliquando deficere.' For anthropo-
    logical and purely philosophical discussions concerning man at Paris university see
    E. H. Wéber, 'Les discussions de 1270 à l'université de Paris et leur influence sur la
    pensée philosophique de s. Thomas' in *Misc Medievalia*, 10(1976), 285–316. J.
    Catto, 'Ideas and experience in the political thought of Aquinas' in *Past & Present*,
    71(1976), 3–21, rightly points out that because Thomas was a profound Aristotelian
    he was sensitive to experience of the physical universe, and that empirical observ-
    ations played an important role in shaping his thought-processes.
15 See 1 Cor. 1:8: 'Knowledge puffs up.'
16 Thus H. Baker, *op. cit.*, pp. 196ff.

ideas to the Romans, had no term for the Greek *politikos*, and the best manuscripts of his relevant works retain the Greek spelling without an attempt at transliteration, let alone translation.[17] It will not have escaped attention that earlier translators of Greek texts, such as Burgundio, rendered the term *politikos* as 'civic' or 'civil', but not as 'political'. It can therefore safely be assumed that the idea and notion of the political made its début in William of Moerbeke's translation of Aristotle's *Politics*, and hence became part of the vocabulary within the orbit of government. Nothing illustrates the new way of thinking more convincingly than this novel term *politizare*, which is evidently linked with politics. From the moment of its entry into the vocabulary concerned with government, a notion of politics (and a political science) emerged which was related to purely human conditions in society, their bases and manipulation. By definition politics[18] was this-worldly and focused attention on the management of public affairs within the State by citizens. The element common to the new triad of State, citizen and politics was natural humanity or, in baptismal language, unregenerated man.

In the present context it is of particular interest to note that Thomas Aquinas created the new science of politics (the *scientia politica*), which he called the *scientia principalissima*, thus establishing its relationship to all other human sciences. This is a most significant nomenclature: of all human sciences this alone was 'architectonic', by which Thomas clearly adopted the Aristotelian idea of the positive and controlling part that political science had to play within a human ambit.[19] For him political

---

17 See Cicero's *Epistolae ad familiares*, 8.1.5 (Loeb, p. 104), where Caelius writes to Cicero: 'Tui *politikoi* libri omnibus vigent' ('Your books on the Republic are universally popular'). Further, Cicero, *Ad Atticum*, 9.4 (Loeb, p. 188): '. . . sumpsi mihi quasdam *theseis* quae et *politikai* sunt' ('I have taken for myself certain theses which deal with high politics and are applicable to the present crisis') ('*en tois politikois*' translated by 'political matters').

18 The term *politicus* was simply a Latin transliteration of the original Greek. The term was not used within governmental precincts, but only in connection with the *virtus politica* of Macrobius (fifth century A.D.). That is why John of Salisbury refers to the 'philosophi' who speak of a 'iustitia quae politica dicitur' (*Policraticus*, I.3). Innocent III in a sermon once referred to the 'virtutes politicae': PL, 217.797D. It was in the same sense that, for instance, Peter of Tarentaise (about him, below, n. 28) used the *virtutes politicae* and declared that pagans and ancient philosophers could act meritoriously (*Sentences*, II.41.1.3, p. 341, *ed. cit.* (below, n. 28) and III.36, p. 289f.). For Petrarch's copy and glosses on Macrobius, see below, p. 155, n. 14. His contemporary Bolognese jurist, Jacobus Butrigarius, the teacher of Bartolus, was one of the earliest to operate with the *virtus politica*, according to the report by Baldus, Commentary on *Institutiones*, I.1.1 (edition Venice, 1615), fol. 2ra. Butrigarius in his Lecture on the Codex (edition Lyons, 1585, fol. 2r) explained this political virtue as 'scientia de regimine civitatis'. Most of the fourteenth-century jurists were familiar with Cicero, cf. also below, p. 161. There is urgent need to investigate the subject of Cicero's influence on the jurists of that age.

19 The term *architektonikos* was used by Aristotle and also by Albert the Great, but not until Thomas handled it did it gain currency.

science was obviously the most important of all intellectual human pursuits, because it helped the building and operation of human society, of the State. It is not without significance, though hardly noted, that he consistently operated not only with the *scientia politica*, but also with the *doctrina politica*,[20] with the *communitas politica*,[21] and the *ars politica*.[22] Moreover, there was the Church as the *congregatio fidelium*, that is, the congregation of the baptismally reborn, as well as the *congregatio hominum*, the congregation of the unregenerate, notably the political community (*congregatio politica*) such as is formed by the members of one people.[23] From a purely historical angle, a correctly understood humanism emerged simultaneously with political science, that branch of learning which dealt with the citizen and the State as organs of humanity.[24] Precisely because Thomas rehabilitated natural man, his doctrines can be said without fear of gainsaying to constitute the opening bars of renaissance humanism. Salutati, the great humanist at the turn of the fourteenth and fifteenth centuries, appreciated Thomist thought fully and was apparently so much impressed by him that he frequently reproduced the Dominican literally.[25]

Without doubt, familiarity with the term *humanitas* greatly assisted its ready acceptance by thirteenth century scholarship. In fact, the term was so familiar that it was to give the whole subsequent period its complexion. Its currency in the christological disputes has already been noted, but it should also be realized that it was once more Roman law which most effectively assisted the acceptance of the concept of *humanitas* in its new environs. Its accommodation within the new cosmology and above all within the precincts of political science, which inherited a very great deal of the earlier jurisprudential thought-patterns, proceeded without any undue effort. The concept of *humanitas* was notably conspicuous in the Digest. It is of equal concern to note that jurists were in the forefront during the early phases of humanism. Moreover, not only was the Roman law concept of *humanitas* coinage with which every academically trained jurist was familiar, but – significantly enough – so also was the very term

20 Commentary on *Eth.* X.16; on *Polit.* I.1a.
21 *Summa theol.* I-iiae, qu. 90, art. 2c.
22 Commentary on *Sentences*, III.3.4.5. ad. 3.
23 *Summa theol.* III, suppl. qu. 26, art. 1: 'qui sunt de uno populo.'
24 In his stimulating *Medieval Aspects of Renaissance Learning* (Durham, N.C., 1975), P. O. Kristeller seems to attach too little importance to the bearing of these and similar Thomist ideas upon political concepts in the age of the renaissance. For a similar development in other branches of learning, cf. U. Kopf, *Die Anfänge der theologischen Wissenschaftstheorie im 13. Jahrhundert* (Tübingen, 1974), especially pp. 125ff and 175ff.
25 See R. B. Donovan, 'Salutati's opinion of non-Italian Latin writers of the M.A.' in *SR*, 14(1967), 185ff., at 199f. See especially E. Garin in his edition of Salutati's *De nobilitate legum et medicinae* (Florence, 1947), p. 347 (inspired by the arguments of Thomas, especially *Summa theol.*, I-ii, qu. 90 and 91) ('ritrovano in gran parte le osservazioni del Salutati' and 'testi e argomenti riprodotti alla lettera').

and concept of *civis* (the citizen) which too had a similarly secure habitat in Roman law and had indeed been employed in thousands of charters throughout the antecedent period, though in a non-technical sense, to mean inhabitants of localities. After all, Roman law – which, it will be recalled, had proved itself as a vital instrument in the process of secularization initiated by governments – dealt only with human (and no other) matters transacted by citizens. Hence just as the citizen was operational in Roman law, so was correspondingly his *humanitas* in all its varying shades of meaning.[26] The full potential of these mutually related concepts came to be realized once they formed part of the new political science. Humanism found its earliest expression in connection with the renaissance of the citizen as an integral member of the (new) idea of the State. Humanism was thus a segment of scholarship that concerned itself with matters of rehabilitated humanity in the context of citizenship, in the context of political science. And once more the indispensable role of Roman law should be noted.

The concept of the citizen was the political expression of rehabilitated natural humanity. As such it paved the way to the adoption of the principle of quantitative majority in elections. This is an aspect of the restored citizen which has hardly been noticed, but assuredly deserves attention. For numerical majority presupposed that, considered from the strictly natural or human angle, there was no difference in the standing of citizens. Indeed, no lesser authority than Gregory the Great in the late sixth century had declared that 'nature created all men equal'. The concept of the citizen did not suffer gradations, precisely because it was based on nature. Gradations and hierarchical ordering came about, as Gregory 'explained', because 'an occult arrangement' intervened, which was a somewhat unconvincing justification for the descending theme. The usual medieval principle in elections was the so-called qualitative majority which was based on the status, office or function held by the electors. But since the electors, such as the cardinals electing the pope, were equals in regard to their office, only counting by heads remained. And because men as natural creatures were born as equals, they were equals when acting as electors. This quantitative principle became prevalent in the thirteenth century, partly because in the lower reaches of society it had in any case always been practised, such as in village communities, gilds, etc.; partly because it was observed in the North Italian communes; partly because it was reflected in current law books, such as the *Mirror of the Saxons*, and

---

26 Cf. Dig. 3.1.1(4); 5.1.36 (pr.); 9.2.27(9); etc. Late Roman emperors were always ready to refer to 'humanitas nostra', cf. Honorius on 14 March 419 in *Avellana* no. 24 (*CSEL* 35.71, line 16). The Roman *conditio humana* came to be employed by the synodists assembled at Orléans in 549 for the place where the bishop died *iure humanae conditionis* (*MGH Concilia* I.103, c.8).

last, but certainly not least, Roman law had clearly enacted the two-thirds majority – after all, the Roman law knew only citizens as full bearers of rights and duties and therefore as equals. The citizen-centred renaissance was greatly facilitated by the medieval familiarity with the concept of the citizen which led to the rationally far more satisfactory principle of numerical majority in preference to the traditional qualitative counterpart. Only on this ground could the requirement of consent as the material ingredient of the law grow,[27] and the idea of representation be put into practice – all of which was necessary for the implementation of the ascending theme of government, germane as it was to the citizen.

Only when it is realized that neither the State nor the citizen nor politics as autonomous structural elements existed in the previous centuries, can one understand why it was that the true character of renaissance humanism found its first and perhaps most important manifestation in a political context. It was the rebirth of natural man, the partial humanization of the (Pauline) 'new creature', which brought with it a new cosmology of which political ideology was the most conspicuous part. Its main concern was the discovery and establishment of principles relative to the ordering and management of the human–natural society, of the State. This humanist orientation capitalized on the immediately preceding practical evolution in an abstract sense and yielded the thesis of bipolarity in the place of the monopolistic unipolarity. It was the principle of bipolarity that was henceforth to determine the path of reborn man, who was able to pursue a natural as well as a supranatural end. It was the prevalence and all-pervading influence of a monopoly resulting from baptismal rebirth that precluded the emergence of the idea of bipolarity, the presupposition for which was the recognition of the natural–human elements as relevant on their own account, that is irrespective of their role in achieving eventual salvation.

The exact contemporary of Thomas and a similarly famous Dominican teacher at Paris university, Peter of Tarentaise (who became Pope Innocent V in 1276 and died a few months after his election), propounded virtually the same thesis of bipolarity which Thomas had advocated. The individual had what he called a *finis proximus* as well as a *finis ultimus*. The 'immediate end' was attainable naturally (*naturaliter*), hence infidels could achieve it, but were unable to reach the ultimate aim of life which was eternal salvation. What is noteworthy in this doctrine – which shows obvious kinship with Thomas's – and what differentiates it from the traditional standpoint, which was based on St Paul, was that the actions and deeds of

27 Gregory I's passage cited in full below, p. 103, n. 30. The papal election decree of 1179 demanded a two-thirds majority, because the cardinals had the same office. For the *Mirror of the Saxons*, see the passage in *PGP*, p. 218, n. 2. For literature on this topic see *LP*, p. 156, n. 1. For Roman law see Dig. 50.9.3.

pagans were credited with full moral value because they flowed from 'a natural sense of righteousness', though eternal life was denied to them.[28]

This citizen-centred renaissance warrants a remark about the accompanying process of atomization. We have already referred to the Aristotelian distinction between the good man and the good citizen, the significance of which was the differentiation between politics and ethics. In his lectures on the *Politics* Thomas Aquinas wholly adopted this distinction and clearly rejected an absolutist standpoint in regard to politics. For, as he says, it is not always the case that someone who is a good citizen, is also a good man.[29] Just as unipolarity was replaced by bipolarity, in the same way the totality principle was to give way to atomism and the consequential autonomy of the political, moral, religious and other sets of norms. This process of fragmentation was eventually to be observed also within the third basic realm, that of universality, which was to yield to national sovereignty.

It seems advisable to point out that the distinction between politics and ethics evidently refers and applies only to the natural–human sphere. Here the traditional vertical or hierarchical ordering of society was to be replaced by an ordering that approximated to a horizontal orientation. The concept of the citizen was therefore not only crucial for a society based on natural–human premises, but also the only one that was possible. There was room for an autonomous, independent citizen only, and none for a subject. But within the religious sphere, where baptismal rebirth mattered, the traditional hierarchical ordering remained untouched.[30] That indeed was the deeper significance of adopting the principle of bipolarity. To the ascending theme of government within the State and its citizen-centred horizontal ordering corresponded the descending theme within the Church and its vertical hierarchical ordering.

Once the implications and ramifications of the new cosmology became crystallized, it began to flood all branches of intellectual disciplines. It was not difficult to arrive at the conclusion that the period between the sixth and the fourteenth centuries resembled a 'dark age'. Whatever had happened, in this period, was not the deed of 'natural men', not of citizens, not of ordinary 'humans', still less of States or the execution of a programme derived from political consideration, but was the work of the (Pauline) 'new creatures', precisely those whose naturalness was said to have been

---

28 Peter of Tarentaise (Innocent V), *In Sententias Commentaria* (Toulouse, 1649, reprinted Ridgewood, N.J., 1964), II.41, art. 3 ad 2, pp. 341f.; here also the statement that 'multa opera infidelium recta et bona sunt propter naturalem pietatem.' For St Paul, cf. Rom. 14:23.
29 See *PGP*, p. 248 and L. Lachance, *op. cit.* (above, n. 12), pp. 349ff.
30 As many centuries earlier Gregory I had declared that 'by nature we are all equals' but 'an occult arrangement' put one above the other (*Moralia*, 21.15.22, in *PL* 76.203). Cf. also *IS*, p. 14.

rendered impotent. All their actions were measured by religious criteria, that is, how far they contributed or failed to contribute to achieving salvation. The ecclesiological unit within which the 'new creatures' operated was not held to be a this-worldly society that followed the laws of ordinary humanity, but one that had its gaze directed towards a future eternity. But as we have seen there were men, such as Otto of Freising in the twelfth century, who quite clearly had perceived that history was the record of men who acted in their capacity as citizens and within a community that somehow or other could legitimately claim autonomy. And that indeed is the significance of Petrarch's famous view of the age between the end of the Roman empire (in the West) and his own time: to him this age was dark.[31] This was a perfectly comprehensible standpoint. Looked at from the humanist angle, that is, from the angle of the reborn or re-habilitated man as a citizen, the antecedent ages were indeed 'dark', precisely because it was not mere natural men but 'new creatures', that is, baptismally reborn men, who were the *dramatis personae*. They were subjects, not citizens, and followed norms and codes which were not of their own making; above all, they were not autonomous and considered their life in this world as merely transitory. This is one more reason why the concept of the State did not and could not arise before the Aristotelian reception.[32]

The concept and meaning of history was bound to undergo a radical transformation as a consequence of the new cosmological orientation. It is perhaps useful to recall our earlier observation that in the 'dark ages' the chronicler began with the biblical account of the creation of the world and worked his way towards more recent times. Now, however, as we shall see, this kind of historiography became thoroughly unfashionable: the view began to prevail that in order to be seriously considered, historicity pre-supposed humanly accountable and responsible measures taken for their own sakes within mundane, secular precincts, so that a humanly perceived goal might be achieved. It was precisely the absence of this *human* element that prompted Petrarch's remark and explains his apotheosis of ancient Rome. History he conceived to be the story of natural–human men, and not of baptismally regenerated creatures. Humanity formed the subject of history and only humanly motivated measures were the stuff of history. History no less than political science began to look back to Rome, which appeared to be the acme of the achievements of which natural, unregenerated humanity was capable. Dante made himself perfectly clear on this point and Petrarch expressed it in the memorable question: 'What else is

31 See T. E. Mommsen, 'Petrarch's conception of the "Dark Ages"' in *Speculum*, 17(1942), 226ff., and below, p. 113. For Petrarch see E. H. Wilkins, *Studies in the Life and Works of Petrarch* (Cambridge, Mass., 1955).
32 See *CL*, ch. XII.

all history but the praise of Rome?'[33] The recourse to history in its ancient Roman setting was a necessary accompaniment of the new politically inspired and orientated humanist ideology. And in this lies the significance of Petrarch's view, whose historical sense had evidently been kindled in his youth by his study of Roman law at Montpellier[34] and Bologna. As he remarked, its numerous references to Roman antiquity never failed to delight him. That Livy was his mainstay in historical matters, and that he even wrote glosses on the text, can hardly cause much surprise.[35] Humanism understandably postulated a history which recorded the actions of ordinary humans as natural men. Citizen-centred humanism called for citizen-centred history – against this background Petrarch's deep and persistent concern with the new perspectives of man's dignity explains itself.[36]

The depth of the problem besetting reflective and thinking men was understandable. Most theories, however new they may appear, had (and have) points of contact with some earlier theories, although the strength of the links may well vary. But here there was precious little in the traditional ecclesiology, in its historical evolution and perspective, from which the new humanist orientation could have drawn some lesson or derived some profit. Now that the State, the citizen and politics had entered the arena and become perfectly legitimate operational instruments, at least in theory, scholarship faced a veritable void as far as the antecedent period went: there was virtually nothing in it that could have been harnessed or could have been of benefit to the new political outlook. All the traditional ecclesiologically based elements – theocratic rulership, the lack of a right

---

33 'Quid enim aliud omnis historia quam Romana laus?'. See on this T. E. Mommsen, *art. cit.*, p. 237, n. 1. For the background see J. Larner, *Culture and Society in Italy 1290–1420* (London, 1971), pp. 221ff.

34 For the contemporary French background see Franco Simone, 'Il Petrarca e la cultura francese del suo tempo' in *Studi Francesi*, 41(1970), 201ff. and 403ff.

35 There is a copy of Petrarch's Livy manuscript in the British Museum, Harley 2493. For a complete list see N. Mann, 'Petrarch manuscripts in the British Isles' in *Italia medioevale e umanistica*, 18(1975), 129–527 (includes also Dublin holdings and ET (where applicable) of his works).

36 For the background, mainly philosophical, see C. Trinkaus, *op. cit.* (above, p. 1, n. 5), I.179ff., especially 192: it was 'the Italian humanists who created this literary genre (of *De dignitate hominis*), elaborating older theological themes'. The argument however was quite different. Either man's dignity was owing to his having been created by God and the counsel of Trinity (this was the view of the Pseudo-Ambrosian tract *De dignitate conditionis humanae*, in *PL* 17.1105ff., and of the Pseudo-Augustinian tract *De spiritu et anima*, cap. 35, in *PL* 40.805), or it was to his being superior to animals on account of his wisdom or religion, the guarantor of eternal life (this was the view of Lactantius, *Divinae institutiones*, 3.8ff., edition in *CSEL* 19 (ET in *FC* 49(1964), 183ff.)). Sometimes both were combined. For rich material in the twelfth century see R. Javelet, *Image et ressemblance au douzième siècle de s. Anselme à Alan de Lille* (Strasbourg, 1967); here also a most useful survey of the relevant patristic literature, I.1–66; cf. above, p. 68, n. 22). The subject of 'man' was treated entirely on a spiritualized level and from a spiritualized perspective.

of resistance, faith as the material ingredient of the law, and all the other satellite features of the descending theme of government – were simply irrelevancies in the new political science, the core of which was the citizen. Indeed, there was extremely little that could serve as a model or could be made use of in the service of the new politics.

It was this void of the dark ages that made men of the fourteenth century turn to the ancients as their masters, teachers and standards. For it is assuredly not sufficient to state a theory of political action, unless one can at least indicate some guidance as to how it can be concretely applied. The strongly secularist complexion of royal and imperial governments, we should remind ourselves, was clearly of crucial importance for the rapid advance of the new political humanist outlook, but was hardly more than a stimulus, important indeed, but no appropriate guide for the implementation of a political programme, such as was postulated by the new political science. The secularism engendered by governments was primarily an instrument against ecclesiastical intervention and still considered individuals as subjects who were given the law by the (secularized) ruler. They were not citizens responsibly laying down the path of their own society by creating the law and thus taking part in government itself. This governmental secularism, overwhelmingly conceived as it was in terms of opposition, contained at best only embryonic constructive elements. One might well be inclined to see here the obverse of the earlier battle-cry of the *libertas ecclesiae*. This secularism of governments did not, and probably could not, develop a coherent and consistent political theory. It still too clearly revealed its former ecclesiological associations, despite all remonstrations and protests against ecclesiastical office holders exercising jurisdiction in mundane matters.

The real and serious deficiency from which the new cosmology, and above all political science relative to the State, the citizen and politics, suffered was the lack of guidance that was usually supplied by the past. But the European period since the Frankish age was perhaps not so much dark, as barely relevant at all to the new political postulates based on the concept of the citizen. The observer is here reminded of the situation which prevailed in the Frankish period. The transformation of the Frankish realms into a Christian society made recourse to early Christian literature necessary, and it was this regress which brought forth the first flowering of a true native Frankish scholarship, hence the numerous copies that were made of the writings of the Fathers of the Church, of ancient ecclesiastical laws, of papal letters, and so on. The essential feature of this Frankish intellectual burgeoning was that it provided and made available ancient Christian source material, which it was necessary to implement if Frankish society was to be reborn. The literary or doctrinal 'renaissance' was merely a means to an end, and not an end itself: it was to supply the basic principles upon which the 'new' Frankish society was to rest.[37] There was precious little native antecedent Christian literature from which a contemporary of the early ninth century could have gleaned relevant knowledge, hence the recourse to the Fathers and other Christian models.

Exactly the same observations can be made about the situation from the fourteenth century onwards. Since for the reasons given the antecedent ages could supply few relevant guidelines, regress to ancient authors as models suggested itself. For about the natural *homo*, about his natural *humanitas*, about his quality as a citizen, medieval literature contained very little information that could be of practical use in the fourteenth and fifteenth centuries. The search was for the true *humanitas* of natural provenance, precisely because this was what was said to have been replaced by baptismal rebirth. The battle-cry 'Back to the ancients' became understandably more and more insistent in the fourteenth century as the new political overtones of more and more human issues became better comprehended. The recourse to the ancients was not therefore an end in itself, but merely a means to an end. This end was in its basic respects as pronouncedly secular, mundane, governmental and social as the Frankish end was religiously and ecclesiologically orientated. Both began on the intellectual level and aimed at providing contemporaries with the kind of knowledge which 'history' did not supply. Because the humanism engendered by the renaissance of natural man and his humanity was secularized religious thought, for which the previous periods supplied few data, the ancient world evidently suggested itself as a source of wisdom and an area of enquiry.

The classical age was the obvious reservoir, not because it was 'classical' or ancient, but because it was wholly unaffected by Christian religious themes and, what is insufficiently appreciated, was easily accessible in the readily available copies of a great number of ancient writers. To use traditional baptismal terminology, the classical age was unregenerated, natural, had a purely human complexion and disposed of the very kind of literature and source material which abundantly described, formulated and evaluated the social, moral, governmental and cultural conduct of an unregenerated society. Here indeed could be found the working of the *humanitas* which the thirteenth century rebirth had revived or restored. That the fourteenth and fifteenth centuries reverberated therefore with the appeal to the *studia humanitatis* can hardly cause much surprise. The study of humanity, understood as the essential being of man himself, became self-propelling. And this was not, as it is commonly understood,

---

37 See above, pp. 19f.

the study of letters, of grammar, and the like, or so-called cultivated pursuits, but the study of the natural essence of man himself, of his 'mere' humanity – in contradistinction to the study of divinity, a distinction indeed to which Cicero had clearly pointed.[38] Ancient authors made contemporaries familiar with the kind of knowledge that medieval authors were unable to purvey. The consultation of the classical–ancient writings consequently pursued definite and practical aims – it was to serve the new political science which had necessitated it. Only at a later stage of the development did this consultation become a literary and cultural pursuit which was an end in itself. The linguistic, aesthetic, artistic and other benefits which accrued were initially mere by-products. In other words, because the political implications of the new cosmology stood in the fore-ground, political science as the most basic of human sciences (or, as Thomas Aquinas had called it, *principalissima scientia*) demanded paramount attention. Politics by definition affected everyone in the purely human society that had human ends to be achieved by human means.

A further observation seems here appropriate. Since, for reasons which should have become evident by now, traditional medieval historical writing was largely concerned with ecclesiastical matters and, moreover, strongly suffused with religious substance, the authors, overwhelmingly clerical or monastic, found ancient Roman history of little use, however much they intended to write history on a universal scale. No doubt a good many ancient historians were known and sometimes also read, but what they had to say was not *au fond* relevant to the substance of the works conceived or written by medieval historians. The ancient Romans had no relevance to the ecclesiological theme which was the focal point of a medieval chronicler or annalist or historian, because they were un-regenerated men, to use baptismal terminology. Roman history entered the purview of medieval historians only in so far as it impinged upon Old Testament history or Christianity,[39] and that was assuredly only a small segment of the history of Rome. The irrelevancy of ancient history to the medieval outlook largely explains why, despite the prolix character of their writings, medieval authors only lightly if at all touched on it. And when they did, it was simply to put forward the Augustinian–Orosian teleology of history, according to which the Roman empire was providentially

---

38 See the scornful remark in Cicero, *De divinatione*, 2.80 (Loeb, p. 462), contrasting *humanitas* and *divinitas*. 'It is your judgement, then, that those devoid of *human* knowledge are the inspirators of *divine* science!'

39 Cf., for instance, Petrus Comestor, *Hist. scholastica*, which quite dexterously weaves some Roman history into his account of biblical history (*PL* 198.1055ff.), especially in connection with the New Testament, at 1337ff., 1413f., 1721f., etc.

created for the purpose of providing a birthplace for Christ.[40] From the medieval standpoint the ancients lived in a dark age, because unregenerated by divine grace and hence unenlightened by Christianity. The very pronounced humanist interest in Roman history reflected on the other hand the strength of the appeal which the rebirth of natural man and of the citizen had made. What was formerly a dark age, became now an age of illumination, and what previously with medieval writers took the centre of the stage, changed into a dark age, precisely because its historical process had been shaped, not by ordinary natural men, but by baptismally reborn men who acted on principles which were not of a natural provenance. Ancient historians now came to be studied, because they provided reliable information on the citizen and his manipulation of public affairs in a society that was not reborn.

It is not easy for man in the twentieth century to visualize fully the revolutionary impact which the new cosmology had made. And it was in the literal sense, too, a revolution, because the wheel had come full circle: it had 'revolved' back to the original natural status of man. That this 'revolution' proceeded on the intellectual level, and not in the streets and on the barricades, does not in the least impinge on its character. Because the 'revolution' was removed from the market place its effects were all the more enduring and went far deeper than any violent means could have attained, not the least reason being that larger and wider circles rapidly came under its spell. Man as a citizen was credited with the faculty of shaping his own destiny and that of his own society. This was a challenge to his innate capabilities, those with which he was naturally born, but which, let us remind ourselves, had no scope of being deployed within the traditional ecclesiological setting – indeed quite properly so: because he was not considered fit to shape his own destiny, he was in the charge of the ruler who was the tutor of the kingdom, and this in its turn was viewed as a minor under age – and every minor under age needed (and needs) a tutor for the transaction of his business.[41]

At this juncture attention should be drawn to the virtually identical effects which the governmental initiative had. It had ushered in the Carolingian renaissance as well as renaissance humanism. Governments were instrumental in setting afoot, on the one hand, the transformation of a naturally evolved Frankish society into a fully-fledged Christian unit on

---

40 A characteristic example is Vincent of Beauvais, *Speculum historiale* (edition Douai, 1624), which attempted to depict the history of mankind from the creation to 1254: a mere compilation which uses Augustine and Orosius (as well as Eusebius, Ambrose, Jerome, Petrus Comestor, etc.) to bring out the teleological standpoint clearly; cf. 6.71, pp. 197ff.

41 For this cf. *CR*, pp. 177ff., and *CL*, ch. VIII.

the model of baptismal rebirth and, on the other hand, the reversal of this selfsame process, that is, the secularization of government, leading eventually to humanism and the citizen's renaissance. Yet in each instance it was the government which reaped the disadvantages of its own actions and measures. As a consequence of the Carolingian renaissance an educated clerical elite emerged which employed its undoubted talents in the service of an ideology. It was to engulf the whole society (one has but to think of the numerous ecclesiastically dominated councils and the large-scale forgeries of clerical provenance in the ninth century) in a sense certainly not intended by the government which had begun this social renaissance, and was to lead to a wholesale clericalization of all public (and private) matters, including the (attempted) ecclesiastical control of the king who, paradoxically enough, having generated this renaissance, became in the end its prisoner. And indeed it is the reaction against the ramifications and implications of this highly successful ecclesiologically conceived renaissance which explains the process of secularization by governments from the twelfth century onwards. But it would similarly be misleading to suggest that the eventual result of this reactive process tallied with the original intentions of the governments. As a result of the citizen's rebirth forces were released which severely taxed secular governments: in the Concordats of the fifteenth century the governments began to ally themselves with the papacy against the rising popular tides. It is undeniable that the initiative taken by governments produced results which were hardly predictable and which detrimentally affected the standing of the governments themselves.

Leaving aside this long-term perspective, there is no gainsaying the erstwhile liberating effect of the renaissance of the citizen which enabled him to employ his natural–human endowment, that is to say, his reasoning power, his faculty of assessing his own needs as well as those of his contemporaries and his own society, the State. No longer was it necessary for the pursuit of what Thomas Aquinas called *bene vivere* – the well-being of the State and its citizens – to depend on the revealed word conveyed by those office-holders who had a special charisma. No longer was man subject to higher authority. No longer was he entrusted to those who claimed to have a special divine mandate and qualification that included the care of the faithful. No longer was he bidden to obey a law in the creation of which he had, and, on the premisses of baptismal rebirth, could have had, no share. No longer was faith a material ingredient of human law, but human consent – in short, his natural birth alone without any additional qualification enabled him to take part in the affairs of the State as a citizen.

Where else but in the ancient world, that is, in the 'unregenerated' world, could contemporaries of the fourteenth and fifteenth centuries find an unbiased description, assessment and account of purely human conduct (of the *humana conditio*) that was not seen through the eyes of baptismally regenerated man? Where else but in ancient Rome could the working of a political system be witnessed that was based on premises similar to those now postulated and formulated in the conceptual triad of State, citizen and politics? In order to understand the motivations for the recourse to the ancients, it is advisable to bear in mind that the 'disappearance' of natural man as a citizen and, through the efficacy of grace, his transformation into a 'new man' with wholly different principles and aims prevented him for centuries from exercising any 'civic' functions. By the turn of the late thirteenth and early fourteenth centuries there were no records nor concrete examples from which the released or restored citizen could have drawn practical lessons. And acting as a citizen with full responsibility presupposes not only a sense of public duty but also a certain training and education in the very matters which concerned the citizen as a bearer of rights and duties.

Yet on closer analysis it becomes clear that, as far as public life was concerned, the baptismally reborn man with his newness of life and the norms derived from it had absorbed a great many features of 'natural man'. It was, in a word, hardly possible, as the historical development had shown, and as we have already indicated, to manipulate and arrange and administer society solely on the basis of the 'newness of life' or of the norms based on divine revelation and grace. Previous history had indeed clearly demonstrated that to regulate public life, the *fidelis*, the Christian, who lived by grace, must needs have at his disposal a number of those very elements which he was alleged to have shed as a result of his baptismal rebirth. The 'old Adam' was not quite as useless as he might at first have appeared. Indeed, it was the 'silent' absorption of natural elements into the 'reborn man' (the Christian), or, seen from another angle, the accommodation of 'natural' unregenerate elements to the Christian framework, which very greatly facilitated the recourse to ancient models.

In this resort language proved itself once again of crucial importance, because terminologically there was very little difference between the old and the new. In such commonly understood matters as *lex, ius, auctoritas, civilitas, nexus, obedientia*, and the hundreds of other linguistic modes of expression, the ancient Roman pattern was too conspicuous and too obtrusive to be set aside. After all, the linguistic equipment of the norms of the 'newness of life' came from the ancient arsenal of language. Once more one can say that linguistic identity of terms does not imply identity in meaning – and the commonly used linguistic terms of the ecclesiological-baptismal framework were now to be returned or restored to their original meaning. In the linguistic sphere, the same process was at work as could be witnessed in the cosmological sphere at large. The umbilical cord with ancient Rome was to be repaired and fully restored. And here too one can say that familiarity with terminology greatly assisted the dissemination of the new cosmology and hence promoted the recourse to the ancient world. Everything, above all institutions and language, pointed towards ancient Rome. Indeed, the paradox is only apparent: it was the Vulgate which had familiarized medieval man with Rome, with Roman law and Roman institutions, and it was assuredly the Vulgate which must also be counted among the forces which facilitated the consultation of ancient authors. It was all so familiar – it was language that evoked well-known echoes.[42]

These reflections should make it easier to understand the renaissance of the Rome idea itself. What had set the tone in the Middle Ages was ecclesiastical Rome, the Rome of the papacy, of the Roman Church, which itself had absorbed a great many features of the 'old' Rome, and precisely those relative to government and rulership. Indeed, the idea of 'Reborn Rome' – *Roma renovata* or *nova Roma* – was very much alive during the Carolingian era, as Muadwin, the bishop of Autun and former member of Charlemagne's academy, testified in his poem (written after 804).[43] Now in the course of the new development in the late thirteenth and early fourteenth centuries Roman antiquity was, like the individual himself or society itself, restored or resurrected. The ancient 'natural' Rome and its eternity in the secular–mundane sense became revivified and to that extent de-clericalized. Eternity therefore was now to be understood in its original, uncontaminated sense as well as in its religious, transmundane meaning. The theme of *Roma aeterna* once more assumed topical value and significance. This also explains the strong appeal which Ovid was to have. His view that nature was the *novatrix rerum*, the renewing agency of all things, was considered relevant to the evolving new outlook. It was the very concept of 'Eternal Rome' that appeared after Troy, Sparta, etc. had vanished from sight.[44] If to this is added the physical absence of the very organ that had given the city its religious–ecclesiastical complexion – the papacy resided at Avignon at the time – one can better grasp the attempt of Cola di Rienzo to implement the very theme of *Roma aeterna* or *Roma renascens* in practical terms.

As we shall see, Cola symbolically enacted, so to speak, the *renovatio Romae*. Ancient Rome was to be reborn, and yet as *nova Roma* it was to be a counterpart, not a contrast to, the traditional ecclesiastical Rome. Never-

42 See for this *LP*, pp. 43ff.
43 See Muadwin (Modoin), *Ecloga*, edition in *MGH Poetae Latini*, I.384ff., at 385, line 27: 'Aurea Roma iterum *renovata renascitur* orbi.' Hence Rome reborn by Charlemagne, was the message: *Nova Roma*, lines 24, 31, which is an independent and first-rate testimony of the Rome envisaged by Charlemagne on his seal and in his imperial title (for which cf. *PG*, pp. 111–15). For the *renovatio* idea here expressed see also J. Szövérffy, *Weltliche Dichtungen des lateinischen Mittelalters* (Berlin, 1970), pp. 395f.; cf. also pp. 469, 492ff. (for Modoin in particular).
44 Cf. K. Burdach, *Reformation, Renaissance, Humanismus* (Darmstadt, 1974), pp. 68f.

theless, the hit at the other New Rome (Constantinople) was certainly not missed by contemporaries. The parallelism of restored, resurrected, reborn ancient Rome and the ecclesiastical Rome (reborn in the baptismal sense) with the individual, notably his function as a citizen, is so striking that one can but be surprised that this has not yet been noticed. And Cola di Rienzo provides in fact a first-class testimony of the thesis here proposed that the governmental and public and political exigencies powerfully stimulated a recourse to the ancients. Rienzo's attempt to govern as a people's tribune was ill-conceived and badly prepared, but it was none-theless highly symptomatic of the practical implementation of a new governmental theme and the ready recourse to the ancients.

Considered from this vantage point it is advisable to recall Petrarch's view that the age between the fall of Rome and the fourteenth century was seen as an age dominated by men who in strictest theory were men moving on the plane provided by divine grace, and not on the natural–human level.[45] Petrarch supplied a symbolic demonstration of his view by addressing himself to Cicero and others.[46] He thereby ostensibly wished to convey the idea that there was no distance between him and Cicero, and that the intervening period was, so to speak, short-circuited. Hence the motto: back to the ancients. And just as the former Carolingian renais-sance exercised an unparalleled and fructifying influence on all branches of learning and scholarship which were in any way associated with Christian principles, in the same way renaissance humanism branched out and fertilized other relevant segments of intellectual activity which con-cerned the study, comprehension and representation of man and his manifold emotions, motivations, reactions, capabilities, attainments, and the functions and phenomena of his mind, his thought and personality. The benefits which accrued to the arts, philosophy, belles-lettres, and so on, from the consultation of the ancients are so well known that all comment is superfluous. But these benefits were ancillary to the original motivation which prompted this consultation: it was undertaken for topical and practical reasons, simply in order to study natural man before his baptismal rebirth had changed him and to learn from the lessons which antiquity had provided for governing the citizen's State. The ancients' views and attitudes and evaluations of the citizen were thus of most immediate relevance to the pursuit of a political theme.

---

45 See T. E. Mommsen, *art. cit.* (above, n. 31), at p. 237: 'In Petrarch's opinion the era was dark, because it was worthless, not because it was little known. The sooner the period dropped from man's memory, the better.' According to Hanna H. Gray, 'Renaissance humanism' in *JHI*, 24(1963), 497ff., at 503, the medieval period was one of darkness, because the light of eloquence had not illuminated man.

46 See *Opere di Francesco Petrarca*, ed. E. Bigi (Milan, 1964), 880ff. He also wrote letters to Homer, Livy, Horace and Virgil.

It is in this context that the common interpretation of humanism falls into its right place. The conventional assertion that it was a literary or cultural or philosophical or aesthetic or educational movement is perfectly acceptable, if it is viewed as a sequel to the (original) humanist renaissance that was primarily, if not exclusively, concerned with the newly advanced political science, itself historically as well as ideologically conditioned. It was the political quest which initially impelled and propelled the search for, and into, ancient literature and sources in pursuit of reliable information relevant to the conduct of man in the ancient world. Man *per se*, his customs, habits, conventions, living conditions, came to be studied for their own sakes. And precisely because in a wider sense political science affected (and affects) basic and crucial conditions of public life and the ordering and governing of society, it came (and comes) to embrace a great many items and issues which were (and are) not in themselves political. What one finds here in the late thirteenth and early fourteenth centuries is the first attempt at integrating various disciplines in the interest of the whole of man and of the total spectrum of humanity.

It is assuredly somewhat unrealistic if not naive to assume that the study of literary or artistic expressions of a bygone age for imitative purposes should be pursued in a vacuum divorced from reality, from the exigencies of contemporary society and its ends. On the contrary, the historical evidence of the period furnishes convincing proof of the exact reverse of the character conventionally attributed to humanist renaissance. Contemporaries were not just manicured men full of affectations, mannerisms, bohemianisms, and pretentious ambitions existing in a world of phantasy, cultivating the art of living, concerned with their inner life and light.[47] Nor were they addicted devotees of a so-called refined culture, and a corresponding style of life, dedicated to the study of ancient literature and art and blissfully unconcerned with contemporary society and its surroundings. Nor, as has been said, was this study of the ancients prompted 'by the glowing, boundless desire and the longing for youth by an ageing generation'.[48] Admittedly, there were some who carried what they thought was true humanism to ridiculous lengths, as when, for instance, during the Council of Constance the Bishop of Fermo, Bertoldi de Serravalle, translated Dante's *Divine Comedy* into Latin hexameters for the benefit of a

---

47 K. Burdach, *op. cit.*, p. 133, who in this same context spoke of a 'Geburtsstunde des Humanismus' (i.e. of a moment (!) at which humanism was born), as if there was no historical evolution that had to be taken into account. My criticism of Burdach does not in the least affect my admiration for his work. But I find it hard to accept his views, though I hasten to add that I merely refer to him because he is the most distinguished of Renaissance scholars of an earlier generation.

48 K. Burdach, *op. cit.*, p. 126.

reading circle largely frequented by Englishmen.[49] During the Council of Florence (1439) the Greeks mocked at the enthusiasm for Plato shown by the Westerners, who apparently could not understand that his philosophy was different in kind from grammar and rhetoric.

But these were merely exceptions which prove the rule that true humanism was *au fond* concerned with something much more serious than these men thought. Overwhelmingly, the humanists were hardened by experience, learned in practical intellectual disciplines and as often as not charged with the management and administration of public matters and communities, where adequate knowledge, the power of public speaking and of persuasively putting forward arguments, in a word command of rhetoric, were essential requirements. It is a romantic–sentimental view to interpret the search for information as an urge to find the golden or ideal age.[50] It was precisely contemporary needs which Leonardo Bruni, the translator of Aristotle's *Ethics* and *Politics*, the outstandingly brilliant chancellor of Florence at the turn of the fourteenth and fifteenth centuries, had in mind when he declared that the study of politics must occupy the central place in any kind of education. For Leonardo, the *studia humanitatis* formed the best and most excellent subject and preparation for a fruitful social life in a fully developed political community. This postulate, however, was only an expansion of the exhortation which Petrarch had already made when he reminded one of his friends in the Augustinian Order that he should not be oblivious of the link between the *studia humanitatis* and the *studia divinitatis*. The demand for conjoining the two *studia* was also re-echoed by Salutati and others who will engage our attention later.[51] The appeal to cultivate the *studia humanitatis* involved an expansion of all knowledge relative to humanity as such, for next to metaphysics there was now physics, next to theology there was now the social–human science. The *studia humanitatis* were to culminate in what the Greeks had called *sophia*. As indeed it was said in the fifteenth century, there is nothing more human than the desire to know man himself, a sentiment that tallied with Aristotle and was very likely garnered from him.[52]

These instances, easily multipliable, would seem to demonstrate persuasively the quite unparalleled widening of the intellectual horizon and the concomitant requirement for an integrated view of man as a citizen, postulated as this was by the rebirth or restoration of natural man.

---

49 Cf. W. F. Schirmer, *Der englische Frühhumanismus*, 2nd edition (Tübingen, 1963), pp. 10f. (among the Englishmen were the bishops of Salisbury and of Bath).
50 K. Burdach, *op. cit.*, p. 105.
51 H. Baron, *Crisis*, (above, p. 6, n. 18), pp. 106ff.; E. Garin, *Italian Humanism* (Oxford, 1965), p. 30.
52 Cf. above, pp. 107f.

This deep impact of what is exclusively a *human*ist development, in which the accent lies on the humanity of man, redressed an imbalance and established a balance between the secular–mundane–natural and the religious–ecclesiological–supranatural. One of the results of this redressing of the balance was the 'demundanization' of the Church, accompanied by the restriction of its jurisdiction, since its influence and field of operation were to be exclusively in the supranatural sphere, and the concomitant secularization or 'naturalization' or 'humanization' of issues and items hitherto enclosed within the precincts of an ecclesiological–religious totality. What had previously formed one undivided whole was now conceptually divided or distinguished, though not separated or severed. To take an obvious instance, property was no longer an issue of divine grace; the law governing a republic or a city or a kingdom or a State was not the outcome of the workings of divine grace and based on faith, but was the result of natural insight into the mundane requirements of the community and based on consent of the citizens; and so on. Yet for the full deployment of all of man's and the citizen's faculties the two spheres – the natural and the supranatural – were held to be complementary. The fullness of life required the inseparable unity of the natural and the supranatural. The 'paganism' or animosity of the humanist renaissance towards religious issues is a figment of imagination. On the contrary, a glance at the epistolary output of, say, Salutati shows how one of the foremost humanists at the turn of the fourteenth and fifteenth centuries sees the mundane, social, this-worldly life ennobled and brought to fruition by heeding the sacral and divinely derived laws enunciated by the Church and especially by the papacy. To Salutati the 'demundanized' Church is a necessary presupposition for the full deployment of true humanity – this is the recurrent theme of his mature political philosophy[53] which presents the core of the new world outlook and of its political and social doctrines in a singularly convincing manner. Upon closer inspection it is a very practical and unproblematic application of the Thomist relationship between grace and nature.

In brief, the initial impetus for renaissance humanism came from the requirements of the new *scientia politica*, which indeed was basic for Thomas Aquinas in more than just one sense. And this humanist renaissance could be said to have completed – on the historical plane – the

---

53 See A. Martin, *Mittelalterliche Welt- und Lebensanschauung im Spiegel der Schriften Coluccio Salutatis* (Nürnberg, 1913), pp. 82–94, with numerous extracts from his letters. For one of his earliest works – *De saeculo et religione* (1381) (ed. B. L. Ullman, Florence, 1957) – see C. Trinkaus, *op. cit.* (above, p. 1, n. 5), pp. 662ff. In this work Salutati still operates with baptismal rebirth (II.2, pp. 97ff.) as the title deed of property (*ibid.*, p. 113). He is a good example of a humanist whose intellectual development can be followed up. Cf. also B. L. Ullman, *The Humanism of Coluccio Salutati* (Padua, 1963), pp. 28ff.

process which began with the Carolingian renaissance. The rigid monopolistic ecclesiological system was broken and was replaced by an elastic, flexible, bipolarity system resting on natural as well as supranatural bases, epitomized by *humanitas* and *christianitas*. The simplicity of the former unipolarity yielded to a structurally more complicated but more realistic system that appeared to take account of the infinite variety of the strands which constituted natural human personality. Seen from yet another angle, the one renaissance ushered in the medieval period, characterized by unipolarity, universality and totality or indivisibility of thought and outlook, whereas the humanist renaissance signified the dawn of the modern age, characterized by bipolarity of ends and aims, in course of time giving way to multipolarity (and eventually to pluralism), national State sovereignty and the atomization and fragmentation of all thought processes. What was common to both forms of the renaissance was their essential social relationship, with all the attendant consequences in regard to rulership, the creation of the law, its contents, scope, jurisdictional extent, and so on and so forth. Empiricism and pragmatism replaced doctrinairism and dogmatism. The former was focused on the natural, mundane–human concerns, the latter still continued to refer to the supranatural, otherworldly, eternal values and items. The humanist renaissance was a reaction to the ecclesiologically conditioned unipolarity, totality and universality. By creating, for the first time, an elastic balance where previously there had been an inelastic imbalance, renaissance humanism accomplished in the widest possible sense a synthesis of nature and grace, of *humanitas* and *christianitas*, of the present and the future life, of mundane secularity and transcendent eternity.

V

Political Humanism

The new concept of the State as an autonomous, self-maintaining, organic entity was the collectivized expression of the individual citizen. The State was, as we have termed it, the citizen writ large. Here it is advisable to bear in mind that the idea of rebirth or renaissance could not properly be applied to the State, because in the antecedent European era there had been nothing that corresponded to this autonomous unit. The State emerged only now (to use Pauline language) as a 'new creature', as a new corporate organism of the political and legal order. This emergence was the consequence of natural man having been restored or reborn into his full stature, which enabled him to function as a citizen. The management and ordering of this 'new creature' was a task that evidently imposed itself upon contemporaries at the turn of the thirteenth and fourteenth centuries. This is one of the reasons why the Aristotelian inspired concept and term of *politizare* – to politicize – had become so indispensable. For the citizen politics was what ethics were for natural man in his private sphere, and what religion was for the Christian.

The turn of the thirteenth and fourteenth centuries makes clear how the search for the identity of the State was powerfully assisted by the concept of the nation. Politics came to be dominated by this concept in theoretical and practical respects. Language once more proved a highly important instrument. For it was held – the most recent exponent of this view was Thomas Aquinas – that the term *natio* actually stemmed from *nasci*, that is, to be born, and this etymological derivation made clear that natural events, such as natural birth, entailed consequences of considerable magnitude within the public law segment. Once men became aware of a common descent, common language, customs, outlook, natural birth (*generatio*) was accorded standing on its own – in fact, it was the exact parallel to the supranatural rebirth (the baptismal rebirth in the shape of a so-called *regeneratio*). And just as within the latter man was incorporated into the Church and became its member through this 'regeneration', in the same way natural man secured incorporation into the nation through natural birth, that is, 'generation'. In conjunction with the new concept of the State the nation could, as indeed it did, become the operational element from the turn of the century onwards. It was the combination of the abstract concept of the State with the factual existence of 'national' groupings which yielded this most powerful unit of the national state.

It will be recalled that by virtue of baptismal rebirth linguistic, ethnic, biological, geographical, and all other physical considerations played, and could play, no role within the ecclesiological unit, precisely because they were of natural provenance. Hence the prevailing concept of the universality of Christian cosmology, which also explains the negligible role accorded to kingdoms in doctrine, if not also in practice. They were essential parts, but no more than parts, of the universal order, and it was this which mattered.[1] But now by virtue of the nation's assuming constitutional and operational character, kingdoms became units with their own identity and complexion, in other words, nation states. As such the nation state contained personal and territorial structural elements which were to form the constituent bases of its sovereignty. The former were characterized by common descent, language, culture, social habits, and so on, the latter by the geographical extent of the physical area within which the personal features were observable. Nevertheless, both these bases had been present in the previous ages, but they had lain dormant: their conjoining was made possible by the confluence of the abstract concept of the State and the concrete living reality of the nation. To make the picture complete, we should recall the importance accorded to the nation in the great ecclesiastical assemblies from the thirteenth century on as well as in the contemporary universities. In both instances voting took place according to nations.

The combination of the personal and territorial–national elements constituted a formidable union which was all the more effective as it had roots in the ancient Roman law. The king was conceived as a judge in the Roman law sense and, like any medieval bishop, had territorially limited jurisdiction. As far as the kingdom was concerned, however, the actual physical boundaries of its territory also became boundaries of the enforceable law. The territory had, so to speak, acquired a juristic personality or, in other words, the king's personal sovereignty was reified, that is, conjoined to the territory itself. If we now recall the essential meaning of *Rex in regno suo est imperator*[2] we can readily grasp the comprehensive

---

1 Hence the pejorative designation of kings as *reguli* (kinglets) in contradistinction to universally conceived emperorship which mattered from the ecclesiological standpoint alone. The term was first coined in the eleventh century, cf. *PG* p. 389.

2 See above, pp. 49f. For some details see W. Ullmann, 'Zur Entwicklung des Souveränitätsgedankens im Spätmittelalter' in *Festschrift für Nikolaus Grass* (Innsbruck, 1974), I.9–27.

power which now accrued to the king as the supreme ruler of the nation state. This indeed was the development in France at the turn of the thirteenth and fourteenth centuries when the mighty influence of the Roman jurists from the southern universities had become manifest.

There is a third consideration which is relevant in the present context. It was at exactly the time at which the nation state made its appearance and became operational that the rebirth of the citizen was to lead to the formation of a new grouping within the State or, as it were, a new class which considerably broadened the base of the State itself. This was the third estate, which took its place next to the ecclesiastical and secular nobility. Its members were (or at least claimed to be) citizens though they were not members of the other two estates. One might go as far as to say that the State was henceforward to rest on a tripod composed of three estates. In constitutional respects the emergence of this third estate – the bourgeoisie, the lower nobility, the wealthy merchants etc. – marked a very real caesura in politics, precisely because of the involvement of people who so far had had no opportunity of taking part in the management of the State. This feature emerged almost simultaneously in England and France as well as in Germany, although the North Italian communes had been chronologically far ahead in this respect. It was the laity which had come to the fore and begun to take an ever increasing share in public matters. The third estate was to change the social and political landscape for centuries. Above all, the third estate was a factor that mightily contributed to the widening of the humanist viewpoint and therefore to the victory of the ascending theme of government over its counterpart. In sheer numbers the third estate by far exceeded the other two 'pillars' of the State.

This is the kind of background which must be adequately taken into account, if some of the political works of the time are to be correctly understood. We may take as an outstanding example a writer who materially contributed to the new political science: John of Paris, a Thomist and a Master at the university of Paris. His book is short but terse and concise, and contains a political theory which is suffused by the theme of rebirth of natural man and the consequential principle of bipolarity. Above all else, John of Paris's book is squarely and firmly based on the purely human foundations of the State and succinctly exhibits political humanism. Indeed, he announced the principle of bipolarity in the very beginning. There was what he called a *finis naturalis* and a *finis supranaturalis*; that is to say, man had a natural and a supranatural end.[3] As a citizen man pursues his natural aim within the *politia communis*, that is the State, which

---

3   John of Paris, *De potestate regia et papali*, ed. F. Bleienstein (Stuttgart, 1969), cap. 1, pp. 78ff.

is a polity of (all) citizens and hence is common to all.[4] Here the humanist orientation comes to the fore: this *politia* operated exclusively by the expression of the human will, that is by the consent of the citizens.[5] There was no room within this entity for the display or expression of a higher or divine authority. The government is made and unmade by the consent of the citizens. The *consensus humanus*[6] (human consent) alone is here operative, and not only in regard to secular government, but also in regard to the creation of the government of the supranatural body, the Church, that is, of the pope and prelates.[7] The creation of law is evidently the sole right of the citizens.[8] All this is only the amplification and application of the thesis with which the book begins, when its author announces his concern for the 'human king' (the *rex humanus*) and 'human matters' (*res humanae*).[9] For his presupposition is not just humanity as such, but what he calls the inherent power of human nature (the *virtus naturae humanae*). This accentuated concentration on the human element reflects the concern of thinking men in the very early years of the fourteenth century.

For John of Paris the structural elements and the fibres of the *politia communis* were the citizens, because the *politia* was theirs – it had not been entrusted to a ruler or government by divinity for particular purposes. The government indeed became a *principatus politicus*. This political government embodied the (human) will of the citizens or of the people at large, and hence political government was government of the people – *principatus populi*, as he calls it – because it was in the people that political power was located. This was, according to him, *democracia*.[10] Consequently, and quite in conformity with the humanist theme, the government provided for all relevant matters of concern to the citizens' life: the *tota vita* was the object of governmental business, the purpose of which was to bring to fruition the common good of the citizens through their greatest possible self-sufficiency.[11]

But because it was humanity as such that was represented in the government, its structure, aims, policies, and so forth were to vary according to the human diversities which in themselves were conditioned by natural

4 *Ibid.*, cap. 3, p. 83, line 12.
5 See above, p. 110, n. 27.
6 *Ed. cit.*, cap. 25, p. 202, line 23.
7 *Ibid.*, cap. 3, p. 82, lines 5ff.; cap. 10, p. 113, lines 8f. and p. 114, lines 32ff.; cap. 25, p. 207, line 8 and p. 208, line 23.
8 *Ibid.*, cap. 17, p. 161, lines 19ff.
9 The essential point here is that the (human) king, no longer a king by the grace of God or the Lord's anointed, was measurable, so to speak, by human standards. He was what he was through election by the citizens.
10 *Ibid.*, cap. 19.
11 *Ibid.*, cap. 4 and other places (the 'bonum commune civium' to be achieved through 'maxima sufficientia').

features: different climatic, geographical or other physical factors gave birth to diverse structures of states (and therefore governments) (*diversae politiae*), simply because there were diverse nations and each expressed its own will according to natural, intuitive, human assessments and evaluations. What is good for one nation, need not be so for another. The emphasis on the natural, human element allowed an alert man of John of Paris's calibre to see the great diversity of structure and aim of the national states which therefore catered for the common good of their citizens in different ways. And the character of this common good of the citizens varied as much as humanity itself varied. Abstract ecclesiological uniformity was replaced by concrete human multiformity. National law began to take the place of a universal law. Bipolarity of man's ends came to be substituted for linear unipolarity. As indeed Thomas had indicated, selectivity was to prevail where previously there had been rigidly absolute principles. In a word, humanity in its infinite variety and multiplicity of manifestations entered the arena of scholarship through political science by taking due account of practical exigencies and contingencies. After all, as Thomas had it, political science was the most fundamental (*principalissima*) of all human sciences and had therefore to start from the foundation of social realities.

How much in fact the human element had become operational in political science can be seen from John of Paris's views on (private) property, which are not properly appreciated by modern scholarship. They abandoned the doctrine hitherto held unquestionable that property was an issue of divine grace. This was a thesis that was directly linked with baptismal rebirth: for the baptismally reborn man lived by divine grace and therefore whatever he had acquired, he held as a trust and as a usufructuary, God remaining the sole owner.[12] But through the process of humanization and the consequential attainment of an autonomous status, property which he had acquired by his own human labour, efforts, industry, thrift, and so on, was to be exclusively his own, and divine grace just did not come into play at all. The citizen's property was restored to its original, natural habitat because secured by human–natural means, and therefore as a citizen he was entitled to dispose of it. It simply was a natural, human right to acquire property, and natural law was at the service of natural humanity. Not despite, but because of his adopting the principle of bipolarity both the unregenerated citizen and the regenerated Christian had in consonance with the Thomist system a legitimate standing. There was now inclusiveness, where previously there had been exclusiveness. The book by John of Paris was a mighty step forward towards the full implementation of humanist theses.

A contemporary of John of Paris, the famous philosopher Durandus de s.

12   For this cf. *PGP* pp. 76f.

Porciano (Saint-Pourçain), who also taught at Paris and later became bishop of Meaux, was far from adopting all the Thomist premisses, but nevertheless adhered to the fundamental Thomist thesis that a layman had a twofold capacity, one as a natural being in which capacity he was a citizen, and one as a Christian, and as such was part of the supranatural order. Evidently, this twofold character was reflected in the jurisdiction exercised by the civic and ecclesiastical courts.[13] The succinctness with which this thought is expressed reveals the maturity of Durandus as well as the influence of Thomas upon another Dominican who was by no means an outright follower of the Angelic Doctor.

Another contemporary and compatriot of John of Paris was Pierre Dubois who, though as a student he had attended the lectures of Thomas and Siger of Brabant, did not pursue scholarly interests, but was a prolific propagandist writer with a marked practical bent of mind, ample experience and a sharp eye for reality. His works – of which an up-to-date analysis is long overdue – set forth programmes and plans which articulately express ideas and points of view current before and at his time. He, like John, follows the Aristotelian–Thomist pattern. He does not however present a scholarly exposition of fundamental ideas, but makes concrete proposals. And these show a remarkable humanist, secular complexion mirroring as they do the ethos of the turn of the thirteenth century. His programmes are *au fond* concrete manifestations of the Aristotelian–Thomist natural law, of bipolarity, of national sovereignty suffused with a good deal of chauvinist French sentiment and the rejection of all universalist conceptions. Since, to take an instance, property was an issue of natural law, he advocated the secularization of all Church property, for which due annual payments or pensions were to be made by lay men: after all, the Church was not a creation of nature, but a divine institution. Because of their occupation and profession, the clerics have no right to ownership of estates. This applies not only to the papacy, but also to the cardinals, the secular clergy and the monasteries. Nunneries should be turned into girls' schools. The abolition of clerical celibacy was an urgent demand, since natural law militated against it. Wars – and clearly he held the just war to be merely a figleaf or a pretext – were an affront to human reasoning. They could be prevented by the formation of a European league of all (sovereign) states – under French guidance.

The king as a territorial sovereign had the right to intervene in all ecclesiastical matters, not because he was a king–priest but because he was the defender of the faith and supreme legislator: 'Did not Moses deal with sacral matters when he gave the laws?'[14] Here is the unmistakable echo of

13   See the quotation in *IS*, p. 140, n. 79.
14   See his memorandum sent to the king, ed. E. Boutaric in *Notices et extraits*, 10(1865), part 2, no. 30, at p. 181.

the (Roman) public law, especially when he refers to those who dealt with the lawyers as 'priests'.[15] Here is Gallicanism in the making. Hence the governmental measures against the Templars. He emphatically insisted above all on the relativity of all law: there was no such thing as a universal law that would be applicable in every place, at all times, and to all persons.[16] Hence the 'statutes enacted by men' vary greatly according to place, time and persons, because the law aims at realizing the *utilitas communis*, that is, the common interest. The works of Pierre Dubois applied axioms which wholly stemmed from the human, secular arsenal and made articulate what large sections of his contemporaries had evidently already accepted.[17]

In unadulterated form the work of Marsilius of Padua presents a political science tract that is a full-blooded expression of the 'human' standpoint, the very consequence of the renaissance of man and of the citizen. There are no more than faint traces of the Thomist synthesis. Marsilius' theme constitutes the culmination of the purely humanist, mundane idea of reborn man within a political framework. It is the basic idea of the citizen as the political manifestation of *humanitas* which is the central item of his closely argued system. To him the State was the aggregate or corporation of citizens, the citizens' body which functions as the *legislator humanus*, where the accent lies on the human (and not divine) character of the lawmaker. New dimensions were thereby staked out for the political activity of the citizenhood, and the traditional landmarks of unipolarity, universality and totality were replaced by bipolarity, state sovereignty within territorial limits, atomism and consequential autonomy of the religious, political and other norms. In this work the idea of rebirth and of humanism, of renaissance and politics, are shown to be indissolubly linked: in virtually classic form Marsilius presents the political expression of humanism that was contingent upon the renaissance of natural man and hence of his *humanitas*. What followed was adjustment and modification of this political theory, and above all the discovery of means with which to implement it. And it was precisely the search for the means which sparked off the subsequent literary and cultural renaissance.

In managing human society 'we must follow nature as a guide', asserted Marsilius, thus avowing his dependence on Aristotle.[18] There is through-

---

15 *Ibid.*: 'Cum dicit lex: est ius ars boni et aequi, cuius quis merito nos sacerdotes appellat. Nonne Moyses cum legem dabat populo, sacra dabat?'
16 *De recuperatione*, p. 39 (ed. C. Langlois, Paris, 1891): 'omni loco, omni tempore, omnibus personis.' Cf. Alexander of Roes, above, p. 78, n. 47, and Dante, below at n. 34.
17 R. Scholz, *Die Publizistik zur Zeit Philipp des Schönen und Bonifaz' VIII.* (Stuttgart, 1903), pp. 391ff.; J. Rivière, *Le problème de l'église et de l'état au temps de Philippe le Bel* (Louvain and Paris, 1926), pp. 343ff.
18 *Defensor Pacis* (ed. R. Scholz, reprinted 1955). ET by A. Gewirth (New York, 1956), I.1.4.

out his work the consistent juxtaposition of animalic nature and human nature.[19] And in constantly postulating the theme of bipolarity he made a clean conceptual break between the two spheres by limiting the citizen's concern to purely human interest. Human society functioned best by the differentiation of human orders or offices or officers, who in their multi-formity constituted the sinews of the State.[20] His main concern was the establishment of general maxims which were to promote the efficacy and validity of purely human volitions and measures, unencumbered by any considerations outside the human purview and comprehension. Any argument based on baptismal rebirth was irrelevant to human society and nothing but a *sophistica opinio*. The supranatural end might be important, but belonged to a conceptually different tier altogether. The citizens, the State, the government and the different orders of government could have a legitimate interest only in limited aims, and yet had a vastly expanded sphere of operation – that of providing the means, not of eventual salvation, but of mundane, this-worldly well-being, which determined the citizens' legislation.[21] The material ingredient of law was the citizens' consent: no longer was faith the kernel of the enforceable law. To be enforceable the law must embody the citizens' consent.

It is therefore understandable why the new category of thought, that is to say, politics, became an essential structural element of his work.[22] Hence the invocation of the ancient Roman law adage 'What touches all must be approved by all'.[23] Hence the solicitude for human well-being by the law-creating organ, a criterion which evidently varied according to different regions and times, so that the principle of relativity of the law clearly emerged. From this followed the relativity of institutions and constitutions, according to differing intellectual, political, educational standards.[24] Here, as in John of Paris and Dubois, was the abandonment of any absolutist universality and the embrace of relativity. Clearly on this basis he does not and cannot advocate any particular form of government: the ascending theme precluded any such advocacy. Whether monarchic, aristocratic or democratic forms of government were eventually adopted was irrelevant, as long as the government was elected by, and remained responsible to, the citizenhood. The main function of government was to guide the *human* actions of the citizens, because for him government was the execution of the law laid down by the *human* legislator: the law was the

19 For instance, I.2.3; I.4.1, etc.
20 *Ibid.*, I.4.5; I.5.1.
21 *Ibid.*, I.12.2: the law as the yardstick of human–civic actions ('mensura *humanorum* actuum civilium'). The State was the corporation of citizens ('universitas civium').
22 I.13.2, quoting the relevant passages of Aristotle.
23 I.12.7.
24 I.9.10.

norm and rule of human actions.[25] The consistent emphasis on the link of political concepts with humanity will not escape notice. Man's gaze had become more modest and was no longer directed to a future, but to the present life. For part of the baptismally reborn man was re-humanized, and it was his humanity that formed the centre of politics and the State. Perhaps no other contemporary work showed so convincingly the profound re-orientation that had taken place in the early fourteenth century: it was the effect of the idea of human rebirth or renaissance that had now opened up new vistas. The replacement of the principle of unipolarity by the principle of bipolarity was therefore basic to the Marsilian system.[26] Or, seen from a different angle, the age-old conjoint unitary character of the earthly and the eternal worlds was broken: there now existed conceptually two disjointed worlds.

One of the most characteristic features of the Marsilian system was the use made of Roman law, which once more proved itself a vital auxiliary means in the implementation of the humanist theme. Other ancient models were soon to follow. Marsilius harnessed the Roman public law which, it may be recalled, was manipulated by the Roman emperor and referred to sacral matters as well as to their administrators, the priests. Now, by propounding the ascending theme of government, Marsilius was perfectly entitled to apply the provision of this Roman public law to the citizenhood: the human legislator alone could create law, and hence the public law was to be manipulated by this organ too. Translated into terms of government this meant that the human legislator could exercise the same rights, that is, the appointment, election and control of clerics, as well as jurisdiction over them.[27] This was the human–populist expression of the ancient Roman public law and signified the culmination of the process of secularization that had begun in the mid twelfth century. What had formerly applied only to the monarch, now applied to the aggregate of unregenerate men, the corporate society of citizens, the State. The wheel had come full circle. It is highly significant that the book was translated into the Florentine vernacular a generation after it had been finished (1324). And it was at Florence that 'civic humanism' was to find its most prominent representatives.

Since the material ingredient of the law was the consent of the citizens, it stood to reason not only that they had to have representative organs, but also that they had to engage in political debate and argument, in a word, had to discuss public issues by *politizare*, by 'politicizing'.[28] The require-

25   I.10.1; I.12.3, etc. Further, I.3.3: 'regula actuum *humanorum*.' Cf. also n. 21.
26   Life can be understood, he says, 'in duplici modo' (shades of the Thomist *duplex ordo in rebus*), in the temporal–mundane, and in the eternal sense: I.4.3.
27   II.17.2ff.; II.21.4f.
28   I.13.2.

ment of consent or, which is the same, the application of the ascending theme of government, compellingly led to an implicit canonization of the vernacular, since only an extremely small part of the citizenhood understood Latin. Political humanism of necessity promoted the vernacular which, as already indicated,[29] strongly contributed to the entrenchment of the concept of nationhood and of the nation State. Consent presupposes agreement on essential matters and this could be expressed only in the vernacular. Public discussion – *politizare* – obviously was not possible without a national language. Against this background the accelerated growth of political propaganda in the modern sense becomes easily understandable – and, eventually, the services which printing could and did render in precisely this context. Here is an aspect of political humanism that has not attracted the attention which is its due.

Even the most cursory glance at the literary output in the first half of the fourteenth century shows how deep and fructifying an impact the renaissance of natural man in his capacity as a citizen had had in the field of political science. It was the rebirth of the citizen and the concomitant humanism which engendered this kind of literature. Its burgeoning proves how fertile the soil was for scholarly expositions which set aside the centuries-old hallowed principles of unipolarity, totality and universality. Conceptually, citizenship endangered, if it did not eliminate, the rigidity of the traditional hierarchical structure of society, and to a not negligible extent strengthened the sense of equality among the citizens themselves. From this angle, it is wholly understandable that in conservative circles a reaction set in, since the replacement of the traditional principles was equivalent to a wholly new cosmology. Indeed in this germinating age of political humanism one can clearly distinguish two schools of thought which opposed the new cosmology. The one was conciliatory and its distinguished representative was Dante, the other school attacked the new political humanism root and branch and rejected all reconciliation: its representative was Boniface VIII and his followers.

One of the main features of the humanist outlook was the adoption of the atomistic standpoint in place of totality (or indivisibility). This standpoint split up the whole into a number of different compartments, each autonomous and independent, such as the religious, political, moral, and other norms. What previously was one undivided whole, now appeared as individual entities, each resting on its own premisses and axioms, in a word, each was autonomous. The collective field showed exactly the same features. What previously had constituted one undivided whole bonded together by the element of faith, had in the course of the thirteenth century split into independent entities of a regional character held together

29 Above, pp. 73, 75.

by linguistic, ethnic and other natural bonds. We have already observed
how much this situation facilitated the emergence of the concept of the
national state, with which was indissolubly linked state sovereignty,
epitomized in the adage *Rex in regno suo imperator* ('The king in his kingdom is an emperor'). National sovereignty however was a ferment of
decomposition, disintegration and fragmentation of what was once a
conceptually undivided whole. In a word, the atomization discernible in
the various autonomous norms (the religious, political, and so on) reappeared in the collective sphere: it was the national state. National
sovereignty was the constitutional expression of humanism. As a product
of nature the citizen had assumed a national identity. And it was merely an
application of the concept of the nation and of national sovereignty that in
due course the appointment of two cardinals from each nation was formally
proposed, so that the interests of the nation could be taken care of in the
papal curia. This would seem to be an irrefutable symptom of the fragmentation of what was once one whole.[30] Only a few years later the
Council of Siena exhibited 'a frightening spectacle of nationalism'.[31]

Dante's *Monarchy* was a clarion call to halt the progressing decomposition of the universal order. He revived the idea of the ancient Roman
empire and attempted a reconciliation of Aristotelian–Thomist principles
with the traditional ways of thinking. He has rightly been acclaimed one
of the earliest humanists, though not for the reason which appears to be
crucial. In order to achieve his purpose to retard the advance of national
autonomous entities and particularism he resuscitated the idea of a
universal State for which the Roman empire served him as a prototype.[32]
Above all, he harnessed to his task the very concept of *humanitas*, now
restored to its pristine meaning, thereby making the *homo* the core of his
political philosophy. For what mattered to Dante was 'the power of
humanity itself' (*potentia ipsius humanitatis*). It was the collectivized *homo*
in the shape of *humanitas* which, in the unsurpassable Dantesque terminology, was the *civilitas humana*.[33] This entity alone possessed the attributes

---

30   The proposal was made by Sigismund at the conclusion of the Council of Constance,
      see A. A. Strnad, 'Konstanz und der Plan eines deutschen Nationalkonzils' in *Das
      Konzil von Konstanz*, ed. A. Franzen *et al.* (Freiburg and Vienna, 1964), pp. 397ff.;
      the formal proposal at p. 428.
31   See W. Koudelka in *ZKG*, 74(1963), 247.
32   That the ancient Roman empire was perfectly acceptable to pagans as well as to St
      Paul (Eph. 1:10), to whom it constituted 'the plenitude of time', was a point specially
      stressed by Dante. For details cf. W. Ullmann, 'Dante's *Monarchia* as an illustration
      of a politico-religious *renovatio*' in *Festschrift für Winfried Zeller* (Marburg, 1976),
      pp. 101ff. The best modern edition of the *Monarchia* is by G. P. Ricci (Milan, 1965).
33   Although John of Salisbury knew the term *civilitas* (see *PGP*, p. 256, n. 1), he did
      not operate with it. Petrus Comestor appears to have used the term correctly in
      connection with St Paul's claim to Roman citizenship, see his *Hist. scholastica*, in
      PL 198.1710B and 1711A ('Romana civilitas': cf. Acts 22:28).

of universality and autonomy, independent as they were of any divine grace or ecclesiastical approval. The succinct term and notion of the *civilitas humana* expressed universal mankind in its natural, that is, baptismally unregenerated, state presided over by the universal monarch, who for Dante represented the abstract idea of justice and law. This ruler was typologically conceived: he typified the rule of law as a regulator on a universal scale. And because he considered mankind a universal entity, it embraced Christians, Jews, Muslims and pagans. What holds mankind together is for Dante the sentiment of community or belonging together, expressed in the identification of man as man, wholly in disregard of religious, ethnic and other divisive factors. It was precisely Dante's humanism that made him view the idea of law in a relativist light by declaring that, because law was a directive of life, the nations and kingdoms must have different laws which take into account the specialities and peculiarities of regional entities.[34] But over and above the nations stands the universally valid idea of law and justice conceived in human terms, the custodian of which is the universal monarch. For the universal monarch no other model or prototype was available to Dante than the ancient Roman emperor. That is also why he resuscitated the idea of the Roman empire: it was a model or a pattern or what was also called an *exemplum*, not to be imitated but an object from which one could learn a lesson.

By operating with the idea of the ancient Roman empire Dante in practice and in theory paved the way to a consultation of the ancients, and showed how greatly the ancients could assist the humanizing process now at work. By resuscitating the idea of an effective universal empire he pleaded for the utilization of the experience and history of Rome. Herein lay the historic significance of Dante as a humanist: not in the sense in which the concept of empire was commonly understood in the medieval period, but in the sense of a unit that at one time had worked well, was providentially chosen as the entity within which Christ was born and had brought peace. The 'Roman empire' that had existed since the ninth century applied the idea of baptismal rebirth on a global scale. This medieval empire corresponded to the 'new creature' in the individual sphere and was created by the papacy as an instrument with which it could effectively oppose the imperial régime in Constantinople. But according to Dante this 'Roman empire' should be seen in its original, pristine, 'un-regenerated' status which had indeed proved a viable political entity for centuries.[35] Hence the empire advocated by him was an essentially human

---

34 *Monarchia*, I.14. For ET of the work see *LP* p. 278, n. 1. For the relativity of the law see above, p. 78, n. 47 and above n. 16.

35 For an explanation of the Dantesque view of the ancient Roman empire, see *art. cit.* (above, n.32). For Aristotelian studies cf. M. Grabmann, 'Das Aristotelesstudium in Italien zur Zeit Dantes', in his *Mittelalterliches Geistesleben*, II(1955), 197–212.

institution embracing what he called the whole of mankind (the *genus humanum* or the *universitas hominum*). His *civilitas humana* expressed this same idea in abstract political language. It was a world State and, in order to show that this was not a fanciful product of imagination but had a factual basis, he invoked the historic example of the ancient Roman empire. It functioned as a model which, according to Dante, held numerous lessons for his contemporaries. The ancient empire pre-portrayed the universal State postulated by Dante.

By the same stroke Dante 'demundanized' the Church as the one universal unit. To the *papatus* corresponded the *imperiatus*, a new and hitherto unnoticed coinage which brought the bipolarity principle into clear relief. This principle of bipolarity was an essential structural element of his philosophy, and indeed in this he clarified Thomist principles very elegantly, as is proved by the frequently misunderstood concluding sentences. The Christian as a member of the universal Church had a supranatural end, while the citizen as a member of the universal State pursued this-worldly aims. In parenthesis it may be remarked that he conceived the Church to be a body exclusively focused on matters of grace, matters, that is, which did not belong to the natural order of things, and in this respect he gave practical expression to the Thomist principle of a double ordering inherent in things. But his main plea was on the mundane level and for a *renovatio* in the sense of a renaissance of a universal unit that transcended kingdoms, nations, empires, because only then peace and fruitful development would be guaranteed. He presented the Roman empire as a model or as a typological pattern, that should be followed. It was a unit that was (in baptismal language) unregenerated, whereas the Church was its regenerated universal counterpart. On the mundane level national states were mere parts of the universal State, and were its emanations, so that they could be comprehended only in a global context, and could achieve their ends only within the universal unit. Autonomy belonged, not to them, but to the universal State, modelled as this was on the ancient Roman empire.

This politically conceived humanism is the incontrovertible matrix and fabric of Dante's philosophy. And this humanism conspicuously showed how essential to it recourse to the ancients was, recourse, that is, to exclusively political models, here not only to the Roman empire, but also to the corresponding universal monarch. No other literary product of the early fourteenth century exhibited so abundantly the very essence and message of humanism in its early phases, which was, not to imitate, but to consult, and learn from, the ancients, in a word, to look at the ancients as *exempla*. Initially the rationale of the message was political, as Dante's political philosophy would seem most persuasively to demonstrate. At the cradle of humanist philosophy, letters, arts, oratory, and so on, stood a plain and unadorned political philosophy which was not the vision of a dreamer, but (as indeed later history was to bear out amply) a realistic assessment of a situation. Nothing sharpens political consciousness and stimulates creative thought as much as banishment and exile do. They above all make man acutely sensitive to the potentially harmful effects of a development that is hidden from the sight of ordinary mortals who are neither the victims of injustice nor endowed with exceptional mental powers.

In stark contrast to the positive, forward-looking programme enunciated by Dante stood his contemporary Boniface VIII, who may serve as a shorthand device for the 'old' school which fiercely opposed any kind of humanist manifestations. While Dante constructively utilized the new Aristotelian–Thomist synthesis for political purposes, Boniface condemned the whole new cosmology altogether. To him – and to many of his contemporaries and later followers – the new principle of bipolarity appeared a prescription for the ruin and collapse of a world order that was exclusively based on Christian principles. The approbation of this new cosmology, involving as it did the adoption of the State, the citizen and politics, would in their opinion have been tantamount to treason committed against the very concept of the universal Church, not to mention against its reality. In other words, the regenerated Christian alone was still to hold his monopolistic position, and in principle the unregenerated natural man was to remain excluded from participation in public matters touching the well-being of the whole Church, and it was these which really mattered. In order to oppose the new doctrines effectively, the Bonifacian adherents laboured hard to fortify the three main themes of the old cosmology – unipolarity, universality and totality.

The Bonifacian standpoint was outright opposition to the new political humanism and was exclusively based on grounds of principle, and on no other. Boniface VIII's bull *Unam sanctam* was not the expression of insatiable papal lust for power, but a papal pronouncement that opened the long line of magisterial scholarly statements by the papacy directed implicitly and sometimes explicitly against erroneous doctrines. *Unam sanctam* was a concise summary of the chief tenets of traditional ecclesiology.[36] It was a product of academic scholarship issued to combat contemporary trends in academic scholarship which, in papal eyes, had assumed dangerous proportions. Paradoxically enough, *Unam sanctam* originated in a first-rate jurist-pope who employed not a single juristic argument. The entry of theologians into the papal workshop – the chancery

---

36 For details and the significance see W. Ullmann, 'Die Bulle Unam sanctam: Rückblick und Ausblick' in *Römische Hist. Mitteilungen*, 16(1974), 45–77, and *id.*, 'Boniface VIII and his contemporary scholarship' in *JTS*, 27(1976), 58–87.

– at this (late) date is not without its deeper significance and would unwittingly seem to lend some corroboration to Dante's – and others' – aim of 'demundanizing' the Church. The entry of the theologians into the papal chancery had its exact counterpart in the entry of the *légistes* into the royal chancery.

What deserves special mention is that none of these theological authors even discussed the topics of the citizen, the State and its autonomy, the renaissance of natural man and the relevance of his humanity in the public field, and other related items. The very silence on these crucial themes is perhaps more significant than any lengthy discussion. Clearly, the conceptual triad of the State, the citizen and politics epitomized a cosmology which was totally at variance with the traditional modes of ecclesiological thought. And, indeed, there was no link between these contrasting cosmologies, unless one adopted the Thomist–Dantesque compromise. As the prolific writings of the first decades of the fourteenth century prove, the opposition to political humanism was total. Yet these valiant efforts to arrest the development were in vain. Political humanism was to usher in wholly new intellectual and constitutional orientations which were to be of direct concern to the Church.

It was precisely in the early phases of political humanism that Roman law became particularly relevant, because it provided perhaps the easiest, and certainly the most readily available, avenue to the consultation of the ancients. It was primarily the academic jurists – laymen they were – who were the first to operate with humanist conceptions on a practical level, precisely because the Roman law and its texts were their lifeblood.[37] The great Cynus de Pistoia – personal friend of Dante and Petrarch, and possibly also of Boccaccio – had greatly profited from his sojourn in France at the turn of the thirteenth and fourteenth centuries, where the most eminent jurists of the day had been lecturing, such as Jacobus de Ravanis, Petrus de Bellapertica, Guilielmus de Cuneo, Petrus Jacobi, Johannes Faber, and so on. The universities of Orléans, Montpellier and Toulouse flourished pre-eminently in jurisprudence and supplied the jurists who have already attracted our attention.[38] Cynus was thoroughly familiar with the most recent interpretations by the French masters and in more than one way gave new directions to jurisprudence in Italy.[39] It is

---

37 See also above, p. 100. Roberto Weiss was the first eminent modern scholar who stressed 'the leading role of lawyers in the early development of humanism in Italy', *The Dawn of Humanism in Italy* (London, 1947), p. 5. But he did not elaborate this highly important insight and mentioned only a few practitioners of the law. Cf. also below, pp. 134f. For very perceptive observations see D. Hay, *op. cit.* (above, p. 2, n. 10), pp. 70ff.
38 See above, p. 49.
39 For Cynus, see *LP* pp. 106ff.

of especial concern that Cynus was the first jurist of name and fame who dealt with the (new) problem of citizenship, and it was also he who on the basis of the Roman law advocated a consistent application of the ascending theme of government and law.

Of course, the so-called *lex regia*[40] in Roman law had been commented upon ever since Roman law had become the subject of serious academic study in the twelfth century and had been a major instrument in the process of secularization of government and in maintaining its momentum. Now however as a result of the emerging political humanism and the new French whiff in juristic thought, the *lex regia* began to assume additional significance. This law, according to which the Roman people had at one time transferred all its own power to the emperor, was now seen in its proper human–political context and therefore proved itself, as we shall presently see, a highly dynamic force in the implementation of the ascending theme of government. The academic glosses and commentaries on this *lex regia* were of an explanatory historical kind without direct contemporary relevance, precisely the role which this law now assumed. Here clearly in the hallowed Roman law books there was the concrete example or model of a monarch who had received power, not by the grace of God or the pope, but from the people itself. It is therefore of special interest that none was more aware of the potentialities of this law than the just-mentioned friend of Dante, the poet and jurist Cynus de Pistoia. He too stood, so to speak, on the threshold of political humanism. His view is perhaps best summed up in his statement: 'Imperium a Deo, imperator a populo' ('the empire comes from God, the emperor from the people'). This is clearly an ingenious compromise that should not hide the intellectual discomfort of its author. But the intrinsic significance was that the consultation of Roman law led to its application in so delicate a matter as the creation of the emperor, always considered to have been the sole prerogative of the papacy. This shows that political humanism had made its inconspicuous entry into a central quarter of traditional ecclesiology. Roman law came to be conceived as the prototype of mundane law, which indeed it was. It is not difficult to see on the not too distant horizon the emergence of humanist jurisprudence, which was shorn of all medieval accretions and marked the 'return' to the 'pure' Roman law – it was the humanist renaissance in the specific shape of humanist jurisprudence.

The unparalleled reservoir of maxims, rules and principles which the Roman law contained, and which were obviously useful in the implementation of political humanism, explains also two features of immediate relevance. First, there was a proliferation of higher educational institutions

40　For the *lex regia* cf. above, p. 42.

in which the study of Roman law was preponderant, and this was the case in Italy (Perugia, Treviso, Verona, Pisa, Florence, Pavia, Ferrara, to mention just a few), as it was in France (Avignon, Cahors, Grenoble, Aix, etc.), in Germany and Bohemia (Prague, Vienna, Erfurt, Heidelberg, Cologne, Würzburg, etc.) or in Hungary and Poland and Spain, not to speak of the exuberant college foundations in Cambridge and partly also in Oxford in the fourteenth century. The beneficiaries of the educational facilities were clearly the laity. This is the other feature, that is, the strong representation of the lay element in the universities – it was perhaps a sign of the times that it was the great Johannes Andreae, the layman lecturing on canon law, who drew up the statutes of Bologna in 1322. Both laymen and the universities evidently pursued interests different from – though by no means hostile to – theological or other divine subjects. They powerfully cultivated the soil for the receptivity of humanist political theses, though the positive contribution which the universities made to political humanism was certainly not overwhelming, as we shall have occasion to observe. But their main function, and this applies with particular force to the juristic academic pursuits, was that of bridge-builders between the new and the old, the *via antiqua* and the *via moderna*, between unregenerated natural birth and regenerated baptismal rebirth. Once more, Roman law proved itself an important factor that assisted political humanism.

To two specific effects of political humanism in the field of constitutionalism some attention should be drawn. The teachings of the great Bartolus, actually a pupil of Cynus, illustrate clearly the consequences of the rebirth of the citizen. He conceived the State as the collectivized prince, and the structural members of the State were the citizens. Bartolus applied the (former) prince's sovereignty to his collective counterpart, the State, so that what previously appertained to the former as a sovereign, was now applicable to the latter, the aggregate of the citizens, expressed in the unsurpassably succinct Bartolist formula *Civitas sibi princeps*: the State is its own sovereign. A corollary of this view was the simultaneous elaboration of the principle of representation which was but weakly developed in Roman law. Bartolus formulated this important principle thus: 'The council represents the mind of the people' ('Concilium repraesentat mentem populi'), because the people, that is, the citizens, elected the council. Indeed this amalgamation of Germanic, Roman and humanist premises had already been impressively at work in the North Italian city-states. There seems little room for doubt that political humanism, the ascending theme of government and representative principles complemented each other rather well – in practice as well as in theory.

Sometimes, and especially in recent years, the observation has been made that in the fourteenth century the constitutional problem of citizenship had arisen.[41] While the observation itself is indubitably true, the question has never been asked why this should be so – or vice versa, why there had been no such problem nor for that matter a theory of citizenship earlier. If the question had been put, an answer could presently have been provided. Precisely because the citizen was now considered as the bearer of power, the problem of citizenship became one of practical topicality. The question of possessing, losing, acquiring it, the criteria and various kinds of citizenship, and related topics, of necessity obtruded themselves. And here the very idea of natural man's rebirth, the renaissance of his humanity, is most strikingly reflected. Constitutional doctrine (and practice) now accorded to the most natural of all natural events, human birth, exactly the same legal standing as had previously been accorded solely to the baptismally reborn man, the Christian. As Baldus, the famous pupil of Bartolus, had it, 'natural man' ('homo naturalis') becomes a *politicus*, and therefore as a citizen a member of the State.[42] Just as natural birth was the presupposition for membership of the State, in the same way baptism was the presupposition for membership of the Church. In other words, the supranatural body of the Church required for membership the regenerative event of baptism, that displayed in the supranatural field the same legal effects as the generative event of birth did within the natural body of the State. Natural birth conferred a *civilitas originaria* or *originalis*, beside which stood a legally acquired citizenship (a *civilitas acquisita*), if certain conditions had been fulfilled, for instance acquisition of citizenship through marriage or through residence in a particular locality for a specified period.

The essential point here is that natural (or carnal) *generatio* now assumed full legal standing and significance. Whether the citizenship was original or acquired, it had reference only to natural man. Because it was tied to a definite territory it reflected the assumption that the natural citizen was a member of the ethnic or linguistic group that predominated in this territory. Evidently, it was in the power of the State, by virtue of the

---

41 See Marvin Becker, 'An essay on *novi cives* and Florentine politics 1342–1382' in *Medieval Studies*, 24(1962), 35–82; further, W. M. Bowsky, 'A new Consilium of Cino da Pistoia (1324): citizenship, residence and taxation' in *Speculum*, 42(1967), 431ff.; W. Ullmann, 'De Bartoli sententia: Concilium repraesentat mentem populi' in *PPI*, ch. X; J. Kirshner, 'Paolo di Castro on cives ex privilegio' in *Renaissance studies for Hans Baron* (Chicago, 1971), 227ff.; *id.*, 'Civitas sibi faciat civem: Bartolus de Sassoferrato's doctrine on the making of a citizen' in *Speculum*, 48(1973), 694ff.; *id.*, 'Ars imitatur naturam: a consilium of Baldus on naturalization in Florence' in *Viator*, 5(1974), 289ff., especially 308ff. On the other hand, P. Riesenberg, 'Citizenship at law in late medieval Italy', *ibid.*, 333–46, is distinguished by its industry rather than its advancement of knowledge.
42 See his Commentary on the Codex, VII.53.5 (edition Venice, 1615) no. 10, fol. 73va: 'homo naturalis efficitur politicus . . .'.

operation of the ascending theme, to limit or to exclude or to suspend citizenship, such as that of insane persons, children, and so on. The jurists had long discussions on the distinctions between citizens, inhabitants and other residents.[43] That the problem of citizenship evidently affected the traditional stratification of society is not difficult to understand. Was the cleric a citizen? Did the citizen continue to be one if he changed his lay status and became a cleric or a monk? These problems need only to be stated to be apprehended in their magnitude and in their impact upon the structure of the State.[44] A glance at the thousands of *Consilia* (that is, expert opinions) given by the eminent academic jurists in the fourteenth and fifteenth centuries shows the multiplicity of other questions relative to citizenship which cropped up throughout Europe: problems of taxation, military service, active and passive electoral rights, asylum, property, and so on, which just could not have arisen in an earlier generation, became matters of dispute. One might say that the principle of bipolarity found its appropriate expression in the citizen as an unregenerated member of the natural State and in the Christian as a regenerated member of the supranatural Church. Political humanism gradually began to assume firm contours.

The concept of the State and of the citizen also necessarily gave rise to the problem of how far a citizen of one State was subjected to the laws of another. Obviously, this too was a question that could not have arisen earlier, precisely because there was neither a State nor a citizen. A further glance at the *Consilia* shows once more the topicality of this very problem from the fourteenth century onwards. Bartolus set forth certain principles which may well mark the beginning of what later came to be called private international law. According to him, statutes referred either to things or to persons or to both. There were *statuta realia* or *personalia* or *mixta*, and hence there were different rules of application to citizens of different States.[45] And since the State was a citizen writ large, its relations with another State proceeded on this same basis, that is, to the internal law regulating the relations between individual citizens corresponded an external law regulating the relations between States as citizens writ large.

---

43   Cf., for instance, Baldus on Dig. 20.1.15(1), *ed. cit.*, fol. 176, no. 3; also Dig. 3.5.3(6), fol. 53vb. Cf. Bartolus himself on Cod. X.39.3 (edition Basle, 1562), p. 881: mere residents cannot be citizens. It is however interesting to note that Bartolus used the locality at which baptism was received as an indication of the birth place: 'sicut per manumissionem quis sortitur forum, et dicitur *nasci*, ita et per baptismum' (on Cod. X.39.9, *ed. cit.*, p. 882, no. 4).

44   The juristic writings of the fourteenth and fifteenth centuries are replete with just this kind of problem. One has but to realize the agrarian character of society, together with the quite rapidly emerging economic changes, if one wishes to comprehend the dimensions of this problem – a veritable result of political humanism. Hardly any research has been done on this topic.

45   For modern literature on this topic, cf. *LP* p. 108.

This indeed is the background to the nascent law of nations or international law, of which the first exponent was a Bartolist, the exiled Italian Albericus Gentilis at Oxford.[46]

In a symbolic manner, not devoid of drama as well as tragedy, political humanism in the mid fourteenth century was highlighted on the plane of practical reality. Indeed, Cola di Rienzo has rightly been acknowledged as a significant figure of the early renaissance scene. However fantastic his programme was, it embodied a number of precisely those elements which the humanist renaissance had brought to the fore in the immediately preceding decades. He, Dante and Bartolus were contemporaries, though there is little direct evidence that Cola was familiar with the writings of Bartolus. Whereas Dante had set forth a political ideology based on the humanist theme, and while Bartolus was a jurisprudential theoretician who with calm, detached and refined scholarship propounded juristic principles capable of application, Cola attempted an accommodation of Dantesque and Bartolist axioms to his programme, and he did this with fiery display, dramatic effort and little discernment. Cola's programme culminated in a radical translation of political humanism into practice.

Cola di Rienzo's brief appearance in the limelight may illustrate a number of the features which we have surveyed. It should be realized that the seven months of Cola's 'rule' in Rome (in 1347) telescoped in an exceedingly compressed form a great many topics of the new political humanism. Evidently, the absence of the papacy at Avignon, the inter-necine strife of the great Roman families, the general instability amounting to chaotic conditions, favoured the emergence of a 'tribune' who by radically departing from the traditional social, governmental and political set-up held out promises for responding to the needs of the people. Aware as he was of the rudimentary requirements of mass psychology and of the advantageous effects of an actor's postures on the crowd as well as equipped with the aptitude for sharp phrases, his vernacular eloquence fired the Romans by the never yet failed appeal to the grandeur of Rome.

As a learned jurist he was thoroughly versed in ancient and contemporary literature, and his programme culminated in the rebirth of Rome with the aim of conquering present difficulties and ensuring the peaceful and fruitful development of the future. This indeed was the message of his various manifestos and appeals. They proclaimed the restoration of secular Rome, *Roma renovata*, cleansed of all accretions not pertinent to it, the 'demundanization' of the Church and its confinement to exclusively

---

46 The term 'international law' was coined by Bentham in his *Introduction to the Principles of Morals and Legislation*, ed. J. H. Burns and H. L. A. Hart (London, 1970), 17.25, p. 296, where he remarks: this new word 'is calculated to express in a more significant way the branch of law which goes commonly in the name of the law of nations'.

supranatural issues, the full restoration of the citizen as the autonomous bearer of public rights and duties, the corresponding application of the ascending theme of government and law, and herewith of the *lex regia*, above all the renaissance of the Church.[47]

Despite the incredibly short span of Cola's activity, his role symptomatically foreshadowed numerous subsequent developments which needed nearly as many generations to come to fruition as it took him months. The dramatically spectacular rediscovery of the *lex regia* on Whit Sunday 1347 in the Lateran after high mass,[48] and the production of the bronze tablet that contained the remnants of the decree of the ancient Roman senate which conferred on Vespasian all the power fully possessed by the Roman people,[49] were the prelude to his address to the crowd. In 'elegant vernacular' he explained the origin of public power and thanked Providence for having singled him out for 'election' by the people[50] and the leadership of the 'sacra Romana respublica'. From the symbolic point of view the bath he took in the tub allegedly used by Constantine and kept in the Lateran must be accorded high significance. It was his symbolic rebirth as the tribune of the people, and this bath was designated by him himself as the *lavacrum militare*[51] or the 'bath of military glory'.[52] Since the ancient Roman tribune was a military commander he called himself *Miles Nicolaus* (Knight Nicholas). The equestrian bath and its symbolic meaning could not be misunderstood by any contemporary present: the *lavacrum regenerationis*, the baptismal bath (Titus 3: 5), was still too near to have lost its meaning. At the same time he announced the sacrality of the Roman people and of the Roman republic – again the point could hardly be lost on the Romans: next to the *sancta Romana ecclesia* there now was also a *sacra Romana respublica*, which he readily extended to the whole *sacra Italia*,[53] that re-echoed Petrarch's *Italia mia* (written about 1345). That he appeared in scarlet, girded with a sword and wearing the golden

---

47   See K. Burdach and P. Piur, *Der Briefwechsel des Cola di Rienzo* (Berlin, 1912), *Ep.* 58, p. 313.

48   See the contemporary account by an anonymous writer: *Vita Nicolai Laurentii*, in L. A. Muratori, *Antiquitates italicae medii aevi*, III(1740), col. 406B.

49   C. Bruns, *Fontes*, 7th edition (Tübingen, 1909), p. 202f., no. 56. The bronze tablet was (or still is) in the Museum of the Roman Capitol, see headnote in Bruns, no. 252. Cf. the report in Muratori, *loc. cit.*: '. . . populum eleganti vulgari sermone apud s. Johannem in Laterano allocutus fuit. Amplam et magnificam aeream tabulam antiquis conceptam characteribus, quod ipse solus legere ac interpretari valebat, in muro retro chorum inseri iussit. Circum eandem figuras depingi curavit quibus modus edocebatur quo imperatoriam auctoritatem Vespasiano populus Romanus dudum contulit.'

50   See *ibid.*: 'Numini tamen sanctissimo gratias ago . . . Finita allocutione descendens universorum publicis laudibus exceptus fuit.'

51   *Ep.* 28, *ed. cit.*, p. 112, line 168; also *Ep.* 50, p. 205, lines 210f.

52   See *Ep.* 27, p. 100f.

53   See especially the manifesto of 1 August 1347, *Ep.* 27, pp. 102ff.

spurs of the equestrian commander, is comprehensible. Everything associated with Roman sacrality was scarlet (hence also the scarlet robes in Constantinople and elsewhere). The 'holy Roman republic' had quite clearly nothing to do with Christianity, the Church or any ecclesiological issues, and hence *Roma renovata* (the reborn Rome) was similarly un-contaminated by these accretions.

Of the numerous manifestos issued by Cola as the people's tribune, the one which proclaimed the *monarchia totius sacri imperii* was perhaps the most significant, because this alone was to guarantee permanent peace. He himself was the *amator orbis*, that is, the pacifier of the world in his new capacity, which gave him an opportunity as well as the right and duty to reform, renew, renovate the world by applying the ancient purely human, secular principles of Rome.[54] Ancient Rome had become the prototype which could teach a lesson.[55] Cola's vision was assuredly inspired by that of Dante. The bipolarity of the citizen's, and hence of the State's, aims and ends was perhaps the most pronounced feature common to Dante and Cola. Hence the progressing secularization of public government and social life and the 'demundanization' of the Church. The citizen's main activity, which Dante and Marsilius had called *politizare*, is for Cola *civitare*, which is no doubt an exquisite terminology, as it brings out the essential meaning most clearly.[56] Although in Cola's programme there was no animosity to the Church or opposition to the papacy, the latter, after assessing the overall significance of his programmatic points, became estranged from him. Yet he had held important papal appointments in Rome, first as notary and later as a Senator. Cola was a symptom of the enthusiasm which humanism in its initial stages as a political ideology and programme was able to kindle. After a meteoric rise his ignominious end does not in the least detract from the importance of this episode.

The dramatic circumstances surrounding Cola's colourful ascent and eventual demise ensured a continuing interest in his programme, and quite especially since Petrarch had warmly espoused the Tribune's cause.[57] And since it was *Rome* that was its core and focus, further interest in Roman history, its arts and actual social and living conditions, became all the more intensified. After Cola's collapse the already lively interest in the Roman past received a powerful stimulus: there was now a very concrete incentive to search for the material that could enlighten contemporaries on ancient Rome, but above all there was a greatly increased desire to study

54 This is the ever-recurring theme of the *renovatio, regeneratio,* etc. in *Epp.* 7, 8, 27.
55 See *Ep.* 50, p. 203f.
56 See P. G. Ricci, 'Il commento di Cola di Rienzo alla Monarchia di Dante' in *Studi medievali,* 6/2(1965), 665ff., at 679ff.; see p. 684: 'sub tyrannide totus populus male civitat.'
57 See E. H. Wilkins, *Life of Petrarch* (Chicago, 1961), pp. 63ff.

in depth the in any case plentifully available records and sources. Certainly, as far as Italy was concerned, Cola's fitful and fleeting appearance showed unmistakably the inspiring character of political humanism, and as such it itself strongly animated and promoted the literary and cultural renaissance. His sojourn at the court of Charles IV at Prague quite unmistakably left an indelible imprint upon the environs of the city and the cultural circles influenced by the emperor.[58] What the second half of the fourteenth century witnessed was an intensification of the searches in libraries and other repositories for copies – almost exclusively of medieval provenance – of ancient Roman authors and books and records. At the cradle of the literary and cultural renaissance stood the political humanism which for easily understandable historical reasons had evidently more chance of practical application in Italy than in any other part of Europe.

The strength of every new theory or interpretation or point of view can be tested not only by its reception, but also, and perhaps even more so, by the kind of resistance it arouses. For the stronger and fiercer the hostility, the more dangerous the new standpoint was clearly considered, for if it were harmless and unrealistic, why oppose it? If a new thesis touches nerve centres, the antagonism will not only be fierce, but also virulent, venomous and violent. This truism can be applied with particular force to political humanism (and also to later theories or even modern scholarly interpretations of the past). If a new doctrine affects unquestionably accepted axioms, it will provoke acrimonious, if not militant, debates, and instead of being stifled and demolished the opposed point of view will thereby be given all the greater currency. An opposition which is incapable of effectively dealing with the adversary's arguments defeats itself and is counterproductive. However unsuccessful this kind of opposition usually is, it renders some service to scholarship. For it is forced to explain itself and to rethink and clarify its own premises which may well have been somewhat inarticulate. This is exactly what happened to political humanism in its early phases. Its strength can best be measured by the talent it released among those who opposed its underlying conceptions, however little constructive or positive the result may have been. To political humanism the opposition from the very beginning was strenuous and determined. The humanist rebirth of natural man let loose a virtual flood of literature which can be called a symptom of a reaction in the most literal sense.

If one looks at the kind of polemical and publicist literature which was produced in the first half of the fourteenth century one notices that it was a genre altogether different in outlook, conception and scope from any

---

58 For this and related topics see S. Harrison Thompson, 'Learning at the court of Charles IV' in *Speculum*, 25(1950), 1ff., at 8ff.

kind of literature composed in the thirteenth or earlier centuries. It was highly professional; it was single-minded; it was hard-hitting, and yet thorough and buttressed with a wealth of supporting material. It was above everything else conservative, again in the most literal sense of the term. Although in regard to the themes pursued by this literature there was very little that was novel or original, its sheer weight and quantity should long have given rise to the question: Why should there have been this outpouring of treatises, books and tracts in the first decades of the fourteenth century? Admittedly, educational facilities had grown, and more of the available sources were being utilized, with greater acumen, than in previous ages. It was also true that there was the conflict between the French monarchy and the papacy at the turn of the century which released a great deal of intellectual talent, but the mention of this conflict recalls the certainly no less fierce battle between Frederick II and the contemporary papacy two generations earlier. Yet the latter produced nothing comparable to the kind, quantity and prolixity of literature emerging in the first decades of the fourteenth century. Why was this so? After all, the great Staufen–papal conflict lasted nearly three decades, punctuated by excommunication and interdict and finally by the deposition of an emperor, while the French–papal conflict lasted only a few years. Moreover, it was only a small portion of the literature that dealt specifically with the Bonifacian conflict – in fact, in comparison with the later output it was only a very tiny fraction. All the more pressing is the question: why was there this unparalleled production of polemical literature?

Part of the answer certainly lies in the stimulus which the revived Aristotelian studies had provided. For they resulted in the atomization of what had been one indivisible whole. The danger which this new outlook, notably the principle of bipolarity, harboured for the traditional world outlook was all too apparent, and provoked the conservatively inclined and traditionally orientated writers to a literally speaking defensive intellectual reaction. They became aware of the virtual overthrow of the accustomed 'way of life'. They knew perfectly well what was at stake. It was not just a conflict between pope and king or emperor, but the challenge of the hitherto unquestioned social and governmental order by the new humanist outlook. It was a conflict between two basically differing views on the ordering of the world. The bonds which held the reaction together were the themes of unipolarity, universality and totality. It should not, however, be assumed that this was a homogeneous 'camp'; far from it. The writers of the reaction came from entirely different backgrounds, educational levels and stations in life. There were as many university teachers as there were members of the secular clergy and of the regular orders, but extremely few from the lay quarter, and this indeed was a portent.

What characterized these conservative writers and scholars was the absence of a thematic, serious and constructive discussion of the Aristotelian–Thomist line of thought, and what deserves special emphasis is that the real target of these writings was the humanist renaissance, that is, the rebirth of natural man with all the attendant consequences which this rebirth implied in the political and social fields. For it was in these fields alone that the humanist impact came first to be felt. What one must guard against is the ascription of any unworthy power complex to these littérateurs who defended the traditional standpoint. They felt, and quite correctly, that to come to terms with the new cosmology or to make compromises would be fatal to the centuries-old outlook and, above all, to the kind of Christianity that had universally come to be accepted. It was a genuine fear of the unknown that motivated these writers. To them any compromise with, let alone acceptance of, the new system of thought would have been considered perfidious and execrable. They were convinced that they themselves would have contributed to the collapse and ruin of a world which to them appeared as the realization, however imperfect, of what was postulated by Christianity. Precisely because they thought that the foundations of society were attacked, their literary productions exhibited a shrillness and sometimes even a venom as well as a penetration and vigour which had not been observable in earlier ages. The concepts of the citizen, the State and politics were anathema to the upholders of unipolarity, universality and totality.

Although as indicated this prolific literature in defence of the traditional governmental and social pattern added in substance nothing that was new, it nevertheless refined, deepened, re-defined and clarified numerous theses of the old ecclesiological system. As one can frequently observe, the (explicit and implicit) challenge made the defenders realize the relevance and importance of a number of points in their own system of which they had hitherto been unaware, because virtually all the fundamental matters had been unquestioningly accepted. Indeed, the 'traditionalists' saw the new system of thought as a challenge (which assuredly it was not intended to be), and challenge requires a reply: it was this situation which brought forth a polarization of the old and the new. There had been no such polarization before. In the traditionalist literature there had been no discussion of the premises and presuppositions upon which humanist political ideas rested. These were simply left on one side without even an attempt to disprove any basic element or strain of thought. Guido Vernani's attack on Dante's bipolarity was as persuasive an instance as was Hermann of Schilditz's or Guilielmus Amidani's on Marsilius. They simply abused their opponents as heretics, only to rush headlong to a re-statement of the old system. But by no means should it be assumed that the scholars defending the ecclesiologically conditioned world outlook were sycophants, or that they merely regurgitated and repeated old and worn themes. Some of them did advocate 'reform' in the higher and highest echelons, but this was hardly a reply to the new orientation and its system. Advocacy of reform is no substitute for argument on fundamental issues. Although the basic assumptions were common to the traditionalist writers, it is nevertheless worth noting that a number of Aristotelian terms began to infiltrate into their writings, as was quite obviously the case with the later Alvarus Pelagius or even with Hermann of Schilditz, but this problem and topic (including the assimilation of Aristotelian ideas) has not even been recognized, and considerable research needs to be done to shed light on the reaction and its gradual succumbing to Aristotelian naturalism.

Because he was an outstanding scholar thoroughly versed also in the Aristotelian–Thomist thought-pattern, Giles of Rome realized how crucial was the theme of baptismal rebirth for the ecclesiological order and society. It can confidently be asserted that this basic feature of Christianity had never before been treated in regard to society, government and public life so trenchantly, insistently and methodically. The tract of Giles makes abundantly clear the vital implications of baptismal rebirth in the public field. He avoided all reference to the State, the citizen and politics, and, in consistence with the old doctrine now much more articulated and presented in the light of topical relevance, claimed that private property, rulership, the capacity to hold public offices, and so forth, were issues of that divine grace which was the kernel of baptismal rebirth. 'It is not sufficient,' he says, 'that for the purpose of holding property or exercising rulership someone should be merely *carnally generated*; he should be *regenerated* through the medium of the Church (as the transmitting organ of divine grace).' Although at the time of Giles's writing there were in any case only baptismally reborn men who ruled and owned property, the statement makes perfect sense when it is juxtaposed to the humanist thesis, according to which baptismal regeneration was not at all necessary for rulership, ownership or any other public right or function. Indeed, the backbone of this tract was the diastasis of natural carnal generation and regeneration through grace. Hence there is the emphatic insistence on the principle of unipolarity and consequently (within the exclusively ecclesiological society) the stress on papal monarchy as the one and only suitable form of government in a Christian society. Hence salvation depended upon the observation of the ecclesiastical norms. There was no room within this system for any kind of humanist renaissance, and consequently there was a highly significant silence on the subject of the citizen, the State and politics – all the more significant as Giles had been the tutor of Philip IV of France and had written a book of instruction for him which was a most competent exposition of Aristotelian–Thomist principles for the benefit of his royal pupil. But in the tract under discussion he reverted to the old theses and elegantly side-stepped any theme suggestive of the natural foundations of public social life. Clearly, the points concerning baptismal rebirth had been known throughout the preceding ages, but there had never been such a pungent thematic exposition of the doctrine which comprehensively dealt with the social implications. Boniface VIII made the issue of baptismal rebirth the central topic in his *Unam sanctam*, which was an official papal presentation of the traditional teaching: it was merely a succinct summary of Giles's tract.[59]

Another writer opposed to the humanist renaissance was James of Viterbo, who quite independently of Giles wrote in the same year 1301–2: his was the first systematic exposition of the concept of the Church, in itself a highly significant feature: not until the beginning of the fourteenth century was the need felt to devote a tract entirely to this concept. After all, the preceding ages had witnessed the ecclesiological system at work – and yet there had not been one monograph or one book or one *summa* or pamphlet that dealt with the concept of the Church *ex professo*. Evidently in James's book there was no room for any human–natural autonomy, and in the working of the universally conceived Church the author saw the sole guarantee for the arrest of the process of decomposition and disintegration. It is a further significant feature of this tract that its author chose the very term and concept *regnum* as his operational instrument for presenting his universalist theme, for thereby from the very beginning he excluded the individual kingdoms as independent units. Being universal – without distinction of nations, ethnic or biological groupings, in a word without any regard to any natural differences[60] – this kingdom could understandably be ruled only by the pope. James considered him the only organ qualified to rule a universal ecclesiological unit.[61] As a third instance of the conservative-minded scholars may be quoted Durandus de s. Porciano (Saint-Pourçain), who composed his tract at the end of the first decade of the fourteenth century. The tract includes a rather strong reassertion of the wholeness point of view, which reaches its apex in his

---

59   For details and references see *artt. citt.* (above, n. 36), at pp. 60ff. and 75ff. That the Thomist view of the perfection of nature by grace was grist to the mills of humanism can be gathered from the opposition to this very point by Cardinal Dominici, the determined adversary of all humanist thought in the early years of the fifteenth century. See Johannes Dominici, *Lucula noctis*, ed. E. Hunt (Notre Dame, 1940), cap. 7, p. 52: 'Naturam non destruit, verum perficit gratia. Sed litterarum secularium studium est naturale, igitur gratia baptismatis non tollit litterarum naturalium usum, potius perficit, imperat, et commendat.' The argument is demolished in cap. 34, pp. 276ff., though the argumentation is quite unconvincing.

60   Thomas Aquinas had declared that the Church can be assimilated to a political congregation: *Summa theol.* III suppl. qu. 26, art. concl., adding: 'quia ipse populus ecclesia dicitur'.

61   H.-X. Arquillière (ed.), *Le plus ancien traité de l'église: Jacques de Viterbe, De regimine christiano* (Paris, 1926).

statement that 'All actions of Christians are directed towards obtaining eternal salvation'.[62] To him man's earthly life was merely a part of his total life: this and the next life were essentially conjoined. Whereas each of these writers singles out a particular theme of the old doctrine – unipolarity (Giles); universality (James); and totality (Durandus) – other writers of the traditional complexion concentrated on wider governmental questions, as in the widely ranging presentation of the monarchic theme by Augustinus Triumphus or Alvarus Pelagius.

For reasons easily understandable Marsilius and Dante drew fire from a great number of conservative writers. Political humanism by no means convinced the generality of the intelligentsia in the earlier part of the fourteenth century, however little its opponents had at their disposal to combat it effectively. Unless one assumes that the bases from which Marsilius and Dante set out were beyond the grasp of their opponents, the only reasonable conclusion one can reach is that they thought opposition consisted merely in spelling out the traditional ecclesiological hierocratic system of unipolarity and totality: the critics did not even realize that the opposed standpoint could not simply be demolished by dubbing it 'heretical', and that an elementary presupposition of a critique is that the opponent's point of view is fully grasped. But there was no attempt to disprove Marsilian or Dantesque premises: they were simply confronted by a logically flawless restatement of a cosmology which was founded on faith and nowhere came to grips with essential themes of political humanism.

Hermann of Schilditz may serve as quite a typical run-of-the-mill opponent of Marsilius. It had apparently never dawned upon him that Marsilius's premises needed some examination if he was to be effectively demolished. But Hermann launched straight into an exposition of what he called the immunity of the Church, because it was impugned. It is as if the idea of a natural and independent end of man, of his *humanitas*, of the principle of the double ordering of things, and so on, had never been aired before, nor, specifically, the *legislator humanus*, the aggregate of citizens, the State, and so forth. Instead, Hermann starts from the *a priori* position that there is but one end of man – and not merely of the Christian – and that is eternal bliss and salvation. Man was created in the image of God, hence was 'naturally' bound to worship God and to seek his salvation, which was attainable by all men of the world only by following the directions of the Church and the pope. The background of this view is what for want of a better term can be called the creational principle, according to which everything was created by God and therefore subjected to God's

---

62 *De iurisdictione ecclesiastica*, edition Troyes, 1516, qu. 3 (no foliation or pagination).

vicar, a thesis first elaborated by Innocent IV.[63] Hence for Hermann everyone's eventual salvation depended on the pope, from whose jurisdiction nobody was exempt.[64] The corollary plainly emerges that naturally created things were merely instruments in the pursuit of the final end of man, with the consequence that the right and proper use of mundane goods could legitimately be fixed only by the Church and the papacy.[65] It can readily be seen that this tract can hardly be considered a refutation of Marsilian themes.

Very similar observations can be made about the opponents of Dante. Guido Vernani may serve as an example. He wrote his invective in the early thirties of the fourteenth century. He obviously never understood the intentions of Dante nor his underlying philosophy. The chief argument against him was that it would be quite impossible to find a suitable world monarch such as postulated by Dante. It was apparently too difficult for Guido to grasp that Dante's monarch represented merely the pure and abstract idea of rulership. And Dante's reason for introducing the ancient Roman empire was similarly beyond Guido's comprehension. In this connection he referred to his opponent as a man who had 'egregiously raved'. Guido questioned whether anyone had so ignominiously erred as Dante, for the argument from the Roman empire was 'vile and derisive'. That for Dante the Roman empire was only a prototype that pre-portrayed a universal State sanctioned by Christ entirely escaped Guido, who towards the end of his tract reveals some slight inkling of the indubitably dangerous principle of bipolarity. There was for him no such thing as a 'double ordering', and consequently Dante's basic argument that man pursued two ends fell to the ground, since God had decreed no mundane felicity as the ultimate goal of man, which can only be infinity and eternity. For the rest Guido operated with stale, old ecclesiological and hierocratic arguments.[66]

Another anti-humanist was Guilielmus de Sarzano of Genoa, who really had no constructive argument at all: his discursive and diffuse tract

---

63 Innocent IV in his Commentary on X: III.34.8, cited in full in *JTS*, 27(1976), at p. 85, n. 3.

64 See Hermann de Schilditz, *Tractatus contra haereticos negantes immunitatem et iurisdictionem sanctae ecclesiae*, ed. A. Zumkeller (Würzburg, 1970). Cf. I.4, p. 14: '... nullus in mundo potest esse exclusus a divina iurisditione ... sed papa est vicarius Dei in terris;' I.11, p. 29: 'Extra ecclesiam nullus salvatur ... sine directione ecclesiae finem ultimum nullus consequitur;' II.5, p. 68: 'de iure habet (scil. Romanus pontifex) omnes mundi homines iudicare, cum sibi omnes commissi sunt ... infideles possunt considerari ut *factura* Dei, sunt ad imaginem Dei facti.'

65 *Ibid.*, I.12, p. 32, lines 18ff., invoking here as in other places Aristotelian terms (mainly from the *Ethics*). For another example of his attack on political humanism, see below p. 160.

66 Vernani's tract called *De reprobatione Monarchie composite a Dante*, ed. T. Käppelli in *Quellen & Forschungen aus ital. Archiven & Bibl.*, 18(1938), 123–46. The expressions cited in the text at pp. 137 and 139, and his attack on bipolarity at pp. 145f.

is little else but an arid regurgitation of ossified hierocratic matter, wholly irrelevant to political (or any other) humanism. It might well serve as a mature exposition of the descending theme of government with its adjunct of the principle of division of labour: to him the pope alone possessed all power as the lord of all who distributed it downwards by mediating it to lower officers, including kings. Even Old Testament history in the shape given to it by Petrus Comestor was at length invoked to erect a counter-thesis. Furthermore, he rejected the Thomist theory of virtues. For the Genoese, grace directed and ordered nature, so that he arrived at the hallowed hierocratic conclusion that the rector of the souls directed the rector of the bodies. Translated into governmental reality this meant that secular laws needed papal approbation.[67]

Numerous other tracts and monographs could be instanced to show how the old themes were now in the fourteenth century refurbished, if not altogether systematically and methodically treated for the first time with all the panoply of scholarship and resources. The obvious conclusion to be drawn is that in the antecedent periods there had been no challenge to the generally accepted assumptions. And it was precisely this challenge that forced a great many scholars to restate basic topics which, in their view, were in danger of being swept away. It is this contingency which gives at least a partial answer to the question of why there was a wholly un-paralleled production of treatises, monographs, tracts, etc., in the fourteenth century. It is no reflection on their quality to say that those who pro-pounded political humanism were livelier and showed a better grasp of reality than the somewhat dogmatic, ecclesiologically orientated writers who, though highly equipped in scholarly respects, lacked something in the appreciation of concrete reality. But it is nevertheless true that the challenge issued by political humanism forced the opponents to draw their lines of demarcation firmly and strongly. The paradox emerges that not until the fourteenth century was there a systematic exposition of the ecclesiological themes of unipolarity and totality, that is, at a time when reality showed itself ready and receptive for the themes of political humanism.

That on closer analysis political humanism and all it implied was the primary target of those who a generation later called themselves anti-humanists becomes clear when one looks at, say, Cardinal Dominici in the opening years of the fifteenth century. Here was quite obviously a man of great erudition, also equipped with a very highly developed sense of fairness, who was genuinely perturbed by the trend which the by then not

---

67 Guilielmus de Sarzano, *Tractatus de potestate summi pontificis*, ed. R. del Ponte in *Studi medievali*, 12(1971), 1020–94. Cf. cap. 7, p. 1091: 'Papa igitur, qui est rector animarum, habet instituere, disponere et ordinare imperatoris officium, dignitatem et regimen et ei omnem, quam habet, conferre . . .'.

so new humanist orientation had taken. He can serve as an example of a scholar who was not opposed to the mere literary kind of classicizing humanism, but to the underlying very real and topical humanism itself. He had no doubt that humanism correctly assessed harboured some grave dangers to the traditionally understood Christian theme of unipolarity, universality and totality. Indeed, this learned cardinal continued on a very much higher plane the line of opposition which in a blunt manner exactly a century earlier Boniface VIII had initiated.[68] But a great deal of water had in the meantime flowed under the bridges of the Tiber, Rhine, Arno and Seine. In order to assess the misgivings of a man of this calibre, it is also vital to take into account the impact which actuality had made upon him: a Europe torn between two popes fighting each other ferociously; England and France locked in fierce battle for the last half century; Byzantium seriously threatened in its existence by the anti-Christian forces of the Turks; all over Europe rampant nationalism which in conjunction with the schism severely impinged upon contemporary religious and ecclesiastical life, so that more sensitive minds may well have believed that all these features were, if not associated with, at any rate aggravated by, the rapidly advancing themes of humanism. Most literally, Dominici can stand as the symbol of reaction against the politically activated humanism.

The abundance of this polemical literature compellingly leads to the conclusion that the first manifestations of humanism in the original meaning of the term were indubitably in the public governmental and political spheres. It was in these that the first reverberations and repercussions came to be clearly understood. It was the humanist orientated *scientia politica* which aroused opposition in the tradition-tied quarters of theology, philosophy and ecclesiastical administrators. The polemics themselves, together with the actual situation in the fourteenth century, in turn created their own momentum and their own ethos. Engulfing as it didthe whole spectrum of human relations, political humanism clearly reverberated throughout literate and intellectually alert circles in virtually all parts of Europe. It was the stirring of a new age which stimulated thinkers and writers to a hitherto unknown degree and forced them to take sides. There was everywhere questioning where previously there had been certainty based on habitual modes of thinking. Indeed, the full realization of the implications of the political themes opened up the prospect of a veritably new world and the collapse of the old.

68   See his *Lucula noctis, ed. cit.* (above, n. 59), chs. 13–17, pp. 126–46, and especially ch. 36, pp. 298ff., with the emphatic plea for the *sacra sophia* as 'sufficientissime' directive for society. Cf. P. da Prati, *Giovanni Dominici e l'umanesimo* (Naples, 1965), especially pp. 164–201. A detailed analysis of this anti-humanist in the light of the new findings would be rewarding.

VI

Humanist Progress and Prospect

An adequate understanding of the literary, educational and cultural revival of ancient literature that indisputably began in the fourteenth century will have to set out from the similarly indisputable premiss that the literature consulted – whether discovered or re-discovered makes no difference in this context – was studied and read and used for purposes geared to the rebirth of natural man and quite especially in his function as a citizen. It was the hallmark of the citizen to play an active role in the shaping of the secular society, of the State, of which he formed an integral part. It is of the utmost interest therefore that this active participation became associated with the very name of *vita activa* which, though certainly no new coinage, assumed a new meaning and function in contradistinction to the also commonly known *vita contemplativa*, the contemplative life of the monk, the religious thinker, the theological scholar, and so on.

In this context it should once more be borne in mind that this nomenclature was not only not new, but indeed had a long and distinguished ancestry. Since the patristic age the different orientations of life had been recognized. St Augustine spoke in fact of two kinds of people, those who worked and those who watched the workmen, the one kind thinking about terrestrial, the other about celestial matters.[1] In the late sixth century Gregory the Great launched the distinction on its long career, but quite in conformity with the principle of unipolarity credited the active life with

---

1 See Augustine, *Enarrationes in Ps. 51*, cap. 6, in *CC* 39(1966), 627: 'Duo genera hominum attendite: unum laborantium, alterum eorum inter quos laboratur, unum de terra, alterum de coelo cogitantium ...' See further *Civ. Dei*, 8.4: 'Studium sapientiae in actione et contemplatione versatur. Unde una pars *activa*, altera *contemplativa* dici potest.' Further, *ibid*. 19.3 and 9. Cf. also in the early fifth century, Pomerius, *De vita contemplativa*, in *PL* 59.415ff.

a lower standing than that of its counterpart.[2] It is similarly not generally recognized, though certainly worthy of remark, that the commentators on the most widely read and studied textbook of philosophy and theology, Peter Lombard's *Sentences* (written about 1150), dealt with the active and contemplative life at great and diffuse length.[3] So far from being a new distinction, as is frequently assumed by renaissance historians, the designation and coinage were of very ancient provenance. The crucial point is that the two styles of life were considered entirely within the framework of baptismal rebirth, that is, within the Christian cosmological pattern. They were, so to speak, two sides of the same coin. One has but to look at the commentaries on the *Sentences* to see that the distinction made sense only within a biblical and theological context and within the terms of an allegorical explanation that was in fact initiated by Gregory I.

Once again, familiarity with the terminology proved of extraordinary value, especially as this terminology was felicitous and could be, as indeed it was, utilized within the new thought-pattern. The twin concept of the *vita activa* and the *vita contemplativa* was easily adjustable to modes of living which rested on premises entirely different from those which had traditionally been applied. The active and the contemplative life came to assume perspectives and dimensions which were infinitely wider and deeper than the traditional, exclusively religious orientation with which they had been associated. They came to answer different sets of norms and each set was valid on its own terms and had positive value in itself. What previously had been part of a whole now became a whole in itself. Or what had previously been two sides of the same coin became now two coins. The distinction was in fact admirably suited for expressing the principle of bipolarity. In other words, because the distinction was so familiar, it greatly assisted the new cosmology by equating the *vita activa* with civic–mundane life and its contemplative counterpart with the concern for supranatural matters. The principle of bipolarity found a secure habitat in this ancient medieval dichotomy. Yet there was – at any rate in the fourteenth century – no rivalry or animosity between the two different forms of life. The designations were simply shorthand devices to disting-

2   Gregory I, *Moralia*, 6.5.57, in *PL* 75.761f. (exemplifying the *duae vitae* as the two eyes in the same face); allegorical interpretation at col. 764, cap. 61, and in many other places. See also his *Homiliae in Hiezechihelm prophetam*, in *CC* 142(1971), hom. 1.5.6, p. 59 and also pp. 261ff. In the Carolingian age cf. Alcuin, *Ep.* 213, in *MGH Epp.* IV. 355; Hrabanus Maurus, *Expos. in Leviticum*, 7.6, in *PL* 108.533; *id.*, *Comm. in Genesim*, 3.21, in *PL* 109.611, dealing with the *vita activa* and *contemplativa*. Thomas Aquinas, *Summa theol.*, I–ii, 57, art. 2c, dealt with the *virtus activa* and *contemplativa*.

3   William of Auxerre, *Summa aurea* (above, p. 19, n. 14), III tract. 8, qu. 4, fol. 190rb; Peter of Tarentaise, *Commentaria* (above, p. 103, n. 28), III.35, qu. 1. arts. 1–3, pp. 276ff.

uish the fully integrated citizen from the fully committed faithful Christian. Although there was no shortage of books, advice, exhortations, enthusiastic and graphic descriptions of the contemplative life, there was on the other hand a distinct shortage of literature relevant to the *vita activa* as it was now understood, that is, the conduct of the citizen in public life. The *vita activa* of the citizen, that is, man's efficacious activity in public life, was nothing else but politics in practice. Politics was the citizen's humanity activated within and for the State, and for this the lengthy commentaries written by the schoolmen in the high Middle Ages did not, for obvious reasons, give much guidance.

If one considers citizenship as the political incarnation of *humanitas*, the pursuit of 'humanist' studies will be easily understandable. We can now deepen our understanding of the *studia humanitatis* and the *studia divinitatis*, to which we have already had occasion to refer. They are, as Coluccio Salutati emphasizes, complementary and supplementary to each other, so that full knowledge of the one cannot be obtained without the other.[4] Once more, these two branches of intellectual pursuit reflect the principle of bipolarity, in the same way as the *vita activa* and its contemplative counterpart do. The *studia divinitatis* had in previous centuries furnished a surfeit of literature, which would appear to have been well-nigh exhaustive, but for the *studia humanitatis* relative to politics there is extraordinarily little evidence that they formed a branch of learning or even evoked interest. But the very idea of the renaissance of natural man and especially in his function as a citizen made the study of his *humanitas* imperative and a foremost task. There is every justification for saying that the *studia humanitatis* began to take their place next to theology, the *studia divinitatis*.[5] In an accentuated form one could here speak of a humanized theology, for it was the essential *humanitas* of reborn man that next to his *christianitas* now began to take its rightful place. Knowledge not only of what the essence of humanity constituted, but also of how people conducted their civic life in public, was the great object of the *studia humanitatis*.

Although a very great amount of ancient literature had been available in the Middle Ages, some new works came to be discovered in the fourteenth century – witness, just to take an obvious example, Petrarch's find at Liège of Cicero's *Pro Archia* and other speeches, or at Verona of some works of Catullus and especially of Cicero's *Epistolae ad Atticum*;[6] or

---

4 *Epistolario*, ed. F. Novati (Rome, 1891–1911), IV.216.
5 About the Ciceronian contradistinction of *humanitas* (understood as the humanity of man, and not merely grammar, style, syntax, etc.) and the *divinitas*, see above, p. 108, n. 38.
6 Cf. here the fine observations by H. Baron, *From Petrarch to Leonardo Bruni* (Chicago, 1969), pp. 30ff.

Salutati's bringing to light Cicero's *Epistolae ad familiares* – but what is important is not the quantity of ancient works, is not the search for new material of ancient provenance (though I hasten to add that there was a continuing search – when is there not?), but the way in which this ancient literature – preserved or discovered or re-discovered – was looked at and to what purpose it was put. Formerly this ancient literature was used for didactic purposes in the very narrow meaning of the term. It formed part of a rudimentary curriculum that was vocational and overwhelmingly, though by no means exclusively, geared to specific ecclesiastical–religious purposes of a devotional, liturgical and doxological kind, to biblical readings, and the like. The ancients were also sometimes employed in order to illustrate or prove some point in a scholarly tract. Further, they formed part of the training in the art of official letter-writing, prose composition and drafting of documents in the various chanceries, and showed historians the technique and style for character sketches.[7] Frequently, however, the use of the classics was merely decorative. Moreover, it is common knowledge that eminent men had always surrounded themselves with writings of ancient authors – witness the books collected by, say, Gerbert of Rheims (Terence, Plautus, Juvenal); Adam of Bremen found Sallust useful; Ekkehard of Aura assembled numerous works of Cicero; John of Salisbury's library contained works by Ovid, Cicero and Quintilian as well as (Pseudo-) Plutarch. But these authors were predominantly used to clothe a religiously conditioned issue appropriately. The contents or substance of ancient writings were of little concern to those who profited from reading them or who wrote with their help. Now this same literature began to be read, seen and interpreted from a much wider angle and in an extensive, comprehensive and material way. Lessons of substance were drawn from it and the main object of consulting the ancient works was no longer of a mere ancillary or auxiliary or didactic kind, but lay in relating what they revealed about the *vita activa* to politics. The experiences, the perspectives, the recognitions of the ancients were to be utilized in the service of politics, because this was what mattered. The *vita activa* of the citizen had become the focal point. The manuscripts discovered by the men of the fourteenth century were overwhelmingly of medieval origin and had lain unused, unrecognized, unrelated to any particular issue, in cathedral or monastic libraries.

What must be borne in mind is that earlier when the ancient works were used, the point of reference had been strictly circumscribed. It had been grammatical or literal or even edifying, and had not been concerned with

---

7   For which Suetonius served as a model. Apart from Einhard, cf. William of Poitiers, Radulfus de Diceto, and especially William of Malmesbury; see A. Gransden, *Historical Writing* (above, p. 61, n. 6), pp. 170f., 234.

any practical issue that touched, or in any way affected, society or government at large, whereas now the point of reference was precisely this latter topic. The works assumed hitherto unknown dimensions as sources of political ideas and therefore were read and understood from a new angle, and their opulence of contents as well as their character as instruments of education in matters of civic, public life were only now fully recognized. Previously the point of reference was the form, now it was the substance. What needs emphasis is the changed perspective from which the ancient works came to be studied and utilized. The use that was made of the ancient authors was new, their utility to social life was newly perceived, not their works, profuse numbers of which, as cannot be stressed strongly enough, had long been in existence and easily available.[8]

There are many modern examples in which certain natural elements already known for a long time acquired wholly unexpected and extraordinary value as a result of new inventions or discoveries. Uranium is one such example, helium is another. Historical scholarship has only in the last decades realized how much new material and knowledge can be obtained from manuscripts or dusty charters or collections of law, and so on: all these materials had somehow or other survived centuries of hibernation and were not in any sense unknown, but their usefulness for historical purposes and for recognizing historical situations or contingencies was new. In other words, the point of reference has changed – formerly these same charters or manuscripts served to show the art of illumination or the change in handwriting or even different hands, such as bookhand and charterhand, but their substance, their subject-matter, came to be understood and valued in its historical context only recently, so that the arenga, the protocol, the eschatocol, etc. came to be valuable means of recognition. They threw significant light on the past, which was now seen from a new angle. They assumed the function of essential and new *Erkenntnismittel* in the service of so mundane a discipline as history. Very similar observations can be made about the study of ancient and medieval symbols which – especially those within the precincts of coronation rituals or of liturgy – served as media conveying vital (and otherwise unobtainable) information. Like the manuscripts, they had been known for centuries and had been listed meticulously, but their true usefulness to historical scholarship came to be understood only in the present century, when they were studied in depth. Previously they were useful to antiquarians, now they were useful to historians. Exactly the same can be said about the

---

8   E. Garin, *L'educazione* (above, p. 5, n. 17), at pp. 30f., points in a general way to the different uses to which ancient authors were put in the medieval period and in the humanistic era: in the former there never was felt the need to get to know the man who was different from the one with whom medieval scholars were familiar. Cf. also above, p. 25.

'search' for manuscripts of ancient authors by the humanists. They were looking for the portraiture of the actuality of living conditions in the ancient world and for the portrait above all of the citizen, that is, for him who was, if known at all, only known in name in the antecedent ages in which only regenerated man mattered, and he lived on a literally different plane from ordinary humanity. The humanists were looking for patterns, for models, which they believed could be found only in the ancient world.

The study of ancient literature from the fourteenth century onwards took the form of interpreting the total work of the respective ancient author. One began to penetrate into the whole matrix of an ancient author in an attempt to comprehend the 'human' cosmology and the 'human' complexion of society and its members, but above everything else the way in which politics had come to be handled. What the ancients revealed, and for which no model in the antecedent ages was detectable, was the mechanics of politics: the translation of political principles into political action by the citizens of Rome. Perhaps in no other ancient author was the combined fulness of humanity, citizenship and politics so profusely and persuasively and also beautifully demonstrated as in Cicero. His works had belonged to the stock of most good medieval libraries, but their immediate relevance to the recognition of *humanitas* and citizenship was not properly grasped until the fourteenth century. Cicero was stylist, jurist, philosopher, epistolographer, purveyor of Greek thought and letters, orator, moralist and much else besides, but all this was overshadowed by him as a *politicus*. He is abundantly shown in all his writings, and especially in his speeches, as an advocate appearing in court, either as a prosecutor or as defence counsel. And perhaps not the least significant point is that it was in precisely the two Ciceronian works recently discovered that the terminology of the *libri politici* and the *theses politicae* were found and put to good use.[9]

It really is very difficult, if not impossible, to visualize the impact which the so-called 'political books' of Cicero made upon fourteenth-century contemporaries. Although he himself used in default of a Latin term the Greek word *politikos*, this term now fell on extremely fertile soil in the fourteenth century, precisely because people had become familiar with Greek thought through the medium of the Thomists and others. *Theses politicae* was the term chosen by Cicero – indeed, two Greek terms conjoined – and in the same letter to Atticus he referred once more to 'political' in the Greek language. And no less significant it is that according to Cicero the Greeks called 'political philosophers' those who possessed 'outstanding knowledge of the most important matters'.[10] Hardly a better

---

9   See above, p. 99, n. 17.
10   *De oratore*, 3.28.1 (Loeb, 1968, p. 86): 'Politici philosophi' are so called 'propter eximiam rerum maximarum scientiam . . .'

qualified and more experienced teacher could be envisaged than Cicero. Himself the expert *en tois politikois*, to use his own words, he clearly presented himself as the fount from which instruction, inspiration and example in politics could be drawn. He was indeed the stimulating and personified pattern *in rebus politicis*.

Cicero's appeal to the humanists is therefore easily understandable. One might be tempted to say that what Cicero aimed to do for the Romans, that is, to transmit Greek thought and patterns and familiarize his contemporaries with Greek, notably Platonic, philosophy, with a view to widening their intellectual, civic and moral horizons, his fourteenth- and fifteenth-century readers aimed to do for their own contemporaries by studying and disseminating and interpreting his works with a view to drawing the appropriate lessons. His writings appeared in a literal sense to illuminate the *humanitas* of the Roman citizen to an exemplary degree. In more than one respect can he be spoken of as a teacher: none of the ancients were to reach this towering height. From a variety of angles he demonstrated true Roman citizenship by throwing light on the variegated complexities, vicissitudes, turpitudes, and also moral excellence and political sagacity of 'unregenerated' natural man – in a word on the concrete reality of *humanitas* which, to him, stood apart from *divinitas*.[11] It was Cicero himself who spoke, significantly enough, of the *artes humanitatis*[12] as well as of the *studia humanitatis*.[13]

By studying Cicero contemporary man was able to see the unadulterated and uncontaminated being of natural man in his *vita activa*, in his prime function as a citizen, that is in his politics, and more than any other writer did he influence the early humanists by the infusion of ethical ingredients into politics. The *vir bonus et civis* (the good man and the citizen) was to them no mere figure of speech. The civic conduct of man seemed to them to portray the civic virtues which, as a specified category of virtues, started on a long and distinguished career. They began to form a set of norms especially applicable to politics, hence also called political virtues, and here once more the link with late antiquity was established.[14] Despite his towering height it should not be assumed that Cicero was the only ancient author who exercised influence. It is true that he was and remained

---

11 See above, p. 108, n. 38.
12 *De republica*, 1.17.28 (Loeb, 1970, p. 50).
13 In his *Pro Archia poeta*, 2.3 (Loeb, 1965, p. 8). Further in his *Pro L. Murena*, 29.61 (Teubner edition, 1961, p. 30, line 27).
14 That is with Macrobius' *virtus politica*, see his *Commentarium in Somnium Scipionis* (of Cicero), ed. I. Willis (Teubner, 1963, 1.8.5, p. 37, line 26); cf. also 1.10.2, p. 42, line 9. Here it should be noted that Petrarch owned and annotated a copy of this work, the manuscript of which is in the British Museum, B. M. Harley 5204.

the most studied and also best understood author, but other writers came to be closely analysed, interpreted and related to the humanist's pursuit of knowledge that appeared to them essential for politics and its mechanics. While in an earlier age – in the Frankish period – it was patristic authors (the Ambroses, Jeromes, Augustines, and so on) who served as founts of knowledge and as models for the ecclesiastically orientated society and for the Christian in the world, it was now the Ciceros, Livys, Ovids, the Quintilians, Senecas and many more who were allocated the same function for a different purpose. In one way or another they all were held to depict true ancient Roman humanity and to paint its portrait in many shades and forms. It was the realistic portraiture of natural humanity that exercised attraction, precisely because it transmitted the type of man who was active in public, civic life, in politics, and could thus serve as a pattern.

Once again the point deserves to be made that this concentration on ancient authors did not imply any break with the past, did not mean any sharp caesura between, say, the twelfth and fourteenth centuries. All there was was a widening of the mental horizon and its enrichment. And once more, it was the Roman law that was a linchpin in this process. As a practitioner Cicero had no equal in his knowledge of Roman law, in his function as an advocate and also in his life-long political career. It is important to bear in mind this feature. There was nothing 'new' in all this. What was 'new' was the use to which the ancient literature was put, its perspectives and relationship to the mere humanity of the citizen, and therefore to politics. Through the continuing influence of Roman law the link with ancient Rome was never broken, but had in fact become the most pronounced social and cultural feature of the Middle Ages. This closest of all close links produced different effects in different situations. For it was first the Vulgate which had prepared the ground for the medieval reception of Roman law and the ready response it evoked, and this in its turn had fertilized the soil for the reception and adequate comprehension of ancient authors and their works. It was the Roman law which, it may be recalled, first set afoot the secularization of government; it was the Roman law which appealed to Dante; it was the Roman law and its *lex regia* which found in Cola its 'discoverer' and enthusiastic follower. The citizen was the centre of Roman law, at any rate in the Digest, and it was here in the Digest that the very term of *humanitas* was conspicuous[15] and therefore thoroughly familiar to contemporaries, denoting as it did not merely the purely human qualities, sentiments and existence, but also the consequences of being human, the nature of living conditions and social as well as legal customs. This role of the Roman law as a linchpin of the historical process is barely recognized. It was perhaps the strongest bond holding

15   For examples cf. above, p. 101, n. 26.

together the ancient, medieval and modern worlds. And conversely the vital importance attributed to Roman law and the role jurists played in government was itself perhaps most convincingly shown in the emergence of a humanist jurisprudence that saw as its foremost task the preservation of the 'pure' Roman law, to the study of which from the fifteenth century onwards it was to give new direction and meaning.

There is further evidence that in its initial stages humanism, with its marked emphasis on jurisprudence, showed how firmly it was embedded in the historical process. It revealed its medieval parentage and, as its primary object, man as a citizen. This was, for instance, the theme of Coluccio Salutati's book significantly entitled *On the Nobility of Law and Medicine*. The work is really a discussion of the relative merits of jurisprudence, which epitomizes all learning concerned with man as a rational being and a member of society, and medicine, which stands for the natural sciences. Jurisprudence had as its object the perfectibility of man in society: it enshrined the rule of law and determined the relations within society.[16] On the other hand, the natural sciences could not provide an answer to questions relative to the State, the citizen and politics. In the early stages of humanism jurisprudence was still the predominant social science, that served as the instrument by which society was to be shaped as a State. To quote just one of Salutati's pregnant statements:

The subject of legal science is the civic work of men directed by the laws relating to the common good and ordering human society.[17]

This same outlook is still more clearly conveyed in his declaration that what matters is man himself in his political capacity, that is as a citizen,[18] whose will alone counts, because he alone is capable of thinking and speculating on the supreme good of society. Jurisprudence informs how the citizen can find his fulfilment in the State. This is *au fond* the expression of a deeply speculative mind for whom divinity (not necessarily in the Christian sense), operating through the natural law, is the determinative principle. The divine law is pre-eminent, he says, the natural law receives

16 *De nobilitate legum et medicinae*, ed. E. Garin (Florence, 1947). In general see B. L. Ullman, *op. cit.* (above, p. 116, n. 53), pp. 8ff.

17 *De nobilitate*, cap. 13, p. 94, lines 1ff.: 'Legalis quidem artis subiectum est civilis hominum operatio quam legum ratio dirigit et in commune bonum ac humani generis societatem ordinat et disponit.' Cf. also E. Garin, *Italian Humanism* (above p. 115, n. 51), pp. 27ff. There is a hitherto unnoticed kinship between this kind of statement and that, say, of Baldus on Cod. VII.53.5 (*ed. cit.*, above, p. 135, n. 42, no. 10, fol. 73va). Baldus lectured on the Codex at Florence university from 1358 to 1364.

18 'Homo est inquantum *politicus* est et *civiliter* operatur' (p. 94, lines 5–7). This too shows great kinship with Baldus, *loc. cit.*, above, p. 135.

what the divine law has enacted, and the human law promulgates and thereby issues a binding rule.[19]

There is every justification for saying that these views represented a not inadequate clarification of the Thomist standpoint – indeed, he refers to Thomas as 'Aquinas noster'[20] – just as Dante would not have dissented from Salutati's thesis that the aim of all political and moral reflection should be the attainment of liberty and peaceful harmonious order.[21] Herein lies Cicero's influence in regard to the bearing of ethics on politics.[22] But what is even more to the point is Salutati's invocation of baptismal rebirth in conjunction with the Ciceronian concept of the 'fellow-slave' (*conservi*).[23] This was no mere operational device, but one that brought into clear relief his strong affinity with Thomism. His opposition to being called 'Lord' (*dominus*) by some of his correspondents resulted from his conception of baptismal rebirth, for by its virtue 'we all are fellow-slaves and brothers of Christ'.[24] Hence there was established an equality among (Christian) citizens who as friends should not use such addresses as 'Lord', nor the plural form 'vos', but the singular 'tu', which was a sign of a state of equality. Only public persons who represented a plurality of people could be addressed by 'vos'.[25]

Since to Salutati law was an agent which directs the conduct of the citizens, it had to be made by them and should not be confused with divine law, for the function of human law was not to compel people to act in a virtuous manner by reason of fear – this was the function of the divine law[26] – but to enact the naturally and humanly conceived sense of justice so that the just and the innocent can be protected. The object which all human law sets itself is 'the common good'.[27] In a word, law is

---

19   Cap. 19, p. 160, lines 19–23: 'Divina lex instituit, naturalis inclinat, humana lex promulgat et iubet.' This tallies with the tenor of his early work *De saeculo et religione, ed. cit.* above, p. 116, n. 53, and B. L. Ullman, *op. cit.* pp. 26ff. It should be noted, however, that he moves not necessarily on a Christian level: 'Ius igitur quod a iuvando dicitur vel forsitan a Iove, qui primus leges constituit, naturalis lex est . . .' (p. 160, lines 15ff.).

20   *De nobilitate*, cap. 5, p. 34, line 14.

21   *Ibid.*, p. 36, lines 26ff.: '. . . ut humani generis societas et communitas non turbaretur.'

22   Salutati refers to Cicero's *De officiis*, 1.3.7–8.

23   Cf. Cicero's use in his *Epp. ad Familiares*, 12.3.2 (Loeb, 1965, p. 526).

24   *Epistolario, ed. cit.* (above, n. 4), II.153, lines 26ff.: 'Unus et idem est Pater, in cuius sacramento et adoptione *regenerati* ambo fratres sumus in Christo . . .' Further, III.376, lines 5f.

25   *Ibid.*, II.163, lines 3ff. A comparative study of forms of address in their historical development would be rewarding. For instance, the English 'you' represents an entirely different social and linguistic parentage, cf. A. C. Partridge's introductory chapter in his *Tudor to Augustan English* (London, 1969), pp. 21ff. ('Social strata and levels of communication').

26   As he expressed it: 'servili metu solum ad virtutes cogere' (*De nobil.*, cap. 3, p. 20, line 10).

27   *Ibid.*, cap. 5, p. 32, lines 17f. Here the Thomist echo cannot be missed.

for him the supreme means of shaping the *vita activa* of the citizens.[28] And for this reason jurisprudence as the science of law is all-embracing – unlike the natural sciences which have a restricted purview – and comprehends all learning, human and divine alike, with the purpose of guiding the path of the citizens.[29] Salutati's humanist philosophy is firmly embedded in the medieval tradition. He readily uses the age-old body and soul allegory in explaining the respective role of the natural sciences (epitomized by medicine) and of jurisprudence as the political science *par excellence*. Here indeed the medieval idea of law as the soul that *animates* the body public[30] revives within the ascending framework, in contradistinction to the preceding medieval descending counterpart. Thus he can well accord a higher rank to political science than to the natural sciences.[31] Politics has become the soul of the State. Therefore politics assumes the function of the governing principle in society and its relation to natural sciences is that of 'imperans imperato'.[32] Transposed to a larger canvas, this is the contemporary expression of the power of the *human* mind over matter. Just as both the soul and the body were considered to constitute one whole in the old ecclesiological framework, in the same way political and natural sciences were now seen as referring to the whole of man's *humanitas*: here as there it was a question of grading. Salutati's humanism reveals its medieval background most exquisitely. The ascription of sanctity to the law[33] is therefore quite in keeping with the Roman law and medieval tradition[34] as well as with the function of law as the directive rule of human actions in society.[35] Politics comprehends the active life of the citizen – his *vita activa* – and, since the law is its core, pursues the one vital aim – attainment of political happiness, conservation of the public order and the achievement of the common good.[36] The praise he reserved for the great Roman jurist Ulpian, because he was the intimate counsellor of the imperial government, is thus understandable.[37]

It was precisely in the context of realizing the *vita activa* to its fullest

---

28 This is the topic of cap. 5, p.t., pp. 26ff.
29 Cap. 28, p. 212, lines 20ff.: 'Necessarium est iuris professoribus artes scire. Quoniam jurisprudentia est rerum divinarum humanarumque scientia . . .'
30 See above, p. 12, and *LP* pp. 27ff., 47, with further literature.
31 *De nobilitate*, cap. 8, p. 50: 'Cum medicina curet corpus, politica quidem curat animam. Ex quo fit, quod quanto nobilior et honoratior est anima corpore, tanto plus debeatur politice quam medicine.'
32 *Ibid.*, p. 50, line 14.
33 *Ibid.*, cap. 9, p. 64.
34 Ulpian in Dig. 1.1.1, and all glosses *ibid.*
35 *De nobil.*, cap. 5, p. 32: 'directio actuum *humanorum*.' Cf. p. 34: 'regula nostrorum actuum.' For Marsilius, cf. above, p. 126, n. 25.
36 *Ibid.*, cap. 15, p. 102: 'Apud leges *finis* iste conservatio dicitur publice societatis et bonum humanum *politicaque felicitas*.'
37 *Ibid.*, cap. 9, p. 64f.

possible extent that the need arose to consult and interpret, meaningfully and in relation to contemporary society, models from which the citizen could draw lessons for himself. But, to the plethora of expositions dealing with divine issues and theological problems in the preceding ages, hardly anything corresponded in the mundane, secular human sphere – hence everything pointed to antiquity. Politics as the formative agent of the *vita activa* and the need for providing political happiness within the State were to all intents and purposes inextricably interwoven. Indeed, the Thomists, Dante and Marsilius of Padua had already unmistakably indicated this link.[38] And this was clearly the mundane, natural limb of the bipolarity principle. It is no doubt of considerable interest that because the *vita civilis* or *negotiosa* claimed to be considered on its own and demanded increasing attention, not because it was preparatory to the *vita aeterna*, but because it expressed the citizen's own inherent style of life, it almost automatically evoked fierce opposition in the 'conservative' quarters. For instance, the already noted Augustinian scholar Hermann de Schilditz, an exact contemporary of Petrarch, Cola, Salutati and many other humanists, made in his attack on Marsilius a special point of the latter's autonomous conception of the *vita activa*.[39] Shortly afterwards and for precisely the same reason, though independently, the noted opponent of humanism Cardinal Johannes Dominici fiercely impugned the very idea of the *bene vivere*, and consequently the consultation of ancient pagan authors.[40]

In substance, however, the *vita activa* was little else but the citizen's *humanitas* activated in a political sense. And here the early humanists of the fourteenth century were in the fortunate position of being able to draw on numerous ancient models, on secular patterns, prototypes or, as they came to be called, on *exempla* provided by the ancient writers. Indeed, as indicated, the search for patterns in the field of politics was an essential part of the *studia humanitatis*: they directed attention to the *exempla*, as the humanists never tired of calling those models and patterns worthy of imitation.[41] And only in ancient Roman – and later also Greek – literature

---

38   Cf. H. Baron, *Crisis*, (above, p. 6, n. 18), p. 7. Indeed, W. Ferguson, *Renaissance Studies*, (above, p. 2, n. 9), p. 101, points out that the conception of the good life the humanists found in the ancient authors was 'based *exclusively* on experience in this world, the experience of thoughtful and responsible *citizens*' (italics mine).

39   Hermann de Schilditz, *Tractatus*, (above, p. 146, n. 64), I.15, p. 42, lines 11ff. and II.12, p. 93, lines 272ff.

40   Cf. above, p. 144, nn.59, 68, and below, p. 165.

41   The concept and use of *exempla* were well known in the preceding ages, but here too the shift is obvious. For medieval *exempla*, see L. Buisson, 'Exempla und Tradition bei Innozenz III.' in *Adel & Kirche* (= *Festschrift Gerd Tellenbach* (Freiburg, 1968)), pp. 458–76. On the model of the old *Florilegia* certain 'moral' or 'moralizing' *exempla* were compiled, and a fair instance was that made by the Paduan jurist Geremia da Montagnone (about 1300), for which see B. Smalley, *op. cit.* (above, p. 96, n. 8), p. 284f.; see further pp. 54, 58, 72, 84.

and indeed history could the *exempla* be found. This in fact was the plea of Salutati in numerous letters.[42] Indeed, among the Roman *exempla* the Roman law was, in time anyway, the first to assume this function. It is advisable to keep in mind that most of the early humanists had studied jurisprudence, and for the transaction of government and for a successful juristic career the facility of expression, the 'science of speech' and mastery in rhetoric, are essential, though once again merely as means.[43]

It was the pursuit of history that was to provide adequate models of politics and of its manipulation, or, seen from a different angle, history was made to serve humanism by presenting relevant *exempla*. The consultation of historical works was therefore merely a means to an end, and not an end itself. What Salutati similarly makes clear is that his contemporaries' vision and perception were to profit greatly from the enlargement of their knowledge. For him the *scientia rerum gestarum* (i.e. knowledge of the past) formed a necessary part of man's equipment, since it shows him how to conduct himself as a citizen in his contact with other citizens and how to act publicly and privately.[44] This enlarged knowledge of the deeds of the ancient nations, tribes, and kings instructs and teaches – hence the constant stress on the *instruere et docere* – so that one can learn from ancestral sources, notably the ancient and tested examples (who were no Christians), how life in society was to be shaped.[45] Historical knowledge thus became a requisite, if not an integral part of the citizen's education. Hence for Paolo Vergerio the classics had recorded the great achievements of men, 'the wonders of nature, the works of Providence in the past which is the key to the secrets of the future.'[46] And Cicero once more proved useful. Salutati quotes his statement that 'History is full of precedents (*exempla*) in so far as it relates to commonly experienced life.'[47] Nor did Cicero's other eulogy of history go unheeded by fourteenth-century humanists, that is to say, history as a witness of the past, as the beacon of truth, as the mistress of life itself (*magistra vitae*) and the purveyor of well-tried customs.[48] Of especial attraction seemed to be Cicero's assertion of the

42 *Epistolario (ed. cit.*, above, n. 4), II.291, lines 2ff. (anno 1392): 'Sed inter alios te precipue dilexisse semper *hystoricos*, quibus rerum gestarum memoriam studium fuit posteris tradere, ut regum, nationum et illustrium virorum *exemplis* per imitationem possent maiorum virtutes vel excedere vel equare.'

43 Cf. the pertinent remarks by J. Larner, *op. cit.* (above, p. 105, n. 33), p. 207.

44 *Epistolario*, p. 292, lines 3f.: knowledge of the past is necessary 'quid cum civibus et amicis, quidque privatim vel publice sit agendum.'

45 *Ibid.*, p. 296, lines 12ff.

46 See J. M. McCarthy, *op. cit.* (above, p. 6, n. 19), p. 38.

47 Cicero, *De div.*, 1.24.50 (Loeb, p. 278): 'Plena exemplorum est historia tum refert vita communis.' See Salutati, *Epistolario*, II.72, lines 6ff.: 'Oportet exempla proponere: plane quidem et ubertim tam divinae quam seculares litterae ... *testimoniis* exuberant et *exemplis*.'

48 Cicero, *De oratore*, 2.36 (Loeb, p. 224).

suggestive power of the *exempla* as demonstrated in law and jurisprudence, which were indubitably sources of inspiration in humanist thought.[49] Indeed, Cicero told his son studying in Athens that whereas the teachers could supply theory, it was the city of Athens which would suggest and provide models.[50] It is as if the later view that jurisprudence without history was blind had been anticipated.[51] Similarly, Seneca's appeal to history as a science from which plentiful *exempla* could be garnered began its triumphant career:

Long is the way if one follows exhortations, but short and efficacious if one follows patterns.

(Longum iter est per precepta, brevis et efficax per exempla.[52])

Indeed, practical examples are more effective educationally than abstract persuasion: 'Life should be taught by examples.'[53] Once he had become available in translation, Plutarch was sure to prove himself attractive and appealing. The avowal of Plutarch that he did not aim at writing history, but life as it is, and that for this reason he was going to attach far more weight to seemingly insignificant deeds, or speeches or even jests, was exactly the kind of stuff which stimulated and excited the men of the early humanist age at the turn of the fourteenth and fifteenth centuries. To Plutarch – and his readers – these manifestations of humanity revealed the character of a man far better than grand deeds. It was precisely his personal details and detached incidents (the so-called *anecdota*) which appealed to contemporaries, and indeed Plutarch's *Histories* portrayed the details of the Greeks and Romans in a human and thoroughly mundane, realistic fashion.[54] Of course, the *exempla* were not viewed as ready-made prescriptions to be applied to entirely different environs, themselves merely the amalgam of varied cultural standards. And it was precisely the richness of experiences, observations and con-

---

49 Cicero, *ibid.*: 1.5.18: 'Tenenda preterea est omnis antiquitas, *exemplorum vis*, nequum legum aut iuris civilis scientia negligenda est.'
50 Cicero, *De officiis*, 1.1 (Loeb, p. 2).
51 For this view of Baudouin in the sixteenth century, see D. R. Kelley, 'Historia integra: François Baudouin and his conception of history' in *JHI*, 25(1964), 35ff., especially 43ff. at 47ff.
52 *Epp. ad Lucilium morales*, 6.5 (Loeb, 1967, p. 26).
53 *Ibid.*, Ep. 83.13 (Loeb, 1962, p. 266): 'Instruenda est enim vita exemplis.'
54 See Plutarch's *Life of Alexander*, cap. 1 (Loeb, p. 225): 'It is not histories that I am writing but lives, and in the most illustrious deeds there is not always a manifestation of virtue or vice, nay, a slight thing like a phrase or a jest often makes a greater revelation of character than battles where thousands fall or the greatest armaments or sieges of cities.' For Plutarch translations, see V. R. Giustiniani, 'Sulle traduzioni latine delle Vite di Plutarco nel Quattrocento' in *Rin.*, n.s.1 (1961), 3–62 (at pp. 14ff. details of translators, manuscripts and early prints).

tingencies reported in the ancient *exempla* which compellingly widened the mental horizons and the intellectual dimensions of man in the early Quattrocento. One might well be inclined to see here an attempt to attain a *plenitudo humanitatis*, not by mere imitation but by creative assimilation and constructive absorption, in a word by positive and intelligent utilization of the historical records.

The postulate to put historical knowledge at the service of humanity rested on the presupposition that historical contingencies provided tangible patterns of behaviour from which the citizen in particular could draw useful lessons. The message was that the ancients as pure humans were essentially no different from their fourteenth-century contemporaries, who indeed had become aware of the dearth of literary products relative to their main concern. This didactic value of historical studies was for instance the explicit interest of Giovanni Conversino da Ravenna who, as an exact contemporary of Salutati and Bruni, advocated the study of history in order to achieve 'a preferable way of life' in which its social and above all its political contents predominated: 'history teaches . . .'; 'the lesson of history is . . .'; 'history holds the lesson . . .'; 'history teaches that more glory accrued to the majesty of Rome under the reign of Augustus than during many preceding centuries.'[55] It is the interpretation and understanding of the a-Christian past which should inform the present, was the prevailing view. It is clear that a sense of history permeated humanist educational tracts and that contemporaries had a real sense of historical perspective.[56] The consultation of the ancient historical works marked 'the growing interest in history as a mine of realistic experience', for what had become essential was the knowledge of the history and the traditions of one's own *patria*.[57]

In short, the *studia humanitatis* were to the early humanists little else but instructional means in the art of civic conduct, and within the precincts of these *studia* the relative importance of history and jurisprudence was unmistakable. The attainment of the full *vita activa* or *vita civilis* or *negotiosa* necessitated the acquisition of historical and jurisprudential knowledge, so as to become a *vita operativa*, to use Salutati's expressive terminology. For in energizing his humanity the citizen relies on his own judgements and assessments and insights when he fulfils his chief task, that is, the creation of the law. Hence the emphasis on jurisprudential knowledge and on experience, that is, the lesson of the *exempla*, in a word, knowledge coupled with understanding and penetration was required in order to manipulate, manage and arrange the citizens' own society, the

---

55   H. Baron, *Crisis*, pp. 134ff., at 144.
56   See J. M. McCarthy, *op. cit.*, pp. 41–2.
57   H. Baron in *JHI*, 21(1960), 141.

State. For Salutati and Bruni it was the accumulated wisdom and prudence of Roman statesmanship that did not fail to become prototypical for the exercise of civic functions.

Clearly, the recourse to *exempla* and the reason for it was by no means new. The medieval sermon literature was replete with *exempla* which served to bring home facets of Christian doctrines, and the plethora of handbooks which set forth the mechanics of preaching (*ars praedicandi*) proved how important the sermon was, but its purpose was different. Here it aimed to teach men how to achieve eternal life, how to direct the Christian's attention to the one end that was set for him, eternal salvation. It was precepts in the literal meaning of the term, moral or philosophical counsels which, together with hagiographical, 'typical' portraits of a more or less genuine provenance, constituted the genre of the medieval *exempla*, whereas in the humanist age it was humanity as such and the ordering of civic mundane life which was the reason for adducing, and learning from, the *exempla* of antiquity. The kinship between fourteenth-century man and the Roman was symbolically demonstrated by Petrarch's writing letters to Cicero, to Livy, Seneca and others,[58] or by Salutati's personal address to Cicero.[59] According to Salutati, what mattered was the life lived by humans, the *vita hominum*[60] for which history was the teacher or *magistra*.

Very similar observations can be made about historical studies themselves. That there were copious historical works in abundance during the period between the eighth and the fourteenth centuries is so obvious that no comment is called for. As we have already had occasion to remark, the chroniclers, annalists and writers of *Gesta* and other kinds of historiographical pursuits *au fond* portrayed the historical process as the external manifestation of the divine plan. Since now, however, historical situations, contingencies and movements were to be explained from the human angle, the view on history as the mistress of life began to have a potent and gripping appeal to fourteenth-century men and succeeding generations. The historical process began to be seen as the totality of human volition and human actions in their individual, social, political and moral contexts. It was the concept of the autonomy of man that became the centre of attention. This makes furthermore accessible to understanding the rapidly increasing impact which the proper study of history made in the fourteenth and fifteenth centuries. Petrarch's thesis of the dark age that intervened between the fall of Rome and his time perfectly epitomized and mirrored the new outlook and revealed like a flashlight his awareness of the distance

58   See above, p.113.
59   Salutati, *De tyranno*, ed. A. Martin (Berlin, 1913), p. XXX.
60   *Epistolario*, II.296, line 12.

between antiquity and his own age. The historical process had been shaped by 'regenerated men', by those who had shed their naturalness and had been baptismally reborn. And it was a very similar sentiment and thought process that animated Salutati in his book *On the Tyrant*, where he owns that he had learned many a lesson from (Roman) history. Ancient history became the staple fare of contemporaries.[61] When in previous ages chroniclers and annalists had referred to historical situations, they had done so in order to prove a point for, quite in consonance with their underlying cosmology, the historical events served as *pièces justificatives*. Now historical contingencies served to enlighten and to educate. It stands to reason that this very function of historical pursuit presupposed, if it did not actually create, a critical appraisal of the sources and of the situations they treated. We will return to this point.

Yet, the feature that strikes the observer and which must be kept in mind is that, because it was conditioned by the antecedent ecclesiological outlook, renaissance humanism demonstrated a quite remarkable continuity with the preceding period. There was not only no break, but precisely because the point of departure was baptismal rebirth, there was continuing and expanding evolution. It was the very idea of rebirth – renaissance – that provided a secure base for continuation: it was the rebirth or restoration of natural man which in no wise touched upon baptismal rebirth. Yet, as already indicated, the effect upon cosmology was far-reaching. To natural man endowed with natural reasoning powers had now been accorded autonomy and a positive, active role in the universe: he had value and standing of his own. But the standing of the baptismally reborn man, the Christian, remained unimpaired within the supranatural order of things. Hence there was an incontrovertible widening of human interests and perceptions as a result of the bipolarity point of view. Whereas in previous ages the use of profane, secular or natural literature was frowned upon, its consultation was now positively encouraged, as the anti-humanist Cardinal Dominici summarized his opponents' view in the first decade of the fifteenth century: these ancient writings contain many truths which should be acquired by Christians, for 'the *human* sciences are not only not to be scorned, but on the contrary are to be used most diligently.'[62] No humanist could have stated his case more succinctly or fairly than this opponent! And of the mere *human* matters that now came to be better understood, none was more important than politics, which was humanity activated in the citizen. The abandonment of the wholeness standpoint made possible the full realization of the individual's potentialities and enabled him to be viewed as an integrated whole with a natural

---

61 See also above, p. 105.
62 Johannes Dominici, *Lucula noctis* (*ed. cit.*, above, p. 144, n. 59), cap. 3, pp. 27, 34.

as well as a supranatural end. He was unregenerated in one sense, and regenerated in another, to employ former and traditional terminology. Differently expressed, he was seen as a microcosm, as the universe *en miniature*. Since this was the very essence of the early phases of humanism which focused attention on the rebirth – the renascence – of man's humanity, the entry of (human) history into the horizon of reflective and thinking man becomes comprehensible.

There would seem every justification for saying that, taken in the widest possible sense, the *studia humanitatis* were subsumed under the heading of education in the service of the citizen. And this education aimed at widening *human* horizons, at enlarging human perspectives, at broadening man's bases of judgments and assessments and stimulating his innate capacities and faculties of evaluation. For an end of this kind, as the discerning reader of the relevant literature soon gathers, education within a public and mundane context was summed up in the concept of *bene vivere*. This term and the idea it denoted was, as we have seen, conspicuous in Thomas Aquinas and numerous others following him, and began to be invested with greater and greater significance by subsequent generations. This *bene vivere* – the good life – was understood, not in any materialistic or hedonistic sense, nor as bourgeois epicureanism, but in civic or political terms, and constituted the end, the very purpose and essence of the *vita activa* which in this same context assumed its proper significance as *vita civilis* or *negotiosa*. In other words, the study of ancient literature, at any rate in the early phases of humanism, was relative: it related to the realization of a full life as was instanced by Leonardo Bruni who specifically singled this out as the object of a full education,[63] in fact in no wise different from the view of Paolo Vergerio and other contemporaries such as Guarino.[64] The significance lies in the crediting of mundane, civic existence with its own *raison d'être* and norms, so that the 'good life' (the *bene vivere*) was merely the teleological expression of the realization of the citizen's own *humanitas* and of his own potentialities as a member of the State[65] – it was the supreme goal of the citizen's politics.

The presupposition was adequate education, that is information on the civic virtues, and for their knowledge and recognition nothing was more conducive and instructive than the study of the ancients, just as the study

---

63 Leonardo Bruni, *De studiis et litteris liber*, ed. H. Baron, *Humanistisch-Philosophische Schriften* (Leipzig and Berlin, 1928), p. 12. Cf. E. Kessler, *Das Problem des frühen Humanismus* (Munich, 1968), p. 209. Hence Bruni's advice to study the ancients *die noctuque*, *ed. cit.*, p. 12, line 6.

64 See E. Kessler, *op. cit.*, p. 209, nn. 19, 20, 21.

65 It may be recalled that for Marsilius the concept of *bene vivere* was crucial, because only the citizens knew what constituted 'the good life'; hence they alone were entitled to make laws in the interests of the public good. See *Defensor Pacis*, I.4.3 and I.5.2; see also above, p. 125.

of religious or theological literature was necessary for obtaining an adequate grasp of the transcendental, supranatural life. Hence the education advocated by the early humanists was a means to an end, and that end was civic, that is the education of the citizen as a politically integrated member of the State. And this indeed was the reason why some early humanists stressed that since boys were members of the State which was in need of governors, defenders, artisans, and so on, it was only right and proper that they be educated in the interests of the State. Obviously these educational aims necessitated the use of the vernacular for the benefit of the citizens.[66] Negatively expressed: education was not what has been termed liberal, but addressed itself rather conspicuously to the needs of the citizen and his conduct within the State. And this very conception of education was one of the reasons why a number of Platonic axioms began to have a new lease of life among the humanists.[67] In the humanist educational curricula there was little on religious or ecclesiastical matters, but all the greater concern was shown for the records of antiquity which became 'records of civilization' in the literal meaning of the term.

The remark is justified that here too there was no dramatic departure from the previous conceptions of the needs of education. Once more, what had changed was the point of reference or, more accurately, a new point of reference was added to the already existing one. Education down to the fourteenth century was quite severely and consistently related to the unipolarity theme and, therefore, ecclesiologically orientated. Life on earth was in any case merely a *vita transitoria*. Since the mid twelfth century these cosmological views had suffered a steady decrease of strength, and now as a result of the citizen's full rebirth his mundane life was no longer considered merely transitory, but an entity on its own: it claimed its due and demanded adequate attention. The bipolarity principle necessarily also involved a mundane orientation, just as previously the unipolarity standpoint concentrated on the future life to which everything was to be subordinated. The exploration of this new human world, of man as a balanced, composite being, opened up vistas and perspectives of hitherto unknown dimensions. There was an approximation to the Greek philosopher's view that man was the measure of all things.

What the restored citizen lacked, and what quite ostensibly was now to become his distinguishing mark, was civic virtue. In the antecedent ages

66 See also below, pp. 183f.
67 Cf. the autograph glosses by Nicholas of Cusa on Plato's *Republic* in a manuscript of the Brixen Seminary Library: G. Santinello, 'Glosse di mano del Cusano alla Repubblica di Platone' in *Rin*, n.s.9(1969), 117–45. Nicholas was thoroughly familiar with Platonism, but did not present it in a comprehensive work: this was done by a less gifted man, Marsilio Ficino, for which see P. O. Kristeller, *The Philosophy of Marsilio Ficino* (New York, 1943).

most literate people were familiar with the doctrine of virtues, of the four cardinal virtues of ancient provenance (justice, prudence, fortitude and temperance) and of the three theological virtues (faith, hope and charity). What now began to make its appearance was civic virtue as a quality specifically germane to man in his civic capacity. Once more one can see that an already existing terminology greatly facilitated the adoption of a new idea, however much the substance may have differed. It may be recalled that the term 'political virtue' had been employed sporadically in an untechnical sense earlier.[68] And we note that, true Aristotelian that he was, Thomas Aquinas had operated with the *virtus politica*, which he equated with the *virtus civilis*.[69]

Effectively employing the inductive method of enquiry, contemporary writers came increasingly to see the civic virtue of the citizen not in any absolute, but in a purely relative, perspective. Its substance could not *a priori* be postulated, but depended partly on the constitution of the state, partly on geographical–physical conditions, and partly on the history that had shaped the respective state. The concept of civic virtue began to have practical and fundamental relevance when once the potentialities of politics were fully grasped. And Northern Italy provided excellent examples of the relativity of the concept: the civic virtue in an oligarchically governed state was different from that obtaining in a republican or democratically governed state or, for that matter, in an elective monarchy. It is, for instance, particularly enlightening to read the tract by Salutati on tyranny where historical knowledge gained from studying the ancients was effortlesslly joined with, and was endorsed by, his practical knowledge of the actual conditions in Northern Italy. Indeed, Salutati's political theory can be explained only by his recourse to the ancient Roman foundations.[70] The notion of civic (or political) virtue became fashionable and pushed the traditional scholastic doctrine of the virtues into the background.[71] Its significance lay in the fixation and formulation of a set of values which were exclusively mundane, secular and human. Just as man's humanity varied according to his natural gifts, in the same way the citizen's civic virtue was to vary: *virtù* was destined to become crucial in the age of the Renaissance.[72]

---

68   See above, p. 99, n. 18.
69   See his Commentary on the *Ethics* (edition Rome, 1969) ad 1141 b22 and 23: VI.7, p. 356, where he operated conspicuously with the *politica virtus* which was *'principativa et dominativa* ratio sive notitia, hic, id est, in genere rerum humanarum.' The creation of law was on a level with the creation of a building by an architect.
70   See A. Martin in his introduction to his edition of *De tyranno*, (above, n. 59), p. 37: 'Aus der Geschichte, nämlich der römischen Geschichte, strömt das Leben, das Salutatis Theorie erfüllt.' Cf. also p. 39.
71   For some details cf. *PGP* pp. 247f.
72   For this topic see H. Baron, 'Das Erwachen des historischen Denkens im Humanismus des Quattrocento' in *HZ*, 147(1933), 5ff., especially 8ff.

This brief sketch should have indicated how much the consultation of ancient literature, taken in the widest sense, was geared to the postulates of the new discipline and category of thought, to politics. What mattered was the acquisition of knowledge relative to politics. To use modern terminology, the *studia humanitatis* constituted an auxiliary science. They were ancillary to politics as a science of its own, which was in need of firmly drawn contours and a sharp profile. The assistance which Cicero above all others rendered in this respect is therefore easily understandable. We may recall that it was what he himself had called the *theses politicae* which supplied the substance of politics, for which the ancients supplied the models. The kinship which Florentine, Paduan or Venetian scholars felt for ancient Rome cannot cause much surprise. Knowledge of *humanitas* became an indispensable requirement for 'political philosophy', especially when it is borne in mind that politics was *humanitas* activated in a civic sense. Hence the close liaison of the *studia humanitatis* not only with politics, but also with history. And both were intrinsically concerned with natural–human, mundane matters; and both stood next to the *studia divinitatis* with which they had a close liaison. What in this very context deserves strong emphasis is the juristic qualification of virtually all early humanists.[73] Moreover, most of them were employed in public service or occupied high political positions,[74] such as Salutati, Bruni, Conversino, Vergerio, Barbaro (of Venice), Palmieri, Poggio, to mention just a few at random. And it was precisely in their public–civic role that they raised the political battle-cry of *libertas*, of which Dante had said that it was the greatest gift conferred by God on mankind.

However much the consultation of ancient authors and their writings was merely auxiliary, because undertaken in the service and interests of politics, it shared the fate of many earlier and later auxiliary or ancillary services. They tended to dissociate themselves from their original purpose, which gradually receded into the background. What had been merely relative, because useful to politics, became progressively detached from the original point of reference and assumed autonomous character with its own premisses and complexion. It was as a consequence of the unparalleled increase in perception and the enlarged width of intellectual horizons that the *studia humanitatis* began to be less and less associated with politics, the citizen and the State. Their utility to politics and the State receded into the background. What became quite clearly discernible from the early

---

73 See also above, p. 161.
74 See E. Garin, 'I cancellieri umanisti della repubblica fiorentina da Coluccio Salutati a Bartolomeo Scala' in *Rivista storica italiana*, 71(1959), 185ff. See also L. Martines, *Lawyers and Statecraft in Renaissance Florence* (Princeton, 1968). Whether all the Florentine lawyers (see the useful list at pp. 482–508) could be termed humanists must await further examination.

fifteenth century was a specialization of several intellectual disciplines which related to the literary, cultural, educational, and aesthetic studies of the ancients. These studies constitute what is commonly understood as renaissance humanism. What had originally been a means to an end, became an end in itself. The original point of reference – the State, the citizen, politics – was so to speak left behind, and the effect was the burgeoning of renaissance humanism in all its multiformity. The original links with politics and so on had become so tenuous that to all intents and purposes they could be considered severed.

It might perhaps assist the understanding of this process – assuredly not peculiar to this topic or period – if one were to cast a glance at an earlier instance of a not dissimilar development in the realms of thought and cosmology. Before the early twelfth century there had been no separation of the various branches which came to make up theology. There was what had been felicitously called a *communauté des matières*. Liturgy came as much under this umbrella as canonical jurisprudence or penitential scholarship or the exposition of governmental themes in the shape of the *Specula regum*. In a way this *communauté des matières* expressed the wholeness point of view. But with the deepening of understanding and the acquisition of ever greater knowledge by the mid twelfth century this undivided theology came to be separated into different segments, such as canonical jurisprudence proper, theology proper, philosophy, liturgy, and so on, each with its own criteria, norms and premises, only to lead to further specialization in each field, such as procedural, matrimonial, criminal studies, etc. as far as jurisprudence was concerned, and moral and pastoral theology, soteriology, and related branches within theology. It was simply no longer possible for a scholar of standing to master all the knowledge in theology as well as in jurisprudence. There was a similar development in the fourteenth century when jurisprudence and politics came to proceed on their own separate lines.[75] And it was exactly the same in renaissance humanism, which demanded the mastery of criteria, norms, and premises as well as intricate and involved thought-processes each virtually independent and self-sufficient. The former *communauté des matières* was replaced by a multiplicity of departments where each part went its own way, established its own norms and criteria and pursued its own germane aims. In parenthesis it might be mentioned that this tendency towards specialization is particularly pronounced in the modern age when what was once one whole, such as physics, chemistry or geography, has

---

75 It is nevertheless interesting that conservative-inclined writers attempted a reuniting of the various disciplines at exactly the same time. Cf. on this W. Ullmann, 'John Baconthorp as a canonist' in *Church and Government*, ed. C. N. L. Brooke *et al.* (Cambridge, 1976), 223–46: he attempted a combination of jurisprudence with theology.

split into different and virtually independent compartments. In the later Middle Ages this process of atomization had profound effects and made a deep impact upon the wholeness standpoint. This is one more manifestation of the process of disintegration and decomposition to which we have already referred.

A few illustrations of how the *studia humanitatis* came to assume their independent status should be given. Because the ancient authors consulted frequently resorted to Greek models, the need was clearly felt to make the latter available in translation. Hence the realization of the importance of rendering Greek works in a Latin idiom that was acceptable to the educated fifteenth-century man. His standard, precisely because he had steeped himself in the writings of authors whose native tongue was the Latin in which they wrote (and not the Latin that was acquired as a foreign language by all the authors from the seventh century onwards), had become far more rigorous and exacting than it had been only two or three generations earlier. The raised standard of Latin syntax, sentence construction, prose, structure, etc., was indubitably a by-product of the perusal of the ancients, but it soon became a study of its own that was no longer satisfied with a mere ancillary status, developing its own criteria, its own norms and standards. For a satisfactory translation of an author from one dead language into another dead language – from Greek into Latin – presupposed the fullest possible command of the Latin idiom. This latter was perfectly adequate for the purposes to which it was put in previous ages, but was clearly seen as insufficient for works which demanded the highest possible empathy in relation to subject-matter and exposition.[76]

It is this widening of interests and horizons – originally conditioned by their close relation with politics – which characterized and explained the detachment of the *studia humanitatis* from their original connection. Their assuming an independent status was directly proportionate to their detachment. The early humanists, such as Salutati or Bruni, became pacemakers in the sphere of translation precisely because they had read and digested the classical authors and had a first-rate command of Latin: it was they who advocated translations from Greek authors, and it was they who themselves heeded their own advice (as for instance Bruni), and it was they who began to evolve what amounted to a textual criticism, as was for instance the case with Salutati. The heightened literary sense now began to develop criteria by which the authorship of a work could be detected, that is, whether or not a work ascribed to, or allegedly written by, say, Cicero or Virgil, was really Ciceronian or Virgilian, and not that of a hack; or a grammar that paraded Donatus as its author, was not foisted upon him

---

76 For the fructifying effects of Greek translations into Latin during the fifteenth century, see P. O. Kristeller, *Renaissance Concepts of Man* (New York, 1972), pp. 64ff., 135ff.

to lend the book an air of respectability and 'authority'. The emergence of literary criticism was in fact almost an exact parallel to that of medieval diplomatic, which concerned itself with criteria by which the genuine document could (and can) be distinguished from the spurious or falsified or plainly forged.

At the same time the penetration into historical works of antiquity and the understanding of historical contingencies in the Greek and Roman world sharpened, if it did not actually create, a proper historical–critical sense. Once the historical process ceased to be seen as the emanation of divine volition, its presentation, explanation and exposition proceeded on purely human–mundane lines and with the employment of purely human–natural criteria of assessment, which is after all the beginning of historical criticism. As Paolo Vergerio had said, Rome and its history cannot be understood without a knowledge of Greek. Textual and historical criticism derived from the same roots and sources. In a sense they were cousins, if not twins, setting out from human premises, with human needs in mind and pursuing human ends: the one linguistic, the other political.[77]

Obviously, seen from the somewhat exalted fifteenth-century standpoint of Latinity and historical critique, neither the earlier Latin translations of Greek authors nor the current historical expositions were considered adequate. It is therefore perfectly understandable that the study of Greek was now seriously set afoot, as is witnessed by Salutati's inviting Chrysoloras to come to Florence with a view to teaching Greek there. Bruni and Vergerio were Greek students of this scholar, and Greek scholarship now began to flourish in Florence as well as in other so-called humanist centres.[78] It is of no little interest to note that in 1406, in the reconstituted university of Rome, Leonardo Bruni (who actually composed the papal charter for Innocent VII) was responsible for the establishment of 'Greek letters and of all Greek authors' as one of the special subjects to be taught there.[79] And it was Bruni who in some of his own translations of Plutarch had laid down certain principles to be observed by any (intelligent) translator. But Bruni also translated Aristotelian works, notably the

---

77 Within the jurisprudential orbit, see the most perceptive study by D. R. Kelley, 'Legal humanism and the sense of history' in *SR*, 13(1966), 184ff.

78 Bruni's early historical *Laudatio Florentinae Urbis* was possibly the first humanist work 'to profit substantially from the knowledge of Greek'. H. Baron, *From Petrarch to Leonardo Bruni*, (above, n. 6), p. 151.

79 See G. Griffths, 'Bruni and the University of Rome' in *Renaissance Quarterly*, 26(1973), at p. 7: 'This fits into the humanists' conception of a rebirth of letters after a long period of darkness.' See the Prologue of Bruni to his translation of Plato's *Phaidon* sent to Innocent VII in 1404–5, ed. H. Baron in *Humanistisch-Philosophische Schriften* (above, n. 63), pp. 3f.

Politics[80] – which he says should be called 'a golden river'[81] – as well as a number of Platonic writings.[82]

The heightened sense of language, the evaluation of the subtleties of meaning attached to terms, phrases and linguistic structure, together with the acute awareness of syntactic rules, were soon to lead to the complete detachment of the *studia humanitatis* from their original nexus with politics: they became a study of their own, concentrating as they did on language and its purity. Or, seen from a different angle, this attainment of a status of its own by 'grammar and rhetoric' was just one more instance of specialization. Indeed, there was a veritable literary rebirth, a literary renaissance, in relation to ancient literature. The former relativity of the *studia humanitatis* was replaced by absolutism, that is, self-sufficiency in their concentration on purely literary topics. The literary renaissance began to enter its own career and gave birth to what is commonly called the humanist style or form of the renaissance.[83] It must suffice to refer to Antonio Corbinelli, an early fifteenth century Florentine scholar, who not only had one of the richest contemporary Greek libraries, but also 'devoted himself entirely to his studies of Latin and Greek letters'[84] – an unmistakable manifestation of the literary renaissance.

Hand in hand with literary and historical criticism went the establishment of the scholarship of history in a professional sense.[85] In the last resort the new kind of historiography was also an offshoot of the enquiries into the models which antiquity had provided. Both historical criticism and

---

80 See the two prefaces (veritable eulogies), ed. H. Baron, *loc. cit.*, pp. 70ff., and his *Vita Aristotelis, ibid.*, 41ff. Cf. further E. Garin, *Le traduzioni umanistiche di Aristotele nel secolo XV* (Florence, 1950); P. O. Kristeller, *Renaissance Thought* (above, p. 2, n. 8), for Aristotelian humanists (pp. 35ff.) and philosophers (Pomponazzi) (pp. 134ff.); and E. Rice, 'Humanist Aristotelianism in France: Jacques Lefèvre d'Étaples and his circle' in *op. cit.* (below, n. 85), pp. 132ff.

81 Ed. H. Baron, *loc. cit.* (above, n. 63), p. 73, lines 30f.

82 For this see H. Harth, 'Leonardo Brunis Selbstverständnis als Übersetzer' in *AKG*, 50(1968), 41ff.

83 According to the commonly adopted view the *studia humanitatis* 'meant a fairly well defined group of intellectual disciplines: grammar, rhetoric, history, poetry and moral philosophy, all based on the study of classical authors' (W. Ferguson, *Studies*, (above, p. 2, n. 9), p. 96); see also P. O. Kristeller, *The Classics* (above, p. 1, n. 3), p. 11.

84 Vespasiano da Bisticci, cited by H. Baron, *Crisis*, p. 321.

85 For most penetrating observations cf. Franco Simone, 'Une entreprise oubliée des humanistes français: de la prise de conscience historique du renouveau culturel à la naissance de la première histoire littéraire' in *Humanism in France at the End of the Middle Ages and in the Early Renaissance*, ed. A. H. T. Levi (Manchester, 1971), 106ff. Cf. also W. Goez, 'Die Anfänge der historischen Methoden-Reflexion in der italienischen Renaissance' in *AKG*, 56(1974), 25–48, especially 29–31, who rightly sees the new historiographical orientation as part of the *studia humanitatis* which search for the 'Muster der Antike'.

(modern) historiography were the offspring of a correctly understood humanism. The new historiography reflected man's active participation in the historical process. Hence his past was seen as the emanation of human volition and therefore as being accessible to human criticism and human evaluation. As long as historic contingencies were said to have emanated from the divine plan that was merely translated into practice by the baptismally reborn man, the 'historical' problem centred in the execution of the divine programme, and not in the programme itself: consequently, criticism had little chance of emerging. As it was said times without number nothing happened 'sine Deo sive iubente sive sinente', the margin of criticism was severely restricted from the very beginning. Further, criticism could be, as indeed it was, levelled at the executing organ – be this pope, king or emperor – but since the organ, itself executive, reflected the institution that was alleged to be of divine origin, there was a very limited scope for criticism.[86]

Moreover, the proliferation of historical productions in the shape of the medieval chronicles, annals, etc., stands in inverse proportion to their value as historical sources, because historiography to be valuable presupposes above everything else distance from the subject. But to the chronicler or annalist the divine plan was ever-present. The naturalist reversal brought about a radical change: it was the human cause and effect that now began to demand attention. For it was precisely here that the *studia humanitatis* had underscored the essential role of humanity in the shaping of the past – and of the present – and consequently engendered a sense of detachment from historical events, and those with which the remote *studia* dealt were in any case, as far as the time factor went, well and truly removed from the contemporary scene. It is, for instance, not without interest that Filippo Villani (the last of the Villani clan) entitled his work 'De origine civitatis Florentinae': it was the origin and therefore necessarily the evolution of the Florentine state that was his historical subject. Begun in 1381–2, the work heralds a different temper and outlook altogether. The employment of rational argument in the utilization of sources was perhaps the outstanding feature of the work, which also breathed a peculiar kind of Florentine patriotism.[87] And the historical work of Gregorio Dati, Villani's contemporary, who wrote in the vernacular on the history of the Florentine war with Giangaleazzo at the turn of the century, is a product in which

86 Cf. here the very apposite observations by W. Ferguson, *Studies* (above, p. 2, n. 9), p. 107: the humanists 'took history out of the theologically oriented framework of the world chronicle in which Augustine had placed it and gave it a purely secular setting and content. In short, they replaced clerical history by lay history.'

87 Exactly the same feature can be witnessed in the astonishingly mature Czech historiography at the time, cf. S. Harrison Thompson, 'Learning at the court of Charles IV' in *Speculum*, 25(1950), 1ff., especially 9,13ff. Here also good instances of the use of the vernacular, both in literature and in historiography.

historico-political reasoning predominated to a very marked degree.[88] Indeed, although the work was written only a few years after the cessation of hostilities, the sense of detachment is quite remarkable here. It is noteworthy that Dati attempted a causal explanation of the war by taking into account the motivating efficacy of strictly political, economic, and psychological elements. In Bruni's famous history of the Florentine people which he began in the second decade of the fifteenth century historical contingencies had to be assessed by the yardstick of antiquity: 'The achievements of Florence,' he says, 'will not appear inferior to those great deeds and events of antiquity which we admire when we read of them.'[89]

The extraordinary advance in historical criticism reached a high water mark in Lorenzo Valla's numerous works, among which none shows his intellectual acumen, nor the effects of the *studia humanitatis*, more convincingly than his tract (1440) exposing the Donation of Constantine as a forgery. What is of immediate concern in our context is not so much the trenchant linguistic, syntactic, etymological, liturgical, symbolic, juristic, constitutional attacks, executed with weapons that had been sharpened by the full mastery of Roman history and constitution and set forth with witty irony, but the tenor of the speech he put into the mouth of Silvester in the early part of the book. In a fictitious reply to Constantine Silvester was made to argue that his function was not to exercise power on a mundane level and in a mundane fashion, and therefore he could not accept a kingdom on earth (invoking John 18: 36) or any jurisdictional powers. The gift offered by Constantine was worthless and useless to the pope.[90] Constantine's powers could not and should not be surrendered, belonging as they did to Caesar: 'I must not accept things that are Caesar's, even if you offer them a thousand times.'[91] Evidently, what Valla wished to express here is that the character and aim of a secular government was incompatible with that of the papacy. The utilization by Valla of some time-honoured arguments should not hide the wholly different framework within which they were invoked: his thesis rested on the bipolarity principle, whereas previously the same arguments were employed to buttress the principle of division of labour which necessarily presupposed the no longer extant ecclesiological unit. Valla laid great stress on Constantine's being a pagan,[92] thereby attempting to show that the subjection of peoples and countries to the government of the pope lay quite outside the end for which Constantine

---

88 H. Baron, *Crisis*, pp. 168ff.; *id.*, *From Petrarch to Leonardo Bruni* (above, n. 6), pp. 138ff.
89 *Id.*, *Crisis*, p. 283. Cf. also *id.*, *art. cit.* (above, n. 72), at pp. 14ff.
90 See C. B. Coleman, *The Treatise of Lorenzo Valla on the Donation of Constantine: Text and Translation* (New Haven, Connecticut, 1922), p. 56.
91 *Ibid.*, p. 61.
92 Cf. pp. 70f.

exercised power and could not possibly have been envisaged by him.[93] It can hardly cause surprise that a man of Valla's calibre endowed with fiery imagination and overflowing zeal re-echoed, in a different key, Petrarch's view of the dark ages and pronounced that, since Boethius, (medieval) writers and scholars had distorted not only classical authors but also Christianity itself: ecclesiastics had been wholly oblivious of the universal mission of Christianity.[94]

The actual historical situation at the turn of the fourteenth and fifteenth centuries presented the unsavoury spectacle of a schism within the Church, the severity and consequences of which had no parallel. It is no doubt interesting that this indubitably serious contingency left only minimal traces in the writings of the early humanists. This is a feature which should long have prompted some investigation, especially as quite a number of them had reached high office in the papal curia, such as Salutati, Vergerio, Bruni and Poggio, to mention but a few outstanding men. What is of immediate concern however is that the very impasse which the schism had reached, and the seeming impossibility of solving the issues it had raised, directed attention to early Church history. The battle-cry of a return to the *ecclesia primitiva* and the often successful attempts by ecclesiastical writers to unearth sources relevant to Christian antiquity are assuredly further signs of the new historical orientation. Cardinal Zabarella, himself the cardinal of Florence, was perhaps the foremost representative of this new orientation. It in fact reflected exactly the same feature as was observable in the precincts of secular politics, that is, looking at antiquity (in this case Christian) so as to learn from it. And indeed the body that terminated the schism – the Council of Constance – was summoned by a king because in Christian antiquity controversial issues were decided by a council convoked by the emperor. Christian antiquity was seen as a model or pattern for curing contemporary ills. This is highly

93   See pp. 124ff., especially p. 126. For Valla as a critical historian see the excellent exposition by D. R. Kelley, *Foundations of Modern Historical Scholarship* (New York, 1970), pp. 21ff. See further S. Prete, *Observations on the History of Textual Criticism in the Medieval and Renaissance Periods* (Collegeville, Minnesota, 1970) (important for bibliographical details). It is assuredly no coincidence that the forgery was exposed wholly independently, by three exact contemporaries; they employed the new historical method: Nicholas of Cusa and Reginald Pecock were the other two scholars. About the latter cf. E. F. Jacob, 'Reginald Pecock' in *Proceedings British Academy*, 40(1953), and Arthur B. Ferguson, 'Reginald Pecock and the renaissance sense of history' in *SR*, 13(1966), 147–65; cf. also J. M. Levine, 'Reginald Pecock and Lorenzo Valla on the Donation' *SR*, 20(1973), 118–43; and for the former see N. Grass, *Cusanus Gedächtnisschrift* (Innsbruck, 1970), pp. 102ff., at 116ff.

94   Cf. E. Garin, 'Die Kultur etc.' (above, p. 5, n. 17) at p. 437. See now also S. I. Camporeale, *Lorenzo Valla, umanesimo e teologia* (Florence, 1972), which shows Valla's intellectual development very clearly.

significant. Brutal reality, in other words, now also turned the attention of alert ecclesiastics towards antiquity. It was the same path which many of their mundane contemporaries had already trodden. It was the search for a pattern which would facilitate the solution of the problems besetting Christianity

The escalation of biographical works in these vital decades around the turn of the fourteenth and fifteenth centuries must also be considered one more effect of the original motive of pursuing the *studia humanitatis*. Previously indeed there were numerous biographies of kings and popes and emperors and bishops, but these were either overwhelmingly apologetic or partisan, or were representations of the deeds of men in the far distant past who were shown as shining examples of saintlihood that itself was worthy of emulation. It can hardly be maintained that the hundreds of *Vitae* approached the subject critically. Biography, if the genre of writing deserves this name, clearly exhibited the basic features of the dominant ecclesiological theses and portrayed the subject correspondingly, that is, as a baptismally reborn creature. His ordinary humanity was of little interest, although there were some notable exceptions, such as William of Malmesbury in the twelfth century who appended brief character sketches of the kings at the end of his relevant accounts. A substantial shift came about as a result of man's natural rebirth and the restoration of his humanity as something worthy of consideration. And the *studia humanitatis* evidently fostered the desire to depict the very essence of the personality itself. In their search for this human reality the *literati* of the fourteenth and fifteenth centuries came wholly under the spell of the ancients. It is hardly open to doubt that Plutarch's *Lives*, once they had become available in translation, powerfully stimulated the development of biographical writing. The attention to personal, human detail, of which only few writers in the preceding centuries could give a lively and full-blooded portrayal, was very characteristic of this new genre. Special mention must be made of the Emperor Charles IV, who himself wrote the biography of a Czech saint, St Vaclav. The tenor in which it was written was 'rational' and 'the critical use of historical sources is truly remarkable'.[95] It is a further significant feature of the biographical literature of the time that it dealt with the personalities of near-contemporaries, such as Dante or even Petrarch. The discussion of historical personalities in classical antiquity, such as Caesar himself, is another characteristic trait. And this discussion as often as not widened into analyses of contemporary (Roman) political and social conditions. In a word, the restoration or rebirth of man led to the critical assessment of what now came to be considered his true *persona*.

95   See S. Harrison Thomson, *art. cit.* (above, n. 87), at p. 9.

Clearly, the ancients could hardly be seen in a different light – and this is also one of the reasons why they attracted so little attention among writers of earlier generations.

In proximity to the emergence of biography stood autobiography. As a literary genre this too was wholly unknown in previous ages, and for perfectly comprehensible reasons. To write about oneself in a critical sense presupposes detachment from oneself and above all the consciousness of the worth of one's own personality – of its being worthy of a critical assessment. But what criteria had baptismally reborn man by which to portray himself as a (natural) man? Anyway, why should he portray what was said to have been rendered impotent and had atrophied as a result of baptism? Knowledge of one's self belonged to God, not to man himself, as Lactantius long ago had expressed himself in appropriately rendering the Christian ethos.[96] It was not indeed for the individual to say how well or how badly he had discharged his function as a Christian – that was to be left to those who governed and laid out the path of the present life as a *vita transitoria*.[97] It was precisely the elimination of natural *humanitas* which was the hallmark of baptismal rebirth – how then should it form the subject of one's self-portrait? This could proceed only on subjective criteria – exactly those which were relegated to the background, and what mattered was the office, the institution, the law: for the human–personal subjective assessment no criteria were available. This is not to deny that there were some autobiographical references by earlier authors – Gerald of Wales at once springs to mind,[98] or even the *Historia Calamitatum* by Abelard – but the genre as such was unknown.

The autobiographical genre took its cue from the ancient epistolary form. Petrarch appears to have been the earliest to do this, modelling himself on Seneca,[99] and it was precisely in these autobiographical letters that he addressed himself (as already noted) to Cicero. He claimed that he was the first to have written an autobiography: 'nobody before me has done this'.[100] Yet at exactly the same time Charles IV, the emperor, had written his autobiography, which was 'a literary effort unique among medieval Rulers.'[101] And the history of families was conceived as an extended

---

96   Lactantius, *Div. institutiones*, III.3.2, edition in *CSEL*, 19.181, lines 13ff. (=ET in *FC*, 49(1964), p. 168). Here also the significant statement that any discussion about natural things can only be conjecture, 3.8, p. 182, lines 14ff. (=ET, p. 170).

97   This, incidentally, was the principle expressed by Gelasius I in his famous communication to the Byzantine emperor. Cf. *PG* pp. 21f. and *PGP* pp. 57ff., where the sources will be found.

98   Cf. above, p. 70.

99   See G. Misch, *Geschichte der Autobiographie* (Frankfurt, 1969), IV.2, p. 579.

100   *Epistolae variae*, ed. J. Fracassetti, in *Epp. de rebus familiaribus* (Florence, 1863), III.364ff., at p. 367: 'De ratione vitae meae integro volumine disputem, quod ante me, ut arbitror, fecit nemo.' This letter was written to Boccaccio.

101   S. Harrison Thompson, *art. cit.*, p. 9.

autobiography. This too was a new departure. The attempt was now made to draw a realistic picture of the family, of its ancestors, its branches and the private and public matters affecting it. An early example is provided by the Florentine Donato Velluti (*c.* 1367), who began his family chronicle by the enumeration of all ancestors known to him and who gave a quite detached account of their deeds (and misdeeds). This, he avowed, he did because everybody is mortal and therefore he wished to hand on useful information to his descendants so that they might draw a lesson from his experiences. The same holds true of Giovanni Morelli's family chronicle: and in Bonaccorso Pitti (died 1431) this literary form written in the vernacular reaches a very high standard indeed. It is a very lively and intelligent account of all his manifold activities, including his gambling, his diplomatic missions to Croatia, Spain and England, his amatory adventures in Brussels, his counsels to princes and their reactions. The work is suffused with a worldliness and a zest for living which makes it a literary gem that allows insight into the humanity of a dynamic personality. What is also quite astonishing is the heightened power of observation which shows itself in, say, Morelli's chronicle, which enters into the description of traits of body and character with verve and skill: height, complexion, colour of hair, eating and drinking habits, health (or ill-health). Especially attractive is the minute detail in his description of feminine appearance and emotion together with the general impression of the persons portrayed.[102] In a word, it was reborn humanity that had come onto the scene: the fabric of the new genre was a realistic portraiture of man's natural personality. It should no longer be open to doubt that this was clearly an effect of the *studia humanitatis*, as originally understood.

It is in this very same context and for the same reasons that personal memoirs and diaries now began to make their appearance. Personal details, personal motivations, personal viewpoints are indissolubly linked with the personality of man himself, hence with his basic humanity. Observational awareness of oneself, as well as self-knowledge, were indispensable preconditions for self-portraits and memoirs and diaries. Petrarch's marginal notes in the manuscripts he possessed appear to be the first modern diaries.[103] These memoirs mirror the self-evident importance which man began to attach to himself. It was a new society of which its members were perfectly aware. Moreover, the epistolary art itself requires not only a highly advanced state of education, but also dimensions of psychological comprehension and penetration which the *studia humanitatis* had furnished as an additional by-product. It is assuredly no coincidence that Leonardo Bruni was one of the first to write a critically inspired history of the *people*

---

102   For all details see G. Misch, *op. cit.* (above, n. 99), IV.2, pp. 582ff.
103   *Ibid.*, p. 580.

of Florence which to some extent approaches contemporary history. Indeed it was during these and the subsequent decades that the history of populations of whole regions and provinces, as well as towns, came first to be treated in a professional way. The inhabitants of a regional entity yielded a portrait, so to speak, of the individual writ large. This was clearly discernible in one of the earliest histories of the Italian people by Dante's contemporary, Albertino Mussato, who wrote what in every respect · amounted to a contemporary history of the Italians after Henry VII: *De gestis Italicorum post Henricum VII Caesarem.*[104] It was precisely the contemporary awareness of the Italian cities as states which explains the proliferation of city-state chronicles, and the quantity and quality of contemporary histories of German towns is equally noteworthy.[105]

What on the other hand needs stressing in the present context is that the Latin of the 'humanists' and the so-called Volgare were not opposed to each other in this phase of 'humanism', but were two sides of the same coin. They were exercising a mutually beneficial influence and complemented each other. It should not be necessary to cite specific examples of humanist vernacular, perhaps the clearest and most persuasive sign of man's own renaissance: Dante's *Vita nuova* or *Divina commedia*, Petrarch's *Can-zoniere*, Boccaccio's *Decamerone* come at once to mind, apart from the plethora of minor contemporary works, and we should not forget Chaucer, *Sir Gawain and the Green Knight*, and Langland in distant lands, nor the exuberant Bohemian and Polish literature at this very same time. Indeed, in his *Vita di Dante*, the classically versed and thoroughgoing humanist Leonardo Bruni defended Dante's vernacular on the grounds that every language has its own perfection.[106] Certainly, in the early stages of humanism there was no rivalry or animosity of the one towards the other. All these vernacular productions conveyed the same sense of humanity though exhibited in different situations, shades and associations. The picture conveyed is as varied as humanity itself. There was, in a word, no norm, no acceptance of, or conformity with, a 'norm of right living' (*norma recte vivendi*). What mattered was the reality and substance of humanity itself, the human emotions, human feelings and sentiments, human experiences, human sufferings, human expectations and aspirations, human failings, human luck and human misfortune, and above all human reactions to vicissitudes of the widest varieties. And that in more than just a minority of vernacular productions religious and philosophic points came

---

104   Edition in L. A. Muratori, *Scriptores rerum italicarum*, X(1727), 571–768.
105   See *Die Chroniken der deutschen Städte vom 14. bis ins 16. Jahrhundert*, 37 volumes, ed. Bavarian Academy (1862–1931).
106   See on this E. Garin, 'Dante nel rinascimento' in *Rin*, n.s.8 (1967), 3–28, with copious literature; for Bruni, *ibid.*, pp. 19f.

to be allocated their fair share of attention needs only to be mentioned for its significance to be grasped.

Yet it was undeniable that in course of time differences between the vernacular and the Latin writers were to come to the fore. Although there was mutual fructification, the cultivation of Latin (and later also of Greek) fostered an intensive concentration on grammar, rhetoric, literary style and expository methods. The distance between the author writing in the vernacular and the student of classical literature began noticeably to widen as the fourteenth century wore on. The former removed himself more and more from ancient models and progressively immersed himself in the cultivation of the vernacular and in the study of contemporary humanity. The purity of Latin and the cultivation of its literature became an end in itself and ceased to be a means to an end. It was the purist, and sometimes also the grammatical pedant, the humanist of the literary and aesthetic stamp, who began to set the tone by frequently writing an artificial, contorted, convoluted, specious kind of Latin that was neither classical nor medieval, but a hybrid. In Italy, the country that gave birth to renaissance humanism, the fifteenth century, as has rightly been observed, produced not a single creative writer who could bear comparison with a Dante, a Petrarch, or a Boccaccio.[107] By a resuscitation of a past that as often as not was the subjectively conceived picture of Roman antiquity, this contrived literary renaissance humanism came to lose touch with contemporary ordinary humanity. The classical purist believed he had returned to *Roma antiqua* and lived in a rarefied atmosphere of clinical, aseptic conditions. It was a pecular kind of classicism that had its own characteristics and had become an intellectual pursuit on its own. The purists emerged as the (commonly known as humanist) *literati*, who indeed set their seal on the literary, intellectual and historical landscape from the fifteenth century onwards and relegated practicability and concrete civic exigencies to an inferior role. Nevertheless, in essence the theme common to both the classicist and the vernacular writer was that of humanity. The former concentrated on what he believed to be the ancient world, the latter on the present, and each referred to the *usus humanitatis* or its *stilus*, a terminology coined by Valla.[108]

It is a frequently observed phenomenon that influential movements in society or in scholarship do not originate, and are not cultivated, in universities or academic circles. This observation applies with particular force to renaissance humanism. Although the background was ecclesiological and

---

107   See E. Garin, 'Die Kultur' (above, p. 5, n. 17), at pp. 519f. But this also applies to other regions; for England, as an instance, see A. B. Ferguson, *The Articulate Citizen and the English Renaissance* (Durham, N.C. 1965), p. 24: 'deadly mediocrity.'

108   For this see D. R. Kelley, *op. cit.* (above, n. 93), p. 34.

religious and the original impetus had come from the study and absorption of Aristotelian ideas by thirteenth-century scholarship, notably at Paris university, the curricula in the universities provided little margin for the cultivation and integration, and above all application, of the new perspectives which the renaissance of man offered. None of the statutes in fourteenth-century universities (and barely a handful of them in the fifteenth century) facilitated or provided for the pursuit of the *studia humanitatis* in the sense in which they were originally undertaken, that is, as a means by which to find models for the conduct of reborn natural man in civic, political matters. The pioneers wrote outside the universities. There was no university that could be said to be in the vanguard of the *studia humanitatis*,[109] and when some educational institutions did in the fifteenth century include them, they were by then confined to the pursuit of classical grammar, rhetoric, and poetry, in other words to the literary and aesthetic species of humanism which had detached itself from the originally very wide humanist embrace. Virtually all over Europe the universities began to decline into second-rate, mediocre factories more or less purposelessly purveying formalized and fossilized matter.

The subject of politics certainly did not figure prominently among academic pursuits, which were academic in more than one sense: politics became a more or less important branch of history. This is a bequest of renaissance humanism that was noticeable well into the nineteenth century, if not beyond. What is worthy of remark is the impact which classicist humanism was to make upon the oldest academic profession – jurisprudence. Indeed, jurisprudence was the first academic study that adopted the purist perspectives and pursued the 'purest' kind of legal studies. But this humanist jurisprudence had no more in common with its predecessor than its name. It was concerned with the restoration of a purified or 'authentic' text of the Roman law that now became the subject of legal education in the narrow meaning of the term. As a governmental (or political) science jurisprudence had ceased to be predominant among academic disciplines.[110] In any case, the leadership in humanist jurisprudence belonged to the French scholars who eagerly responded to the stimulus of Alciatus. King Francis I was to Alciatus and Bourges what Countess Mathilda had been to Irnerius and Bologna. The Italians were left behind and brought forth mere compilers of the stamp of Jacobus

---

109   This includes the English universities too, cf. W. F. Schirmer, *op. cit.* (above, p. 115, n. 49), especially pp. 54ff., 91f. For some qualifying remarks see A. L. Gabriel, *art. cit.* (below, n. 134), at pp. 443–6.

110   D. Maffei, *Gli inizi dell' umanesimo giuridico* (reprinted Milan, 1964); H. E. Troje, *Graeca leguntur* (Cologne and Vienna, 1971), especially pp. 3–190 and 301ff. (on Guillaume Budé). Further, D. R. Kelley, *art. cit.* (above, n. 51), 35ff., and *art. cit.* (above n. 77) at pp. 187ff.

Menochius and Jacobus Farinacius. Creative and 'pure' jurisprudence was to become and remain a French domain.[111]

The situation at basic educational levels was somewhat different. There were in any case numbers of new educational foundations and endowments by town corporations, guilds, wealthy merchants and barons,[112] and the rudiments of education were conveyed in schools which were later to become 'grammar' schools. Where, however, the humanist outlook began to manifest itself most clearly, as far as primary education was concerned, was once more in Italy. It was the need to provide the necessary equipment which prompted a considerable widening of the educational horizon. How could the ancients be models, if one could not understand them properly? The ecclesiastically controlled and religiously motivated kind of primary education was clearly inadequate but, as so much else in this context, it was an important base upon which educational advance could be made. By virtue of the equalizing effects which, as we have seen, citizenship involved, larger and larger sections of the populace were drawn into the 'humanist' precincts. After all, it was ordinary natural humanity that had been 'reborn' or 'rehabilitated', and this was virgin territory, fallow ground, only too ready to be cultivated. Hence it was the 'bourgeoisie' in the form of merchants, skilled artisans, estate and land owners, bankers, and so on, who took a genuine interest in the 'humanizing' process. There was a widening and deepening of interests and teaching, one consequence of which was the provision of educational facilities for women and girls,[113] who had already by the mid fourteenth century been full members of some guilds and who in actual fact formed sometimes predominantly female guilds, such as the embroiderers or illuminators of manuscripts; other guilds, as in the textile industry, were mixed. Indeed, Leonardo Bruni proposed the inclusion of women in any comprehensive educational programme.[114] But since the Latin of the new 'liberated' classes was quite clearly insufficient, it was felt necessary to write for them in the vernacular – and the appearance in the vernacular of purely political tracts is highly significant and goes only to confirm that by the early fifteenth century the original roots and traits of renaissance humanism were still rather conspicuous. Thus, Manetti in his *On the Dignity of Man* (*De dignitate et excellentia hominis*) opposed the pessimistic view of human life. The insistence by Leone Battista Alberti (1402–73) in his tract (written in

111 Cf. also D. R. Kelley, *art. cit.* (n. 77), pp. 194ff. on the strongly national French character of this legal humanism.
112 For English schools of the time see N. Orme, *The English Schools in the Middle Ages* (London, 1973), especially pp. 198ff.
113 For England, *ibid.*, p. 203.
114 See Bruni, *De studiis, ed. cit.* (above, n. 63), p. 12, lines 7ff.

the vernacular) *Trattati della cura della famiglia* (about 1430) that the
citizen had an inescapable obligation to do public service is characteristic
of the original humanist trend. And in the famous and most significantly
entitled tract by Matteo Palmieri, *Della vita civile*, the educational ideal put
forward was that of the well-informed, if not learned, statesman whose
vita activa was wholly absorbed in the service of the State and in the
administration of public–civic affairs.

Yet it would be quite misleading to think that this development was confined to Italy, or that men had a monopoly of political matters. In this
context Christine de Pizan merits a few observations. Born in Venice of
Italian parents, she migrated at a tender age to Paris where her father was
employed in the court of Charles V. She became a widow at the age of 25
and had to care for her three children. She certainly was a remarkable
woman in a remarkable age. Not only was she a woman of extraordinary
intellectual gifts, erudition and initiative, but she also had controlled yet
uncommonly well-developed imaginative powers. Having assimilated a
great deal of variegated literature, she put it to good use by writing a
number of works on subjects which included poetry, history, education
and politics, and social welfare.[115] She handled her knowledge quite
dexterously and to good advantage, though on the whole her works, at
least as far as the political ones go, are compilatory. At any rate, she must
be one of the earliest women to have made intelligent use of Aristotle's
Politics and *Ethics* – in the works which are of immediate interest here.
They are *Le Livre de la paix*[116] and *Le Livre du corps de policie*,[117] written
between 1404 and 1407. This latter work was soon translated into
English.[118] The former was a response to the challenge of the issues underlying the Hundred Years War; it was written in 1413. It was suffused with
a good deal of moralizing reflections on the use of arms for the settlement
of quarrels, contained a great many definitions and explanations concerning
warfare and settlements, but had also pertinent and acute observations on
contemporary matters. The work was dedicated to the Duke of Guyenne.

In both these works Christine used as *exempla* not only Aristotle,
Cicero and Ovid but also the *Policraticus* of John of Salisbury, who thus
becomes a staple source of information for humanist and renaissance

---

115   There is a very good survey of her work and life in M.-J. Pinet, *Christine de Pisan*
(Paris, 1927), and in P. A. Becker, *Zur romanischen Literaturgeschichte* (Munich,
1967), pp. 511–40. For her literary works see also C. F. Bühler (ed.), *The Epistle of
Othea* (*EETS*, Oxford, 1970), pp. XXXIIIff.

116   Ed. C. C. Willard, *The 'Livre de la paix' of Christine de Pisan* (s'Gravenhage, 1958);
details of historical background, pp. 17ff.

117   Ed. R. H. Lucas, *Le Livre du corps de policie* (Geneva, 1967).

118   The manuscript of the ET is in ULC (Kk i.5, set 1). The French original is in the
British Museum, Harley 4410.

writers,[119] as well as Dante and Boccaccio. Indeed, it was only through her that Dante became known in France.[120] The work on *The Body Politic*, clearly modelled on Giles of Rome's *De regimine principum* (originally written by him as tutor for Philip IV), was a political–educational tract consisting of three parts – for the ruler, the aristocracy and the people. There are few, if any, original ideas in the work, which is rather eclectic.[121] It is intrinsically valuable since it shows how a sensitive and alert woman, with a considerable command of literature at her disposal, had absorbed and digested the sources in order to make a contribution to the solution of questions which beset all thinking contemporaries. Admittedly, she aimed high – the work 'est un miroir d'un état parfait'[122] – though she falls short of the aim she had set herself. Nevertheless, her book – it had in fact a companion volume specially written for women, and dealing with their education and domestic life,[123] while *The Body Politic* was intended for men – reflects the intellectual and ideological liveliness that was quite clearly a feature of this excitable age. For a woman to have written in the vernacular on highly explosive topics of the day shows what a rapid advance political humanism had in actual fact made. Even more surprising is her protest against the traditional discrimination against women which makes her one of the first fighters for female emancipation.[124] Her works obviously appealed to a great variety of readers, as some of the annotations in the manuscripts still reveal. Although it was never printed in France there were several editions in England.[125]

This is an appropriate point to suggest an answer to the long-standing problem of why renaissance humanism – in the commonly understood sense as a literary, linguistic, aesthetic, educational movement – found the

119   Cf. W. Ullmann, *The Medieval Idea of Law* (reprinted London, 1968), pp. 31f.; *CL*, ch. XV. The instances cited could now easily be multiplied.

120   See now Yvonne Batard, 'Christine de Pisan' in *Dante nel pensiero e nelle esegesi dei sec. XIV e XV* (Florence, 1975), pp. 271ff.; see p. 276: 'Le trecento français ne connaîtra pas la Divine Comédie. C'est l'oeuvre de Christine qui marque la première étape d'une très lente découverte de Dante par les Français.'

121   The most recent discussion is by G. Mombello, 'Quelques aspects de la pensée politique de Christine de Pizan' in *Culture et politique en France à l' époque de l'humanisme et de la renaissance*, ed. F. Simone (Turin, 1974), pp. 43–153. Here also further literature.

122   G. Mombello, *art. cit.*, p. 65.

123   Entitled *Le livre de trois vertus*, written 1408. A finely executed and miniatured manuscript of the book (mid fifteenth century) is in the Beinecke Library, Yale University (MS 427): see the facsimile in the catalogue to the exhibition *The Secular Spirit: Life and Art at the End of the Middle Ages* by T. B. Husband and J. Hayward (New York, 1975), no. 177, p. 161.

124   Cf. also A. L. Gabriel, 'The educational ideas of Christine de Pisan' in *JHI*, 16(1955), 3–21.

125   The editio princeps is in ULC (London, 1521) (by John Scott on vellum). Her *Feats of Arms and Chivalry* was printed by Caxton in 1489.

English soil in the fifteenth century originally so unreceptive. It has long been noted that humanism did not strike roots in England before the last decade of the century.[126] Poggio stayed in the country some four years in the earlier part of the century and left no trace, and although he made some flattering remarks Erasmus in the later years of the century was still somewhat critical of English learning and letters in comparison with their counterparts across the Channel. If renaissance humanism is viewed from the historical angle as an initially politically motivated intellectual move- ment concerned with the rebirth or rehabilitation of man as an autonomous citizen, there is a possibility of explaining the English situation in the fifteenth century and the slow adoption of 'humanist' learning. The answer must obviously set out from the historic reality and its premisses, and they of necessity include feudal government and feudal kingship which had set their seal on the complexion of the kingdom and its society. For no intellectual movement can progress in a vacuum, but needs a receptive soil in society in which gradually to evolve.

Since the feudal contract was in essence, as Marc Bloch once observed, a political contract, feudal kingship and government meant first and fore- most team-work between the king and the tenants-in-chief: after all, feudal lord and vassal had mutual rights and duties. This is a basic con- sideration if one bears in mind that there was nobody who did not hold what he had from someone else, so that all 'freemen' came within the feudal network.[127] The result was that government and therefore the making of the law proceeded on a far broader groundwork than where theocratic kingship prevailed, or, as Maitland said, law was a joint effort. This feudal system was intensely practical, pragmatic and unsophisticated and had arisen out of the natural exigencies of social and public life, with the consequence that the laity had certainly from the late twelfth century a correspondingly large share in the transaction of public business. The significance of this was that there was little need for any theories which rehabilitated or restored natural man, because he was already quite active in numerous spheres of public life. To all intents and purposes he acted in an, as it were, pre-citizen capacity, notably in the shaping and making of the law through the instrumentality of parliament, and quite especially after the separation of the House of Lords and the Commons in the early decades of the fourteenth century. It was precisely the unsophisticated natural character of the feudal system which enabled it to strike deep roots. The common law, originally the law common to the king and the barons,

---

126 The best guide is still Roberto Weiss, *Humanism in England during the Fifteenth Century*, 3rd edition (Oxford, 1967). See now also D. Hay, below, p. 202, n. 3.

127 For details on the following points cf. *PGP* pp. 150ff., with additional material in Appendix 1 and 2, supplemented in *IS* pp. 68ff., with further literature and material in IT (1974), pp. 81ff., and in GT (1974), pp. 66ff. Cf. also above, pp. 58ff.

was a mighty instrument which brought about the cohesion of society that harboured far less tension arising out of social stratification than was the case in contemporary regions on the Continent, where a stern hierarchical system predominated. There was on the whole a homogeneous society with little polarization, which could hardly be said of some neighbours across the Channel.

The members of the community assumed functions in the public field which were in essence not substantially different from those of citizens. The presupposition of the working of parliament, in fact its very substance, was debate, discussion, argument – talking *(parlare)* – concerning topics which touched all. This is exactly what in a large measure *politizare* meant. One may well advance the view that politics and the concomitant politicizing activity were built-in elements of a system of government which went back to the feudal contract: this was the nucleus out of which the constitution developed. The humanist theories of John of Paris, of Marsilius and others, had in fact been effectively anticipated by the actual practice of government. That is why the reception of these doctrines in England caused none of the reverberations they did on the Continent. And that is why humanism never encountered any opposition in England. No preachers denounced humanism from the pulpits.[128] Here the importance of the vernacular also comes into prominence: it was a force that in the political field immeasurably contributed to the welding together of the nation which itself had developed its national (common) law. Furthermore, the role claimed for the ancients – that is to act as guides, models or *exempla* – had little topical relevancy in fourteenth- or fifteenth-century England: they – not unlike, say, Marsilius, and others – could merely serve as confirmatory pieces of evidence. They corroborated in theory what had been realities in practice. But they could hardly act as guides. Political humanism had already struck firm roots without highfalutin theories. Apart from that, the ancient world could make only a very limited appeal to a society and government built on foundations which had little in common with that of ancient Rome. It was hardly to be expected that *Roma antiqua* could get such a grip on the imagination of contemporaries as it did in, say, Italy.

Whereas on the Continent, especially in Italy, the literary brand of humanism was a sequel to the politically inspired humanism which in the interests of citizenship had prompted the *studia humanitatis* in the first instance, in contemporary England there was therefore very little incentive to study the ancients from this angle and for this purpose, because reality had to some considerable extent achieved what they had set forth. And

---

128   Roberto Weiss, *op. cit.*, p. 183. One has but to think of men such as Dominici in
      Italy.

since the presupposition was missing, it is not incomprehensible that this kind of renaissance humanism met with native indifference.

The works of Sir John Fortescue[129] – which were written partly in Latin and partly in the vernacular – show how a man of the appropriate intellectual calibre, not burdened with too great learning but all the greater in practical experience, was able to present the historically and naturally evolved English government at work in a Thomist guise.[130] Fortescue fused Aristotelian–Thomist principles and those of English government as they were in actual practice. He clothed the latter in a Thomist garb, because he desired a clarification of the principles underlying the government.[131] Indeed, the operation was not as difficult as might be imagined. The English development did not call for a rebirth of natural man to make him a fully-fledged citizen, because the feudal contract as applied in government had already ensured what in theocratically governed communities was postulated by the rebirth or rehabilitation of the citizen. Fifteenth-century England had indeed no cause to go through the stage of political humanism, because it had long been there in practice. That therefore there was an initial indifference to the literary kind of renaissance humanism is perfectly understandable: the presupposition did not exist. Renaissance humanism in England omitted the political phase and began the literary, linguistic and educational kind of humanism by way of importing the humanities from abroad. Hence their influence and spread in England was late, slow and restricted.

In whatever shape or form renaissance humanism spread, it displayed conspicuous effects also within the religious precincts. The observer of the fourteenth and fifteenth centuries witnesses striking evidence of the search for an adequate expression of the individual's supranatural ends and aims. And here indeed the theme of bipolarity is reflected in an accentuated form which as a consequence brought about a veritable and total renaissance of religious life. The period shows beyond a shadow of doubt that the institutional character of religious life had experienced severe jolts. Despite repeated prohibitions of the translation of the Bible and of religious tracts into the vernacular, the progress could not be halted.[132] Avignon and all it stood for was as much a symptom of the age as the great vogue of mysticism that swept the whole of Western Europe at the turn of the century. And it is not always sufficiently appreciated that this pro-

---

129 Some details in *PGP*, pp. 192f.; *LP*, pp. 300f.
130 Hence his reliance on Thomas Aquinas's *De regimine principum* and on the tract with the same title by Giles of Rome.
131 This is rightly pointed out by A. B. Ferguson, *op. cit.* (above, n. 107), pp. 113f.
132 Charles IV prohibited a German translation of the Bible and confiscated religious tracts written in the vernacular in 1369. About his anti-heretical measures in Bohemia, see now A. Patschovsky, *Die Einführung der ständigen Inquisition in Böhmen* (Berlin, 1975), p. 73.

nounced mysticism owed a very great deal to women – the three Catherines of Siena, Bologna, and Genoa – as well as to Juliana of Norwich and lesser beacons of mystical religiosity. The immediate impact which women began to make upon the religious mode of living is certainly a sign of what one may well call an embryonic emancipation of women, as it showed itself also in the spread of the so-called double monasteries (such as those of the Bridgettines).[133] That most of these manifestations were linked with the new humanist outlook would be no rash conclusion. What was common to the new religious movements, including the Friends of God, was an individually orientated appeal to the religious sentiments of their contemporaries. The variegated movements emphasized the weight to be attached to the supranaturalness of man's life, which apparently was seen by some contemporaries as in danger of receding from man's vision altogether.

Evidently, this renaissance of religious life easily absorbed some traditional religious, doctrinal and ecclesiastical ideas and thus underlined a continuous development. Yet some elements in this new religious outlook at least potentially harboured features which could hardly be accommodated within the traditional framework. The very emphasis on the supranaturalness of man's end was apt to cause people to look askance upon the external ecclesiastical structure and organization and its adjuncts of power of enforcement through a hierarchically ordered machinery and above all the mechanics of law. Indeed, one could go further and say that this renaissance of religious life received a good deal of its stimulus and impetus from anticlericalism, although the advocates of the new orientation may not have been fully aware of the implications. A characteristic feature was also a pronounced aversion from rigid dogmatism: this in its turn incurred the opprobrium of the professional exponents of dogmatic theology in the universities.

The tenet that held the various new movements together was the urge to seek direct divine guidance: they desired to restore the essence of Christianity without necessarily adhering to any external apparatus. This presupposed a far greater internal involvement of the individual Christian than had been customary in the preceding period. The individual was to seek direct communion with God, which meant that the mediatory role of the official clergy was proportionately reduced in importance. The Friends of God no less than the Brethren of the Common Life, and others, were convinced that the Christian truths could be apprehended by intuition and introspection or meditation, even if they were beyond human articulation. This too tended to weaken the importance of the mediatory role of the priests as administrators of sacraments. The relationship between divinity and the individual was outside the traditionally fixed structure and frame-

133   Cf. *PPI* ch. XII, concerning their recognition by Martin V.

work. And this intimacy of relationship reached its culmination in the book by Thomas of Kempis, *The Imitation of Christ*, which was to serve as a guidebook for many generations. Its advocacy of the traditional medieval exhortation of *Nosce teipsum* – self-knowledge – could not but fall on particularly fertile soil in the somewhat changed circumstances of the fifteenth century. Moreover, the very plea to imitate Christ presupposed knowledge of the Bible, and the translations of the Bible from the late fourteenth century onwards in virtually all parts of Europe was partly a reflection of this new orientation, partly a response to its needs, partly an implied challenge to established ecclesiastical authority, and partly a symptom of the Christian's reliance on his own capability to understand the Bible itself.

It is not difficult to realize why these new movements and trends strongly appealed to the laity who in the meantime had in any case come to the fore. The laymen – and laywomen – began to plead for a greater share in the life of the Church than they had hitherto had, on the grounds that they were just as much necessary members of it as the ordained clergy. The growth of vernacular religious literature was one more effect of this appeal by and to the laity. And it was not only sermons but also tracts and professional theological literature that came to be written in the vernacular. This was accompanied by a somewhat strongly tinged emotionalism in religious matters. The relevant literature addressed itself to the individual's conscience as the supreme tribunal and authority in matters which touched the individual's eventual salvation, and thus unwittingly stressed the theme of bipolarity, if indeed it did not, by its very emphasis on the supranatural elements, exacerbate the tension between the individual's conscience and the external ecclesiastical organization. The *Devotio moderna*, as this new orientation came to be called, had many facets, of which the perhaps most significant was the concentration on the individual's own religious assessments and his own direct approach to God. In some respects one might speak here of a humanized theological orientation when one considers the concrete manifestations of the renaissance of religious life. It will presently be seen how the *Devotio moderna* was a phenomenon that must on no account be confused with 'modernity' or 'modernism': the term expressed nothing like progressivism, but on the contrary the return to, or a renaissance of, what was considered primitive Christianity or the manifestation of religious life in Christian antiquity.[134] Here once more there was

---

134 See on these aspects H. M. Klinkenberg, 'Die devotio moderna unter dem Thema Antiqui-Moderni betrachtet' in *Misc. Medievalia*, 9(1974), 394–419, with a slight difference in accentuation. Cf. also N. W. Gilbert, 'Ockham, Wyclif and the via moderna', *ibid.*, pp. 85–125. The antithesis of the *via antiqua* and *moderna* also referred to the question of the universals and did not necessarily imply adherence or opposition to humanism; see on this A. L. Gabriel, 'Via antiqua and via moderna and the migration of Paris students and masters to the German universities in the fifteenth century', *ibid.*, 419–83, especially pp. 442–3.

recourse to ancient models – to *exempla* – in the search for the uncontaminated norm of the Christian way of living. That there sprang up sects and
conventicles which exhibited remarkable tinges of libertinage clothed in a
religious garb, should at least be mentioned in passing.

The marked inclination towards independence from the institutional
organization of the Church on the part of the mystics and other contemporary movements and sections harmonized well enough with another
trend in the religious and also ecclesiastical field which too was a direct
effect of the concentration on man's humanity. It has long been observed
that one of the most crucial features of medieval government and politics,
if not indeed of medieval cosmology, was the objective standard that was
imposed. Evidently, if the law was to rule supreme, no other standard was
possible. Vice versa, the validity of the law did not depend on the moral
excellence of the lawgiver. What mattered in public life was the office, the
institution, the depersonalized institutional organ, and not the personal
features, such as the personal morality of the office-holder. Precisely
because virtually all medieval public life rested on the distinction between
the office and the personality of the office-holder, the objective norm held
sway and had great success, as the history of the period persuasively
showed. The concentration on the humanity of man, on man's inner
natural being, on his personal features, on the core of his personality and
individuality, gradually undermined this objective standard, not indeed as
a result of any particular doctrine, but partly because the new humanist
attention released forces which in any case had been latent, and now
became merely patent; partly also because the gulf between what was
taught and what was done by contemporary ecclesiastical authorities was
too glaring to be overlooked by the in any case greatly stimulated critical
capacities of the laity. Finally, it must not be forgotten that private–
subjective assessments had never been, and could never be, eliminated,
not even in historiography, where writers frequently enough resorted to
personal–subjective criteria (including vituperations) when they could not
otherwise explain historical situations. In a word, the 'human' point of
view became humanist – a conclusion which is particularly relevant within
the religious field proper.

Thrown against this background the subjectivized standpoint quite
rapidly gained ascendancy. In some respects, when methodically and
systematically pursued, the personalized thesis that concentrated on the
character of the man and evaluated his public measures by setting them
against the norms of an ethical code was necessarily to lead to a perforation of a social order that had for centuries been based on purely objective
standards and norms. Moreover, the subjectivized standpoint was not only
quite evidently a threat to the social order, but above all most directly
involved religious issues. The personalized or subjectivized view found

perhaps its clearest articulation in Wyclif and Hus, for whom the valid administration of sacraments depended upon the moral standards of the ecclesiastical office-holder. Hence a 'bad' priest or one who had committed a sin or was in any other sense a *malus sacerdos* was not credited with the right to administer any sacraments. In other words, the sacraments no longer displayed effects by virtue of their own inherent qualities (*ex opere operato*) but as a result of the merits of the administrator of the sacraments (*ex opere operantis*),[135] a thesis which, as can readily be seen, spelt the death knell of a good deal of medieval Christianity. Some such views had of course been expressed earlier, but the soil had not yet been ready to receive them. For instance, in the twelfth century some people said that what mattered was the meritorious life of the priest, not his office – 'meritum dat potestatem, non officium'[136] – whereas the Oxford Master Vacarius said: 'Priesthood is a matter of the law, of the constitution, and has nothing to do with the man's mind.'[137] Now, however, circumstances had radically changed through the humanizing process, and these person-alized views were held by men learned in theology, who set forth this subjectivized standpoint and thereby gave it standing, respectability and endorsement. Clearly, what is a 'good pope' or a 'bad king' rested on definitions and criteria which varied as widely as human personalities did (and do). How was one to know whether or not, say, the pope lived up to the standards which St Peter had observed?

In close proximity to these features stood a further development. There is abundant evidence that a not inconsiderable and certainly articulate part of contemporary Christendom viewed the traditional external ecclesi-astical order with reservations or misgivings, if not with outright animosity. That the schism could last as long as it did – and this despite its all-too-obvious calamitous and catastrophic effects – is a symptom that cannot be ignored, just as it was symptomatic that some twenty years after its termin-ation the last-ever anti-pope (who played a pitiable role by any standards) came to be elected: this too must be taken into account if the forces at work are to be adequately assessed. Hence it is comprehensible that there was a search for models with the aim of finding out how the renaissance of

---

135 As Innocent III had classically expressed it in his *De sacro altaris mysterio*, in *PL* 217.844: a sacrament is not founded 'in merito sacerdotis, sed in verbo creatoris conficitur ... quamvis igitur *opus operans* aliquando sit inmundum, semper tamen *opus operatum* est mundum.' This was old Augustinian theory as transmitted by Ivo of Chartres, *Decretum*, II.100, in *PL* 161.187, and in his *Panormia*, III.79, in *PL*. cit. col. 1147; it was also incorporated in Gratian's *Decretum*, I.1.96, and his own view is expressed in D.a.c.96.

136 This is what, according to Alan of Lille, some heretics held: *PL* 210.385.

137 Cited by Ilarino da Milano, *L'eresia di Ugo Speroni nella confutazione del Maestro Vacario* (= *Studi e Testi*, 115(1945)), pp. 550f.; cf. also pp. 476, 484, 500: 'sacer-dotium *res iuris est*, hoc est administrationis.'

religious life was best and most adequately to express itself. Now the significance of this search was that it greatly assisted the study of ecclesiastical history and fostered historical as well as biblical criticism. In fact, one can go further and say that the more contemporaries penetrated into the matrix of Christian antiquity and began to read the available and relevant records, doctrinal expositions and biblical exegeses, the more their critical faculties developed and with all the greater facility were they able to detach themselves from the accustomed modes of religious expression. More and more the realization began to dawn that there was a time in Christian antiquity without a papacy, and without ecclesiastical institutions armed with the panoply of the law and the means to enforce it. And the longer the schism lasted the stronger the appetite grew for further critical examination of the existing ecclesiastical structure and the traditional religious views allegedly based on the Bible. Question marks often replaced the certainty of faith. It was the employment of man's critical faculties that was powerfully engendered by the actuality of the historical situation. This indubitably stimulated personal religiosity and fostered an aversion from the external legal order. The slowly emerging and as yet still vaguely conceived distinction between the *communio fidelium interna* and the *communio externa* or *corporalis* pre-portrayed the kind of renaissance which was to grow under the guise of the Reformation.

What is of no little weight in this context is the dexterity with which new theological themes as well as religious views could be combined with sentiments which to all intents and purposes stepped into the place left vacant by the decay of the traditional objective standards. It was, for example, the confluence of Wycliffite theological theses with national Bohemian tenets which characterized the Hussite movement, partly religious, partly nationalist, but in any case a very powerful ideological combination. As already indicated, the nationalist sentiment had made great strides all over Europe. It was, perhaps, more pronounced in Bohemia than, say, in France or England, but it was everywhere of essentially the same substance. Neither pure religious sentiments nor pure nationalist sentiments could have achieved popular reactions: it was the combination of the two elements – the religious and the national – which was so potent by the late fourteenth century. It was, for example, by no means uncommon in England, France or Bohemia to find statements asserting that priests were not necessary, that laymen had power from God to preach and hear confessions and to give absolution, that the decrees of the Roman Church need not be heeded, let alone obeyed, that the host was not the body of Christ, that any 'just' man could administer the Eucharist, as there was in any case no difference between bishops, priests and laymen, that there was no such thing as hell, because it never existed in nature, and so on. And what is especially noteworthy is that this kind of statement could be heard from the mouth of the scholar, the literate graduate and the illiterate peasant. At the same time it must be stressed that the expression of such views was by no means proof of membership of a heretical sect or organization. What these views prove is simply that more and more people had begun to think and reflect about hitherto accepted matters. But when this kind of questioning of hitherto unquestioned axioms persists and begins to embrace larger and larger sections of the populace, it clearly assumes the proportion or dimension of a heretical movement when measured against the yardstick of the law. It requires very little historical imagination to visualize how easily nationalist sentiments especially could spread and absorb, or be absorbed by, these religious views which if they denoted one thing, it was a tendency to nonconformity.[138]

The abstract concept of the State was concretely reflected in the strongly expressed national sentiments. And here is a feature which is, from the historical angle, far more significant than the theological disputes or the character of individual religiosity. For in the aftermath of the schism the papacy itself had come to terms with the principle of the nation state, which assuredly was outwardly the most conspicuous sign of the disintegration and decomposition of what had once been held to be a universal entity. The papacy began to conclude treaties with the individual kingdoms and these came to be called concordats. To be sure, this was an evident result of the national grouping during schismatic times, but the significance of the concordat development lay in the papacy's solemnly recognizing the individual national states as separate, sovereign, independent entities. And this papal accommodation with the new national states occurred exactly a century after the full blast of Boniface VIII against the incipient state sovereignty. This change convincingly shows the strength of the new 'human' forces that had affected virtually every organ, institution and establishment. The fragmentation of Europe had come to be formally sanctioned by the papacy itself and marked the abandonment of the traditional Christian universalism. The acceptance of the national sovereign State however involved at least implicitly the possibility, if not the virtual certainty, that the king was to act as an emperor in his realm.[139] The application of this principle was thus unwittingly authorized by the papacy itself.

Considering it from a wider angle one has no difficulty in realizing that

---

138   For England cf. *PGP* pp. 103ff.; A. G. Dickens, *The Lollards and Protestants in the Diocese of York* (London, 1959), and E. F. Jacob, *The Fifteenth Century* (Oxford, 1969); for France, cf. J. Duvernoy (ed.), *Le registre d'inquisition de Jacques Fournier*, 3 vols (Toulouse, 1965–6); for Bohemia, see A. Patschovsky, *op. cit.* (above, n. 132), p. 131.

139   For the significance of this, see above, pp. 49f.

the decomposition and disintegration concerned nothing less than the gradual perforation and eventual disappearance of the corporational character of the ecclesiological unit – a body understood as an organic, organized, juristic, visible entity – which needed authoritative guidance, government and hence the law. To the divestiture of the corporational character of the ecclesiological unit corresponded, in the individual field, a growing awareness of man's own faculties. Greater and more comprehensive powers of judgment and self-guidance and self-reliance came to be attributed to, or were asserted by, him, with the consequence that in politics the ascending theme of government came to be applied, and in the religious sphere mysticism and the other new manifestations of religiosity were adopted. But above all, within the religious precincts, there was an incontrovertible alienation from the external, legal–constitutional order of Christendom: at any rate in some circles the Pauline statement that 'We are one body in Christ' was no longer encapsuled in the Roman law corporation but understood in a purely invisible, supranatural, if not mystical or pneumatic, sense. The loss of the universal corporateness of the ecclesiological unit also helps to explain the religious feature that could well be termed introversion. On the not too distant horizon appears the Christian who was no longer considered an integral part of a unit, but who constituted a unit himself. He was his own priest.

It is precisely at this juncture that the *Devotio moderna* requires a few more remarks. The concept epitomized the religious renaissance that began in the fourteenth century and gained momentum in the fifteenth. It was characterized by the attempt to restore religious practices to that level which had existed in primitive Christianity, or what on the basis of their own critical reading of the sources the adherents of the movement believed to have been the state of affairs in early Christianity. Hence all the institutional overgrowth, as well as the accretions and 'decorations', which liturgy and also theological doctrine had acquired were targets for opposition. Similarly, a somewhat individualistic perception of religious sentiments could not but help viewing the law and all the legal apparatus and measures which were said to be necessary for salvation with detachment, if not animosity. The intimacy of the Christian's relations with God was characterized by his meditation, his self-knowledge, subjective apprehension and personal experience. There was to be an intimate, direct link between God and the Christian, precisely that dedication to divine service that was a veritable *devotio* unencumbered by external decrees, laws or organization. It is not therefore a purely coincidental postulate that among the advocates of the *Devotio moderna* there was a strong subjectivized strain, as well as the postulate for equality of the laity to the clergy. Although there was as yet no specific articulate opposition to the traditional hierarchical structure,[140] the function of the clergy as mediators of sacraments was seriously doubted, if not also in some quarters rejected. The important significance of this religious development was that it was the exact counterpart of that in the secular field: in both, the return to ancient models was to be the means with which the future was to be fashioned. Here as there the observer witnesses very similar features. The consultation of, and the recourse to, the ancients still proceeded within the traditional framework, and was to have been merely a means to an end, which purported to be a purer form and a deeper kind of Christianity than that which throughout the preceding centuries had been suffocated by externalism, ritualism and legalism.

But what was intended to be a mere means to an end became an end in itself. The humanism that was engendered by the renaissance of natural man, and consequently of the citizen, detached itself from its original base, emerged as an independent intellectual pursuit, and saw its fulfilment in the imitation of the ancients in grammar, rhetoric and style. And in the religious field the *Devotio moderna* postulated a similar consultation of and recourse to the ancients as a means to an end, so that ancient Christian examples could function as models in the service of a revivification or a true rebirth of the Christian faith and practice: and this too detached itself from its base, became separated, and reappeared as an independent movement in the shape of the Reformation.

---

140   See M. Ditsche, 'Zur Herkunft und Bedeutung des Begriffs der Devotio moderna' in *Hist. Jb*, 79(1961), 124ff. Numerous details with much relevant material in H. M. Klinkenberg, *art. cit.* (above, n. 134), pp. 396ff.

Epilogue

The attempt to lay bare the historical and ideological foundations of what is commonly called renaissance humanism will have shown that it indisputably had strong roots in the medieval period and that the commonly accepted view of a 'new era' or a 'break with the medieval past' is not tenable. As it was a movement within space and time, it must be seen from a historical perspective, and it is precisely this perspective which demonstrates beyond a shadow of doubt firstly, that renaissance humanism was firmly embedded in the preceding historical and ideological process, and secondly, that it cannot be adequately understood without taking into account the intellectual, and above all the religious–ecclesiastical, forces which had shaped the age out of which renaissance humanism was to grow.

The initial impulse to renaissance humanism was the challenge with which the traditional world order was faced in the Investiture Contest. Secular governments were exposed to fierce ecclesiastical attacks, and herewith not only their standing, but to an equal degree the standing of the laity as such, was severely impugned. Harnessing the Roman law – and also Roman law scholarship – to the cause of secular government opened up entirely new dimensions which tuned in perfectly with the numerous secular manifestations detectable in society at large. The welding together of Roman law based secular government with the secular manifestations in society presented a most fertile soil for the reception of Aristotelian philosophical themes in the thirteenth century.

The focal point had now emerged – man himself. The concentration on his *human*ity became predominant and formed the central interest of thinkers and writers. As Otto of Freising said in the mid twelfth century, '*human*itas' was 'the very substance of man himself' ('quae est integrum esse hominis'). The deep significance, unnoticed by modern historians, of this concentration on man's humanity is that the effects of baptismal rebirth were quite considerably reduced. According to the unquestioned doctrine, divine grace in baptismal rebirth had reborn or regenerated natural man, who became 'a new creature'. His natural humanity, he himself as a mere natural *homo*, was thereby rendered harmless and neutralized. It goes without saying that it is not within the sphere of human competence to assess the effect of baptism on the individual human being. What admits of no doubt however is that public life and public government were fundamentally affected by this idea of rebirth. Without taking it into account the period between the eighth and the thirteenth centuries would be well-nigh inexplicable, and this applies to governments and their standing within an exclusively ecclesiological framework.

The combination of governmental changes with the already existing and influential practical contingencies, together with newly arising intellectual forces, resulted in the rebirth of natural man. Man's natural humanity was credited with the very thing which baptismal rebirth had claimed to have done away with: it was credited, that is, with autonomous character. Aristotle provided the theory for practice which, as we have seen, reflected the continuing process of secularization. Natural *human*ity had now come into its own, natural man had been restored, restituted or reborn, and with this rebirth went the rehabilitation of the citizen as an autonomous and integral member of the self-sufficient State – like himself a product of nature – and the introduction of the new dimension, in the shape of politics, which was the category of thought and activity appropriate to the citizen. Herewith, quite evidently, the effects of baptismal rebirth were radically curtailed: they were confined to the supranatural sphere. Bipolarity replaced unipolarity; territorial State sovereignty came to be substituted for universality; and the totality point of view gave way to the atomistic autonomy of the religious, political, moral and other norms. Over and above all these changes was the theoretical claim to apply the ascending theme of government in the natural–mundane sphere, whereas its descending counterpart remained within the supranatural realms.

Modern historians all too rarely realize that the citizen in his rehabilitated status was, to use traditional baptismal language, 'a new creature'. Both the terms of *humanitas* and *civis* (citizen) were of course well known throughout the preceding ages. And nothing helps a new theory more than familiarity with the terms it employs, however much their meaning may have changed. There was a plethora of doctrines, writings, counsel, statements, laws, dogmas, and so on, relative to the Christian, baptismally reborn man. But about the citizen there was precious little in medieval writings. To the studies of divinity or of Christianity – the *studia divinitatis* – nothing corresponded on the human level, because interest in man's humanity had lain dormant. For his political conduct the citizen could find no model, no pattern, no prototype in the literature of the preceding ages. Yet the running of the State presupposed appropriate instruction, guidance and acquisition of knowledge. Hence the recourse to the ancients suggested itself. Their study became an essential part of renaissance humanism, which in this very context assumed educational dimensions of a magnitude hardly appraised by modern historians. Indeed, it was these studies which were the *studia humanitatis*. They concerned the understanding, evaluation and recognition of ordinary humanity within its ordinary environs, for which the ancient works, uninfluenced as they were by Christianity, proved easily accessible mirrors and consequently provided reliable guidelines for conduct. This was ostensibly an educational issue of major proportions. Education was then (as it is now) concerned with instruction in matters essential to society, its well-being, its progress.

The *studia humanitatis* had the same comprehensive educational function as the earlier *studia divinitatis* (or *christianitatis*). In the course of the eighth and ninth centuries Western Europe came into being as an ideological concept that replaced the purely geographical–physical connotation hitherto associated with it. A whole society was to be shaped according to Christian principles. The Frankish–Carolingian governments vigorously pursued this aim, which in the last resort was a social rebirth conceived on the model of individual baptismal rebirth. But in order to transform this raw, natural society into a Christian body, knowledge of the main principles relative to Christian doctrine was needed – hence the search for ancient Christian writers and works that were to serve as guides and books of instructions for the transformation of society. This Carolingian renaissance produced its corresponding educational aims and ethos. In substance the resultant new European society was an ecclesiological unit which explains the overwhelming and decisive part played by the *studia divinitatis*, the pursuit of studies most germane to it.

Exactly the same feature, only in reverse, can now be witnessed from the thirteenth and fourteenth centuries onwards. There had been a very real dearth of knowledge relative to the management of society and the State by the citizen – hence the rapidly advancing *studia humanitatis* were to supply knowledge relative to the principles of citizenship and its manipulation, and reliable knowledge could be obtained only through the study of Roman (and later Greek) *exempla*. These were means to an end. They constituted an educational programme that corresponded to the needs of humanism, in which the accent lay on the human aspect of man (as distinct from the supranatural aspect, of baptismal provenance) and on his handling of his *human* society, the State. Instruction in the essential needs and in the mechanics of citizenship and the State was an indispensable requirement. Reborn or restored humanity was the citizen's material ingredient. The German Mutianus (= Conrad Muth) expressed proper

renaissance sentiments when he declared that thanks to the *studia humanitatis* 'we have been truly reborn' ('vere renati sumus').[1]

Of course, readily available as most of the Latin works were, they had in
any case been studied in the preceding ages, but the reason for studying
them was different and the perspectives differed. They were used for
purely didactic, vocational purposes in the narrow meaning of the term,
that is, for Latin composition, prose writing, drafting of documents,
church services, and the like. Now, however, the purpose and perspectives
were infinitely wider and broader and referred to the substance of these
works. They were mirrors of ancient societies, of purely human complexion, from which essential and fruitful lessons could be drawn. The
point of reference had changed, though the transition was smooth enough.
By no means should it be assumed that the earlier purpose was abandoned.
What happened was that they were used for additional and widely
expanded purposes, perspectives and designs. Humanity as such was
studied in them. The civic conduct of man was observed in them. Politics
at work was realistically conveyed by them. They were the educational
means of renaissance humanism which were to assist the attainment of the
end. And the end was the reshaping, the rebirth, of society on principles
derived from natural humanity as depicted in the works which formed the
centre of the *studia humanitatis*, and not on those principles which were
extracted from the *studia divinitatis*. The end was certainly not, as is
commonly assumed, the recreation of the ancient world. The end was the
creation of a human society, of the human State that had, conceptually,
not existed before, and for the building and manipulation of this human
community the consultation of the ancients was an evident necessity.
Nobody studied 'the humanities' (there never were *humanitates*) but what
was studied was *humanitas*, humanity itself, though not for its own sake,
but for the sake of utilizing the knowledge acquired in the service of the
citizen, the State and politics. And precisely because the core of humanism
was humanity itself, which in different shapes and forms had become the

---

1   For this see H. O. Burger, *Renaissance, Humanismus, Reformation: deutsche Literatur
    im europäischen Kontext* (Frankfurt, 1969), p. 365. See Muth's own characteristic
    expression: 'Sum Mutianus homo' (ed. K. Gillert, *Der Briefwechsel des Conrad
    Muthianus* (Halle, 1890), no. 76, p. 111, lines 5f. In former ages it was common to
    address the ruler as 'Christianitas vestra' or refer to a king, notably the French, as
    'Rex christianissimus', but in the full flood of humanism letters written by Muth to
    his intimate friend the Abbot Henry Fastnacht (Urbanus) address him: 'Pater . . .
    philosophorum (or presbyterorum) *humanissimus*' or 'humanitate studiosus', see *ed.
    cit.*, no. 272, p. 357; no. 29, p. 39; no. 158, p. 229. There were of course several
    variants, of which 'in omni genere *humanitatis* perfectus' (no. 328, p. 421) is perhaps
    most significant. In mocking at the Latinization of surnames Muth shows how ready
    at hand lay the idea of rebirth: the bearers of new Latin names believed that they had
    been reborn: 'Postquam vero *renatus* es et pro Jheger Crotus, pro Dornheim Rubianus
    salutatus . . .' (no. 260, p. 342).

focal point of interest all over Western Europe in the fourteenth and fifteenth centuries, Italian, and notably Florentine, humanism readily assumed the function of a model. It presented on an unsurpassably advanced level the mature humanist reflections drawn from practical experience and the theoretical study of *humanitas*. What Bologna was to Europe in the twelfth century, Florence was in the fifteenth.

Yet renaissance humanism began to undergo some changes as the fourteenth century advanced. The mass of material that had come to be studied was of such complexity, comprehensiveness and quantity that, for the best use to be made of it, specialization was virtually forced upon thinkers, scholars and officials. The result of this intensive study in depth of the ancients was departmentalization[2] which – and this is a vital point that ought long to have been realized – involved a crucial change in the meaning and function of the *studia humanitatis*. They were no longer a means to an end, but became an end in themselves. Mere instruments of education changed into full-scale educational programmes. It is super-fluous to comment upon this momentous change of function. The original concern of renaissance humanism – *humanitas* as the kernel of man, and therefore of the citizen and the State – receded more and more into the background. While originally the *studia humanitatis* – the counterpart of the *studia divinitatis* – aimed at a better understanding of man's conduct as a citizen, for which the ancient works were classical witnesses, these same *studia humanitatis* came now to refer to the study and cultivation of the means by which the essence of humanity was expressed. The accent had shifted from the substance to the apparel which enveloped it.

Specialization concerned itself above all with language and, indeed, the traditional medieval Latin left a good deal to be desired when compared with the original Latin which was now studied and absorbed in depth. That the attempt at purification of the language led to controversies which may seem strange to us today, such as those concerned with the correct orthography of *michi-mihi, nichil-nihil, civalier-chivalier*, and so on – was probably thanks to overzealous enthusiasm for the restitution of an unadulterated Latin. The *studia humanitatis* became the study of literature and of letters, and gradually came to embrace the whole spectrum of intellectual activity within which the problem of citizenship, of the State, of politics was no longer accorded its originally commanding position. What is more, the change of meaning and function that affected the *studia humanitatis* reacted upon the meaning of renaissance humanism, the substance of which was originally the rebirth of *homo* and the consequential rehabilitation of the citizen. But this original sense of renaissance humanism

---

2 The same feature was noticeable in the twelfth century, when juristic theology came to be compartmentalized, about which cf. above, p. 170.

receded into the background and gave way to a secondary renaissance humanism. For in the fifteenth century renaissance humanism engulfed educational, ethical, aesthetic, linguistic, rhetorical, philological aspects, and created its own momentum by leading to new branches of learning, such as the *theologia platonica* in the hands of Marsilio Ficino. The fifteenth-century humanism constituted a supreme effort to imitate the classical style, attended by the consequential and sometimes acrimonious debates concerning the role of the vernacular as an appropriate literary medium of expression.

This secondary renaissance humanism became a fashion, if not also a profession for highly educated and erudite, sensitive and subtle scholars, some of whom even began to classicize their own names. As has rightly been observed, a good deal of this renaissance humanism was imitative and has little originality. For imitation is hardly conducive to creative, original and constructive work. But in an overall assessment due consideration must be given, on the one hand, to the role of this secondary renaissance humanism as an incubator of the very idea of the rebirth of the citizen which, after passing through various stages, became highly topical again from the late seventeenth century onwards, and most effective from the eighteenth as a result of the French Revolution – only to be re-enacted in this century in the Revolution in Russia which for historical reasons had been left behind. On the other hand must be remembered the fructifying character of this secondary renaissance humanism in numerous branches of the human intellect and its profound impact on European culture, learning and philosophy.[3] But in no other field did this humanism leave such an enduring imprint as in the arts proper, which burgeoned forth as the Renaissance proper – the unique European phenomenon that traversed political frontiers, disregarded religious differences and set aside natural boundaries, and in its full-blooded form gave to the world at large products of beauty which were inimitable, because they were at once creative, original and constructive and reached artistic heights unsurpassed in any period of European history. The Renaissance was the proud, sublime and noble heir of that rebirth which culminated in the rehabilitation of man as a citizen, whereas the long-term effect of this same rebirth was the modern democratic State in its pluralist configuration.

---

3 See most recently the admirable surveys and studies in *Itinerarium Italicum Dedicated to P. O. Kristeller*, ed. H. Oberman *et al.* (Leiden, 1975). For England see D. Hay, pp. 305ff.; for France see S. Dresden, pp. 119ff.; for Germany, L. W. Spitz, pp. 371ff.; for the Low Countries, J. Ijseijn, pp. 193ff.; for the Italian reactions to Erasmian humanism see Myron Gilmore, pp. 61ff.

Index

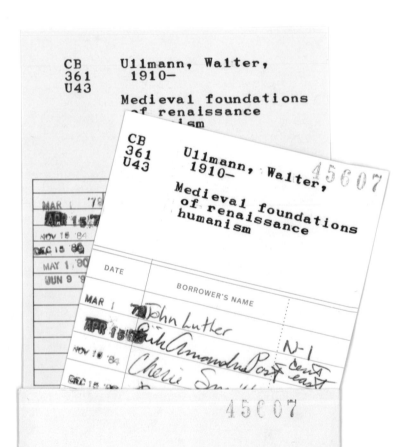